SOCIAL AND POLITICAL HISTORY OF NEPAL

Social and Political History of Nepal

B.D. SANWAL

MANOHAR
2026

First published 1993
Reprinted 2026

ISBN 978-81-7304-021-4

Published by
Ajay Kumar Jain *for*
Manohar Publishers & Distributors
4753/23 Ansari Road, Daryaganj
New Delhi 110 002

Printed and bound in India

Contents

Part I

Part II

Introduction

There is great dearth of books on the history of Nepal. The first authoritative book on Nepalese history by Sylvain Levi was published between 1905 and 1908. This work is a classic study but is now outdated. The volumes of Nepalese history by D.R. Regmi are more recent but they are voluminous and do not cover recent history. There are, however, some new books on Nepalese ethnography, political system and present day geo-political milieu of Nepal by Nepalese, Indian, British and American authors.

Nepalese history has generally been divided into the ancient, medieval and modern periods. The ancient period extends from the earliest times to the middle of the eighth century when the Lichhavi dynasty came to an end. As no epigraphic record of the Lichhavis after 740 AD has come to light, 750 AD seems a good approximation for the beginning of the medieval period. There is general agreement that the modern period of Nepalese history begins with the year 1768 AD when Prithvi Narayan Shah of Gorkha conquered Kathmandu. In this pattern, the study of history becomes a set of chronological lists of rulers compiled from epigraphical and numismatic studies. The social and economic condition of the peoples of Nepal has generally remained static since times immemorial. We can call it the traditional or primitive or Asian (Himalayan) society where agriculture and trade were rooted in the geographical and ethnic contours of the country and changed little from the times of the Buddha to the middle of the twentieth century. The beginnings of modernisation in Nepal can be traced to Jung Bahadur's war with Tibet and his later visit to Europe. In Tibet, the Gorkha army overcame old taboos about eating yak flesh and in going to Europe. Jung Bahadur discarded the Brahmanical injunction about crossing the seas. In both cases, it was contact with conditions in foreign countries that ushered in change from the top. Nepal also became a State governed by law so far as power and succession to the highest echelons of power were concerned. This process of modernisation finally became operative after the over-throw of the Rana regime and is continuing unabated since then. Despite the ruling elite wanting to keep power to themselves and denying the same to the common people, Nepalese society has been opening up. Contacts with foreigners, tradesmen, tourists, social scientists and political analysts, businessmen and thousands of others have brought better understanding of world forces and developments. The emphasis by the monarchs since 1951 on education, and economic development has strengthened this process. The inevitable consequence is that Nepal is fast losing the character of a closed society and is definitely though slowly emerging as a modern society governed by the Rule of Law, respect for human rights and the need for better living conditions for the majority of the peoples.

This book is a pioneering effort to examine the social conditions obtaining in a traditional society which is beginning to open up for change and modernisation. The "Sanatan" or eternally valid norms of living now do not appear to be sufficient for preservation of national identity. The account gives in detail the contemporary perspective of social and political conditions in the country. The directions of change are visible but the process itself is slow. The emphasis is on recording a land-mark survey for the second half of the present century where a closed and traditional society is passing through a period of transition and transformation. Levi called his history of Nepal an account of a Hindu Kingdom. Nepal is still the only Hindu State in the world. Social, economic and political change in Nepal is a significant part of such transformation in the larger Hindu environment in India as also in other less developed parts of Asia. The basic theme of the book is that despite the various means to keep Nepal a closed society, there is simply an inevitability of change over-time.

One

The Geography of Nepal

Nepal is properly the name of the valley of the Baghmati wherein lie the towns of Kathmandu, Bhatgaon and Patan. The name, however, was applied to the entire political area administered by the Gorkhas after the conquest of the valley by Prithivi Narayan Shah in 1767.

Nepal is said to be derived from the word NEWAR. It is claimed that Nepal denotes the country of the NEWARS. There is also a legend that the valley of the Baghmati had been blessed by a great saint called NE when the valley came under his special protection and since then it has been called Nepal.[1]

Nepal is situated in the central portion of the Himalayan ranges which extend from the Pamirs in the west to the great gorges of the Yang-tze-Kiang, Mekong and the Salween in the east. Its boundaries are now defined on all her frontiers. Nepal is separated in the west from the districts of Pithoragarh and Naini Tal of the State of Uttar Pradesh (U.P.) by the river Mahakali and the Sarda. In the east, the Mechi river separates it from the district of Darjeeling in West Bengal and the watershed from Kanchanjungha to the Singh Leela range is the boundary between Nepal and the State of Sikkim. In the south, the frontier has been defined by treaties between Nepal and the East India Company in 1816 and between Nepal and the British Government in India in 1860. In the north, the boundry has recently been demarcated between Tibet and Nepal by a treaty signed by the People's Republic of China and Nepal in 1962. The boundaries generally follow the traditional boundaries between Tibet and Nepal. Mount Everest is accepted to mark the boundaries and the south face of the mountain is admitted as Nepalese territory.

The southern boundary of Nepal has been marked by fixed boundary pillars extending from the river Sarda in the west to the river Mechi in the east by a joint Commission of Indian and Nepalese officers between the years 1900-1905.

In shape Nepal is a long narrow country, the length lying east to west, and as one proceeds to the west, the country inclines northwards. The average length is about 840 kms and the breadth 160 kms. The area is 141,181 Sq. kms and the latest estimate of population is 19 million. This gives an average density of 13.45 persons to the Sq. km.[2] The density of population is roughly three times that of Sikkim or Bhutan. The density in neighbouring Tibet is estimated to be less than 2 persons per sq. km.

The topography, climate and vegetation in Nepal are similar to those obtaining in the neighbouring Himalayan ranges of Kumaon in the west and Sikkim and Bhutan in the east. Similar physical features, climatic conditions and natural vegetation are found in Nepal as are obtaining at similar heights in the neighbouring Himalayan ranges. The lofty peaks of the Himalayas separate Nepal from Tibet which we could say lies in Inner Asia. But there are significant links and few barriers between her and India. To that extent Nepal is part of South Asia. The links that connect India with Nepal are mainly the rivers that arise in Nepal and flow down to join the Ganges in Uttar Pradesh and Bihar. This has led to the present state of affairs where Nepal has to depend excessively on India for her trade and cultural activities with the world outside her own frontiers. Her export and import trade is mostly with India and Hindi books, magazines and newspapers provide her peoples with cultural contacts with the outside world. There is a constant flow of her educated men to the Indian Universities in Benares, Bihar and Calcutta and of her martial races to the Gorkha recruiting centres in India.

In her climate, Nepal is "typically monsoonal with the regular cool, hot and wet seasons". Owing to height, the climate in the hilly areas is pleasanter and healthier than in the plains of India.[3]

Little is known about the geology of Nepal because of the indifference of the ruling circles to the sciences of the west and the policy of exclusion of all foreign nationals from intercourse with the Nepalese. It is, however, presumed that Nepal should generally have the same geological features as Kumaon and Sikkim.[4] After the Second World War, Nepal is taking steps to organise geological and other scientific surveys and the results are eagerly awaited. A north-south section through the Baghmati Valley near Kathmandu would give us a broad picture of the geology of the country. From the alluvial plains, we would rise to the Bhabhar area with coarse gravels and then come to the Churia Ghati range, which is the exact equivalent of the Siwalik range south of Dehra

Dun, being composed of soft sands and conglomerates of coarse river boulders. The dip is gentle and towards the main range, flattening out in the dun or mari of Etoundah, which corresponds to the Dehra or Patli duns. Beyond, harder but still soft sandstones of Nahan type form the lower spurs of the main range by a reversed fault, as is the case further north-west. The whole of this Sub-Himalayan series, which aggregates three to four thousand metres in thickness, is presumed by analogy to be of upper tertiary age. The valley of the Baghmati contains representatives of the Karewas of Kashmir and of the baggar and khadar alluviums of the Ganges valley. These surface deposits have been laid down in the valley basin within recent times *i.e.* post pliocene times. With them occur beds of peat and phosphatic blue clays which are used for fertilizing the fields. North of the valley are older rocks of the main range comprising a much-folded sequence of earthy schists, with their blue limestone beds, black schistose slates, white massive crystalline limestone, quartzschists, and gneissose granite, the last being porphyritic, and containing mica and schorl. The general strike is with the main Himalayan chain, and the apparent dip is towards the north-east complicated by inversion and over-thrust.[5]

One further point may be adverted to. Earthquakes are of frequent occurrence in Nepal, and time and again the valley of Nepal and other areas have been rocked by severe earth shocks, resulting in numerous deaths and great damage. The last great earthquake was in 1935 which affected large areas of North Bihar also.

The study of a mountainous country like Nepal is profitably attended to in two ways. Firstly, we might study the country as we ascend from the low lying areas to the higher mountains. Secondly, we might study the geography of a mountainous country by looking for the drainage system of its rivers.

Accordingly, Nepal may be divided into four geographical regions; namely the Tarai and the Bhabar at the foothills, Inner Himalayas, the Great Himalayas and the Trans-Himalayas.

The country below the foot of the hills is called the Tarai and is the most fertile part of the country. Its height varies from 150 to 500 metres above sea-level. The narrow belts of country to the north and immediately below the hills are generally covered with shrubs and are remarkable for absence of water. In these areas, called the Bhabar no water can be seen except where one of the largest rivers takes its course. There is but a thin covering of alluvial soil on a vast dry bed of boulders and shingle through which all rain that falls seeps rapidly and which absorb in the same way all the minor streams from the hills. Below the Bhabar the streams again appear on the surface but the soil is generally similar in quality. Instead of weeds and grasses, tall trees above a tangled undergrowth of creepers, shrubs and thorny bushes present a barrier to movement which an elephant alone can surmount. The width of the waterless tract is from 8 to 15 kms. South of this lies the Tarai which in general is a tract of forest and swamps with scattered patches of cultivation. The Tarai as we proceed southwards merges into the plains of India.

The Tarai has monsoon climate and the rainfall varies from 120 to 240 cms a year, the eastern portion of the Tarai getting more rainfall than the western portion. The Tarai is the rice and sugarcane producing area of Nepal. At places where the forests have been cut down the Tarai is densely populated and produces food for the country as also for export to Tibet and India.

In the Bhabar and Tarai plains and before the beginning of the inner Himalayan ranges appear at places the low sandy hills called the Churia Ghati Hills. Geologically they are a continuation of the Siwalik ranges in India. Between these smaller hills and the inner Himalayan ranges lie the famous Sal forests at the height of nearly 600 to 900 metres above sea level. The inner Himalayas vary in height from 1000 to 4000 metres above sea level. This region should be considered as a part of the great Himalayan mountains which have been cut in innumerable forms and designs by the forces of nature.

At places the rivers in this region flow east and west. These longitudinal valleys are the most important geographical features of Nepal. The climate of these valleys is salubrious and all types of vegetation prosper according to height. Near the river bed people cultivate rice. They grow wheat, sugarcane, corn, pulses and millets in the terraced fields in the gently sloping hillside. In the hilly areas and away from the valleys the farmers turn to barley, high altitude wheat, potatoes, beans and coarse millets. The smaller rivers collect the rainfall, latitudinally near the highest mountains and longitudinally in their middle courses. They then join together to form great rivers which force their way through the lower hills onto the plains of India.

The Great Himalayas consist of the highest peaks in the world. True to their meaning they are the abode of permanent snow. They present an almost impenetrable barrier between Nepal and Tibet except for a few convenient passes; e.g. (i) the Takla Khar pass, (ii) the Hatia pass, (iii) the Mustang pass, (iv) the Kerong pass, (v) the Kuti pass, leading to Lhasa from Kathmandu, and (vi) the Wallong pass. There is hardly any vegetation in these altitudes and there is hardly any animal life.

The Trans-Himalayas are regions north of the Great Himalayan ranges especially in the Humla and Mustang districts in west Nepal. The Himalayas keep out the monsoon and the rainfall is never more than a drizzle. The vegetation is Tibetan and the main occupation of the people is sheep-rearing and trade between Tibet and the market-centres to the South.

We can now turn our attention to the watersheds and drainage systems of the rivers. There are three great river systems in the country from west to east-namely the Karnali or the Gogra, the Naraini or the Gandak and the Kosi. Sandwiched between these great river systems are the minor valleys and drainage areas of the Kali in the extreme west, the Rapti between the Gogra and the Gandak, the Baghmati between the Gandak and the Kosi and the Mechi in the extreme east. The valleys of the Rapti and the Baghmati had developed the culture and civilisation of the country in past years, particularly in the areas surrounding Palpa and Kathmandu, respectively. These minor river valleys were comparatively larger in area than the great river valleys and were correspondingly richer. Both these valleys were of volcanic origin and, as legends have it great lakes existed there in ancient times.

The area of the Kathmandu valley is about 800 sq. km. and that of Palpa about 450 sq. km., and both are at an elevation of 1200 to 1600 metres above sea level. Both have been rich and prosperous valleys from times immemorial and both have been the seats of great and wise Kings.

Because of its importance, we would describe in some detail the valley of the Baghmati or the Dun of Nepal as the inhabitants call it. It is an oval plateau crossed by numerous streams with an average height of 1500 metres above sea level. It is a gently undulating plain, having an average length of about 32 km. and an average width of 20 to 25 km. The valley is surrounded by mountains on all sides. On the north are Ghyanche (2400) and Shivpuri (2800), to the east Manichur (2200) and Nagarkot (2150), to the South Phulchok (2850) and to the west Champadevi (2450), Chandragiri (3500) and Nagarjun (2100)

The Baghmati rises near Shivpuri and is joined by many streams before it leaves the valley at Pherping through a narrow gorge. The Baghmati is joined by the rivers Vishnumati and Bhadrawati from the west, Rudramati, Manimati, Hanumati and Ikshumati from the east and Prabhawati from the south.

The valley has several places sacred to the Hindus and the Buddhists. There are the Hindu temples, of Pashupati Nath, Guhyeshwari, Telaju, Surji- Binayak, Ganesh and Changa Narain and the

Buddhist shrines of Swayambhu Nath, Buddha Nath and Maha Buddha which are visited every year by thousands of devoted pilgrims from India and Tibet.

The flora of Nepal varies from the tropical to the alpine and on the whole may be said to correspond in the east with the species met with in Sikkim and the west with those of Kumaon; both of which have been extensively studied by the Botanical Survey of India.[6]

As regards her animal wealth Nepal is richer than contiguous areas in India and the wildlife is better preserved. Wild elephants, the tiger, the rhinoceros, the wild buffalo, the sloth bear, the hog deer, chital, and the pig are all found in abundance in the Tarai forests and the leopard in the minor Himalayas. The musk deer and the Nepal dog are to be found nearer the permanent snow-line. The Himalayan birds, continue to enjoy their environment and are not faced with wanton shooting as in several parts of Himalayan India. For those who love plants, birds and animals, Nepal continues to be a paradise and is now better accessible than in the past.[7]

Nepal is greatly handicapped by lack of rapid internal communication systems. There are few telephone and telegraph lines and radio-communication is the main link between Kathmandu and the outlying regions.

There are few motorable roads in Nepal. Kathmandu is now connected by road with Raxaul on the Indian frontier and with Kuti on the Tibetan frontier. A road also connects with Pokhara and Palpa in the west and with Biratnagar in the east. The towns in the Tarai areas are now connected with one another by jeepable fair weather roads. In the interior most roads are merely tracks negotiated by men's feet or on occasions with mules or hill ponies. The cheapest and quickest way to travel from Ilam in the east to Doti in the west is to travel from inland to the nearest Indian railway terminus then by the Indian railway system to the terminus nearest to the other Nepalese town and then negotiate the rest of the way on foot, horseback or jeep. The lack of internal lateral communications is now receiving government's attention and two motorable road systems are planned to span the country from west to east, one along the foothills and one in the inner Himalayas. These two road systems with inter-connecting roads at several points will add to easier and quicker travel facilities.

A description of Nepal's geography cannot be complete without reference to the most prominent Himalayan peaks. The highest peaks also demarcate the three main drainage areas of Nepal; Nanda Devi in

Kumaon (India) and Dhaulagiri peaks skirt the Karnali river system. Dhaulagiri and Gosainthan mark the Gandak system and Gosainthan and Kanchanjungha the Kosi rivers. A little towards west of Kanchanjungha is Gauri-Shankar, Sagarmatha or Mount Everest.[8] The names of these peaks embody the cultural aspirations and history of the people of Nepal. Nanda was the daughter of an ancient king of Kumaon who was gored to death by a buffalo. The peak is named after her and annual fair is held to this day in Almora in memory of that tragic event and young buffalos are slain with one stroke of the Kukri or light sword. The ice-wall round Nanda Devi reminds the local people of the folds in the skirt of their princess who, after her death, was consecrated as the deity of the most magnificent rounded peak in Kumaon. Similarly, Gauri-Shankar or Sagarmatha or Everest reminds the Nepalese of Shiva and his consort, the daughter of the holy Himalayas. Gosainthan is the Abode of the Lord and Dhaulagiri connotes the white Mountain. Kanchanjungha or the Golden Thighs remind us how the seers amongst the ancient Nepalese named their beautiful landmarks as human beings with celestial characteristics. Angular peaks were the homes of the gods and rounded peaks those of the goddesses. Even the rivers were named after celestial damsels and the auspicious 'seven' or 'sapt' designated them as a multitude and not as strictly seven in number. Thus the Nepalese always refer to Kosi and Gandak river systems as 'the sapt Kosi' and the 'sapt Gandiki' and all rivers share the epithet Ganga-the holiest of rivers. Ganga itself connotes that which goes; from the Sanskrit root ga meaning to go.

Lastly a few words are necessary about the influence of geography on the history of Nepal. This can be summarised in the words of Prithvi Narayan Shah that Nepal is a hardy plant embedded by nature between two giant rocks. Nepal, as King Mahendra used to say, is an Himalayan country between India and China. Inspite of the mountainous terrain and the difficulties in inter-communication Nepal has interacted with both its neighbours. Nepali and Hindi are linguistically close to each other and most of the Nepalese near the Tibetan border can speak Tibetan and their own dialect. Every year thousands of Nepalese come to Hindu and Buddhist shrines in India and even greater number of Indians go to Nepal to visit the sacred shrines there. Tibetan and Nepalese Buddhists also travel to each other's countries and are equally welcome in both countries. Nepal's borders on both sides are open and to this day the Nepalese and the Tibetan Bhotias or Highlanders cross and recross the demarcated boundaries with their flocks of sheep, yak and goats. Nepal being poorer than India, every year thousands of Nepalese citizens come as seasonal labourers to the hills of Kumaon, Darjeeling and other neighbouring States. The rich in Nepal and India also find the other country as the cheapest tourist attraction. Nepal also shares with Northern India the rich heritage of Hindi literature.

Nepal has received from eastern Tibet streams of immigrants in the past and the culture and ethos in eastern Nepal has accepted several Tibetan traits. The Tarai has also received hundreds of thousands of immigrants from the neighbouring Indian districts who have now been there for generations. We could well say that Nepal is the meeting ground of the Tibetan and the Indian languages, races and cultures.

Nepal has always been an open country to inhabitants of both her neighbours-Tibetans and Indians alike. For Indians, Nepal was part of the Himalayas studded with holy temples, mountain peaks and valleys. For Tibetans the pony tracks in the valleys formed the corridors through which traders, shepherds and devout Buddhists travelled in winter months to the prosperous trading centres in the plains of India and the Buddhist shrines there. Travel and trade have always been unrestricted. But the Great Himalayas were a barrier to the movement of armies. Thus Nepal, throughout the ages, had large number of dynasties in different principalities which were of Indian princely descent. On the other hand, we do not know of any dynasty in Nepal of Tibetan origin.

Secondly, being mountain country, Nepal has always had small tribal areas or princely territories, concentrated mostly in river valleys. The valleys had wider tracks for ponies and cattle whereas the rest of the country had merely pathways for sheep or goat. There were hardly any tracks for bullock-carts or warrior's chariots. Thus the world of the common people was limited to the area a day's journey from their own village. These areas were controlled by the tribal elders or the local rajas. Like the Swiss cantons, these small principalities had enjoyed sovereign privileges throughout recorded history. The classic examples are the baisi (20) and the chaubisi (24) principalities of medieval Nepal in the Sapt Gandaki and the Sapt Karnali regions. In the eastern part called Sapt Kosi Pradesh by the Nepalese there were as many small rajas and Kiranti tribes.

It was only after Prithvi Narayan Shah that the Nepal Raja's authority was accepted from the banks of the Satlaj in the west to the banks of the Mechi in the east. Even today, the Kingdom of Nepal is governed from Kathmandu only because of the network of radio communications, Nepal Airways and the motor road running throughout the length of the Kingdom in the Tarai. In the mountain county there are hardly any motorable roads and the administrative and political divisions still follow the Gandak, the Karnali and the Kosi basins. The latest reorganisation of administrative regions has also emphasised the importance of river valleys. At present there are, the anchals or regions of Mahakali, Seti, Karnali, Bheri, Rapti, Gandaki, Narayani, Baghmati, Kosi, Mechi (all after names of rivers), Dhaulagiri, Sarmatha (after mountain peaks), Janakpur and Lumbini.

Lastly, we would like to point out that geographical conditions have provided shelter to countless warriors and others who fled to Nepal for fear of their lives and possessions. The near impenetrable Tarai and the trackless mountains provided excellent cover and succour. In very early times the Kirat rulers of north Bihar plains appear to have been driven to the mountain hideouts by the more resourceful Indo-Aryans. Similarly several rulers with their retinues escaped to Nepal because of the pressure from the Saka and Hun invaders from Kashmir and beyond. After the defeat in the first battle of Panipat, the Rajput rajas from the Gangetic plains fled with their women-folk to the sancturies in Nepal. In a short period these warrior rajas displaced the local rajas in the different principalities by marriage, adoption or conquest. Thus most of the baisi (20) and the chaubisi (24) rajas claimed Rajput descent and even Prithvi Narayan Shah traced his ancestors to Chittor-the most renowned Rajput principality in Rajasthan. This trend continued and prominent Lamas from Tibet, Nana Saheb of Kanpur and Begum Hazrat Mahal of Oudh escaped to Nepal when defeated in battle by their adversaries. Thousands of Tibetans also sought refuge in Nepal after the flight of the Dalai Lama to India. And the Nepalese rulers have granted asylum to these refugees on purely humanitarian grounds.

Notes

1 NE = Name of the Saint; Pal=blessed, cherished; hence Nepal. Capt. Eden Vansittart, Notes on Nepal (1896) page 1.

2 The 1981 census registered a population of 15,022,839; male 51.45% and female 48.55%. At that time the ethnic composition was Nepalese 58.4%, Biharis (including Maithili and Bhojpuri) 18.7%, Tharu 3.6%, Tamang 3.5%, Newar 3.0% and others 12.8%. The religious distribution was Hindus 89.5%, Buddhists 5.3%, Muslims 2.7% others 2.5%.

3 Lyde. Continent of Asia, p. 373. In Kathmandu the mean temperature is 15°C and the mean rainfall 150 mm.

4 The only note on the geology of Nepal to be found in the Records of the Geological Survey of India is by H.B. Medicott who visited Kathmandu Valley in 1875. Records of the Geological Survey of India Vol. VIII, part 4, pages 96-101.

5 Article on Nepal in the Imperial Gazetteer of India, Vol. XIX (1908), pages 28-29.

6 The Imperial Gazetteer of India, Vol. XIX, page 29.

7 "Fauna of Nepal" by S.H. Prater, Curator Bombay Natural History Society published as Appendix XIII and "Flora of Nepal" compiled under the authority of the Director of the Royal Botanical Gardens, Kew; published as Appendix XIV to Landon's Nepal, Vol. I.

8 The British Indian Survey of India triangulated the heights of these peaks as follows: Nanda Devi (25,700 ft.), Dhaulagiri (26,826 ft.), Gosainthan (26,305 ft.), Kanchanjungha (28,146 ft.) and Everest (29,002 ft.).

Two

The People of Nepal

A study of the different races that inhabit Nepal is both interesting and rewarding to a student of Nepalese history. Many travellers who have visited no other part of the country except the Kathmandu valley have tried to give us pictures of the racial complexity of Nepal. These attempts have not been quite successful, because, out of the scores of travellers who have written about Nepal, only two were serious students of ethnology, namely Brian Hodgson and Sylvain Levi. It is in their writings only that one finds a scientific attempt at classification and arrangement of the knowledge we have of the different races of Nepal and an effort at essaying their achievements and drawbacks in the pages of history. Other writers merely give us catalogues of some of the representative races and, at the most, unconnected and incomplete accounts of their physiognomy, marriage customs, military aptitudes or religious predilections.[1]

In fact, however, the ethnology of Nepal appears to show to a certain extent the results of the same historical processes that have changed the racial characteristics of the Indian subcontinent. In a way, the study of the ethnology of Nepal helps to a great extent, the study of the ethnology of South Asia. The mountain fastnesses of Nepal have afforded shelter to the aboriginal inhabitants of pre-historic South Asia and still there may be found in out-of-the-way places in Nepal men, women and children living in a state of primitive savagery that could never have been possible in the plains of Hindustan; partly because of over-population there and partly because of competition from superior types. The struggle for existence would by itself have exterminated this early type of humanity in most parts of India. Only in unapproachable places could the bow and arrow still survive as among the Veddas in South India. And in Nepal have been found people who approach the Veddas in the use of primitive weapons and in primitive standards of living. Again, Nepal has provided a refuge for all those races from India which preferred to adhere to their own manners and customs and preserve their identities distinct from the militarily superior races who were forcing their own culture upon the conquered. Also, Nepal has been over-run in part, especially from the north-east, by the Tibetan races, who, in search of warmer valleys, left their homes in the snow covered plateau of Tibet, and migrated with all their flocks to parts of northern and eastern Nepal. In short, we find that geography has introduced Tibetan blood into Nepal from the north and through Sikkim, and history has sent stream after stream of fugitives from the keen struggles for existence, and annihilating conflicts of cultures and values, into the different river valleys, mainly from the south-west.

As a result of these processes Tibetan blood is predominant in the north and east of Nepal and Indian Rajput and Brahmin blood, as distinct from earlier Nepali blood, in the valleys of the Karnali and the Rapti, while some other parts of Nepal preserve to a certain extent the same racial complexion that they did say about 3,000 B.C.

The earliest known inhabitants of Nepal are the Chepang, the Kusunda, and the Hayu tribes. Hodgson thought that they were "like fragments of an earlier population". Their numbers are very small and, like the Veddas of South India, they are decreasing in numbers, as the civilisation of a more vigorous type approached their homesteads in its gradual expansion and search for more living space. These tribes live in the wildest imaginable state of nature. They do not pay any taxes because they have no material possessions except their bows and arrows and skins used as warming material for their bodies. They do not even acknowledge allegiance to the Maharajadhiraj of Nepal or do the bidding of the officials except under threat of immediate punishment. They themselves claim to be the masters of the uncultivated wastelands they subsist in, and decline to have anything to do with the Maharajadhiraj's domain where fields are cultivated and administrative authority is accepted. They, however, sometimes procure arrow-heads made by the village blacksmiths near their forest homes in return for the "Kastura" of the musk deer or other produce of the jungles. Their homes are mostly in the mountain caves which are closed and opened every day in winter with the help of tree trunks, branches, pieces of rock, etc.

Sometimes as Hodgson noticed "boughs torn from trees and laid dexterously together constitute their houses, which they are perpetually shifting according to the exigencies of the hour."

They do not use any implements known to primitive mankind except the bow, which seems to have been their invention. Their only means of subsistence is hunting wild beasts with the bow and arrow, snaring them and catching wild fowl. Cultivation is an art unknown to them. So also are the arts of spinning threads, weaving cloth or pressing wool into felt. Little also is known about their social life and customs and they are said to bury their dead. These nomadic forest tribes have their homeland in the river basins of the Kali, the Seti and the Tirsuli rivers. Some Chepangs are even known to have got themselves enlisted in the Gorkha regiments, calling themselves Magars. Their figures are not very pleasing to the eye and people who have seen them say that they are actually a dirty and ugly race. Hodgson thought the Chepangs to be slightly above the Kusundas and recorded that the former were beginning to hold some slight intercourse with civilised beings and to adopt the most simple of civilised arts and habits. He added that "compared with the mountaineers among whom they are found, the Chepangs are a slight but not actually a deformed race; they are about the same in height but in colour are very decidedly darker or of a nigrescent brown". In one respect, however, Hodgson seems to be wrong. He thought that "linguistically these tribes were allied to the Lhopas of Bhutan (Lho is the native name for Bhutan and hence Lhopa, an inhabitant of Lho). Their language, however is allied to the language of the Mundas and the other Kolarian races found in India. This, however, requires the attention of a good philologist. This work, unfortunately, has not yet been brought to an authoritative conclusion. However, one is led to think that these primitive races represent the "fragments", as Hodgson has so well termed it, of the protoaustraloid races which inhabited the South-Asian mainland in very early times. It is difficult to decide whether the Kusundas, the Chepangs and the Hayus are all representatives of the protoaustraloid race or whether the Kusundas represent an even earlier race-the Negritos-and the Chepangs and the Hayus the protoaustraloids who inhabited parts of South Asia either at the same time as or after the conquest of the Negrito race by them.

The Kusundas and the Chepangs are rarities in Nepal. They are like backwashes of civilisation that linger against the processes of evolution and assimilation in human history. The main and the underlying elements in the Nepalese population are formed by the second groups, namely the Austric race. The most important representatives of this race are the Newars in the valley of Kathmandu, and the Khas in the rest of the country who have contributed most to the culture of Nepal as we know it. The bulk of Nepal's population is either Austric with very little admixture of foreign blood or the product of foreign male mating with the Austric type of female from the higher social classes. These vigorous conquerors from outside with their Vedic learning have given a note of superior culture and manners to the whole community. It is thought by some that the Boksas from Western Nepal, the Newars in the valley of the Baghmati, the Tharus in Western Nepal Tarai, the Mechis in Eastern Nepal Tarai, and many others, are all representatives of the pre-Austric races which points to a different classification. According to this view, the Chepangs, the Kusundas and the Hyus belong to the Negrito race; the Tharus, the Boksas, and the Mechi belong to the protoaustraloid race; and the Newars and the Khas belong to the Austric race. There has been little scientific work done on the subject and definite conclusions cannot be given. On the whole, however, it seems the latter classification will stand up to the test of further investigation.

The Tharus and the Boksas are found in the Tarai and the Bhabar areas. They call themselves Hindus, and Brahmins officiate in their religious ceremonies. They usually burn their dead but are also known to bury them especially if the death is due to snake-bite, cholera or smallpox. Their main occupation is the cultivation of rice.[2] Most Tharus, Boksas and Mechis now live in permanent settlements, cleared in the mid of the dense Tarai forests. They are averse to meet strangers and keep to their primitive self-sufficient economy. They keep pigs and fowl and make their own drink to which they are greatly addicted. They assert that a diet of meat and their strong drink gives them immunity from the dreaded malaria of the Tarai.

Their women are known to rule the household, and to have a more privileged social position than the men. The tribal panchayats are very powerful and all disputes regarding succession, divorce etc. are settled there.

These tribes live in the hills to about 800 metres above sea-level. They inhabit also the hottest valleys with immunity to malarious fevers. They call themselves Hindus, but little Brahminism is in evidence among them. They use no sacred words or prayers and the old men of the tribe themselves officiate as priests. Most of them are illiterate, and, therefore, have great respect for learning and the Brahmins who possess that learning. Hodgson said of them: "In their dark-hued skin, slender forms, oval faces, elevated features and peculiar dialect-barbarous patois as the last now is-may be traced, however, the indispensable signs of a southern origin."[3] The Mechis are akin to the Tharus and Boksas, and it seems that their material difference from the Tharus and the Boksas is that of habitat-the Tharus inhabit the western half of Nepalese Tarai and the Mechis the eastern half. All these races resemble closely the Newars of Nepal, except that the Mechis and the Tharus "have no towns and rarely even live in permanent villages, generally quitting a clearance after having had two or three successive crops from the land, to take up their abodes in a fresh portion of the forest."[4]

The Newars are a civilised people. They are agriculturists and cowherds by occupation and they devote their lives to the arts of peace and the enjoyment of life rather than to military glory. The similarity between Newars and Nayars and the looseness of sexual morality among both these peoples is a hint that at one time the greater part of India was inhabited by these polyandrous tribes of the Austric race. However a common origin for the Newars and the Nayars is not claimed but it seems that both these peoples originally sprang from different branches of the same race.

It seems that before the people with the Vedic civilisation became the masters of the South Asian mainland, an earlier civilisation was flourishing in most parts of India and a people having the same or related blood and civilisation were inhabiting Nepal. These people were of the Austric type and form to this day the largest component of the Nepalese and Indian population. Some remnants of their speech and forms of worship are still to be found throughout Nepal. The temperament of the Newars and their psychological make-up owe a great deal to their early civilisation which must have flourished at the same time as the Mohanjodaro and Harappa civilisation.[5]

Afterwards new races invaded Nepal. The snows of Tibet sent the Bhotias across the mighty Himalayan heights. They came mostly as peaceful settlers from the North, and settled in the upper regions of the Himalayas at heights ranging from 3,000 to 4,000 metres above sea level. Their only possessions were flocks of sheep and yak and their occupation was to look for supplies of food. They also brought their own culture and language with them but in course of time many of them became bilingual. Every year the Tibetans came down in winter to sell wool, borax, salt, musk etc. to the people inhabiting the lower Himalayas as can be seen in trans-Himalayan Nepal to this day, and they returned to their country in spring. It might be that some of these nomadic tribes remained in the Upper Himalayas by choice or in certain years the rigours of the weather forbade their returning home or perhaps the head of the clan fall ill south of the Himalayas and the whole party had to remain with him or perhaps some chief with his followers fled from the fury of his rivals in Tibet and took refuge across the Himalayas. Whatever the particular reason might have been, one thing is certain, that in these altitudes the migrations of the Tibetans have been peaceful and with the tacit permission of their neighbours below them.

But Tibet also sent a number of conquerors to Nepal mainly through Sikkim and the North-Eastern passes. These swarms of Tibetan manhood which moved down in search of warmth upon more fertile soils involved larger numbers than the migrations across the Himalayas. In both cases, however, the Tibetans came with their womenfolk and children (as they do to the present day in their winter sojourns). This custom enabled them to retain their language and culture, and to keep their identity separate. The newcomers through Sikkim, however, were partly absorbed by the conquered. Murmis, Limbus and Rais are all, to some extent, the descendants of Tibetan newcomers to Nepal. They have gradually submitted to Brahminical influence and are now almost completely Hinduised and rank as Kshatriyas. At present any member of those races will feel offended if he is not called a Hindu. It is an honour to be a Hindu Kshatriya in Nepal and, although these races have a great deal of Tibetan blood and a large number of words of Tibetan origin in their vocabularies, yet they all call themselves and want others to call them Hindus. And, therefore, they are Hindus now.

Dr. A. Campbell was interested in these tribes and his investigations may be summarised in his own words as follows:

> I have not met with any Murmis who could give me particulars of their Tibetan origin, all being satisfied with the knowledge of their tribe having at some remote period migrated across the snows from Bhote (Tibet).[6]

Dr. Campbell was also informed by Ilam Sing (Dewan of the Sikkim raja) who was a Limbu himself that "the original country of his tribe was the province of Chung in Tibet". Also about the Magars, he added "they are unquestionably a people of this side of the snows, and the original country is Sikkim from which they were first driven west by the Lepchas across the Mechi and the Konki rivers and thence further west by the Limbus beyond the Arun and the Dodh-Koshi.... As to Gurungs, we people of Tibetan origin have nothing to do with them".[7]

The result of Hodgson's incomparable experience and study deserves the greatest respect and the following is a resume of his main conclusions as regards the races of Nepal.

The "physiognomy exhibits no doubt generally and normally the Scythic or Mongolian type of human kind; but the type is much softened and modified, and even frequently passes into a near approach to the full Caucasion dignity and beauty of head and face, in the same perplexing manner that has been noticed in regard to the other branches of the Allophylian tree, though among the cis or trans-Himalayas there is never seen any greater advance towards the Teutonic blond complexion than such as consists in occasional ruddy mustaches and grey eyes among the men and a good deal of occasional bloom upon the cheeks of the children and women. A pure white skin is unknown, and the tint is not much less decided than in the high caste Hindus; but all are of this pale brown or isabelline hue in Tibet and the Sub-Himalayas, whilst the many in the plains of India are much darker."

The evidence of comparative vocabularies also shows that most of these races are partly of Tibetan origin. Further the creeds, customs and legends of these races also point to the same conclusion. Their legends indicate a transit of the Himalayas from 35 to 45 generations back-say 1,000 to 1,300 years ago. Hodgson preferred the remote period, because, in his view, the transit was certainly made before the Tibetans had adopted from India the religion and literature of Buddhism in the 7th and 8th centuries A.D. This fact is as clearly impressed upon the crude dialects and religious tenets of the Sub-Himalayas as their Tibetan origin is upon their peculiar forms and features.[8]

Lastly we come to the penetration, through South-western Nepal, of the Brahmins and the Rajputs from different parts of India. Tradition has it that most of the high caste Brahmins came to Kumaon and Nepal from Maharashtra or the Gangetic Doab. The Pants are said to have come from Maharashtra, the Joshis from Jhansi, the Tripathis from Kanauj and the Pandes from Kangra. Even today the Gurus of the Nepalese royal family and the nobility in Nepal are Kumaoni Brahmins who themselves trace their original homes outside the Himalayas. Similarly, the high caste Kshatriyas trace their origin back to the Surya and Chandra Vanshi Rajas of Udaipur and other States of Rajasthan. The facts seem to be that Rajputs and Brahmins, of great tenacity and full of idealism, voluntarily retired from the plains of India after they had been defeated by Muslim soldiers on the battle-fields. Some of these refugees were very capable men, and succeeded in creating honoured places for themselves among the people of Nepal. The Rajputs sometimes carved out petty principalities for themselves and the Brahmins, by their learning, established themselves as the ministers and preceptors of the local chiefs. Gradually by the mixture of this foreign blood with the local blood a number of sub-castes of Brahmins and Rajputs grew up. At the same time a number of hill people slowly adopted the titles and manners and creeds of either Brahmins or Rajputs, and inter-marriage sometimes followed between these new Brahmins and Rajputs and the outsiders on terms of equality. But still the main distinctions remained. The hill Rajputs and Brahmins were considered to be not quite their equals by the Rajputs from Rajasthan and the Brahmins from Prayag (Allahabad) and Benares. Thus arose in the Himalayan principalities innumerable sub-castes of Brahmins and the large groups of Kshatriyas collectively called the Khasiyas or the Khas.

The Khas are in fact the backbone of the Himalayan population. They might be called Khasiya Rajputs in Kumaon, and Gorkhas in Nepal (Gorkhas include Khas, Thakurs, Gurungs and Magars). In Doti the Khas blood is more mixed with Kshtriya blood from India than elsewhere in Nepal. The Thakurs claim royal descent, *i.e.* they claim to possess the blood of royal houses from Rajasthan or Nepal itself, and outside marital connections are supposed to show higher social standing.

The Khas race is mentioned in many ancient books. Asoka is said to have given his daughter Charumati in marriage to Devapala-The King of Nepal-who was most probably a Khas. It seems that the Newars and the Khas were two branches of the same Austric race that in early times inhabited the Eastern and the Western parts of the modern kingdom of Nepal. The Khas came more into contact with Hindus from India, the Newars were partly overwhelmed by Tibetan invaders especially in the Eastern extremities of Nepal, and the Tibetan influence in language and blood penetrated even to the tribes which we now call as Gurungs and Magars to the west of the valley of Kathmandu.

Not much is known about the lower castes of Nepal. They are called Doms, and represent perhaps the remnants of the protoaustraloid inhabitants of the country who were subdued by the Austric race (Khas, Newars etc.) and who accepted a lower and servile position in the social organisation of their conquerors. They thus became parts of the dominant Hindu or Buddhist communities and shared some of the benefits of their civilisations whereas the other members of their race who retired to the hills are still as primitive as they were about 1000 B.C. or even earlier.

We should mention the Muslim segment of the population who now number nearly half a million in all. They live almost entirely in the Tarai belt. When Muslim commandars of armies and local potentates rebelled against their superiors in the Gangetic plain, they invariably fled to the Tarai jungles to escape the fury of their suppressors. There has been a significant population of Muslims on both sides of the Indo-Nepalese border ever since the Uzbeg and other Turkish Chieftains were defeated by the Pathans about 1400 A.D. and in turn the Pathans were defeated by the Mughals about 1550 A.D. The gift of part of the Tarai lands to Nepal after 1857 by the British has made a sizeable number of these Tarai Muslims as Nepalese subjects.

This brief account of the races of Nepal brings into focus the presence of several racial elements in most parts of the country. What is to be emphasized is that in Nepal several distinct ethnic sub-groups live side by side in most territorial areas. This is different to what we find in most other countries of the world outside South Asia. Ethnic groups practically monopolise their habitats. Only in South Asia do different ethnic groups live cheek by jowl in the same village, district or region. For this the caste system evolved by the South Asians must take the credit. By segregating people into caste groups on the basis of race, occupation and social habits, South Asians provided an example of deep respect for human life and values. What we now call as human rights were generally upheld by the elders in tribal or territorial groups in the countries on either side of the Himalayas. The ancient sages called it "Sanatan Dharma" or universal and immemorial respect of certain moral values; the Buddhists, the Jains and Mahatma Gandhi called it Ahimsa or Non-violence. Gandhi also phrased this principle as Truth or perception and acceptance of Reality. There are several instances of ethnic conflicts in the history of our world. The Red Indians were totally exterminated in the U.S.A. between the Mississipi and the Atlantic.

In recent history the Armenians and the Jews were sought to be exterminated even in their traditional habitations by the Sultan of Turkey and by Hitler. Amir Habibullah of Afghanistan forced the people of Kafiristan to accept Islam or be done to death. However, the great South Asian tradition has been of tolerance and respect for basic human rights in racial or religious or political conflicts. And the mechanism for achieving these human rights has been the caste system which elevated the status of conquerors, learned men and moral leaders and depressed that of the vanquished, the unlettered and the moral offenders. This complex system organised mainly by the Brahmins has stood the test of time and saved the cultural, moral and peculiar values and traits of hundreds of thousands of human beings throughout these countries. Nepal is a living example of this. And the country is none the less strong or beautiful because of this.

The same values of tolerance and realism are exhibited in the ruling dynasties. They include all members of the caste system from cow-herds, Ahirs, Kiratis, Lichhavis, Thakuri Rajputs to Suryavanshi Rajputs.

From the above, however, we should not conclude that there have been no ethnic or caste conflicts in Nepal. Broadly speaking these conflicts, however, have changed the supreme rulers with little bloodshed and the changes in the caste hierarchy have taken place in an amicable manner thanks to the flexibility in the decisions of the Brahmins and Buddhist monks. But struggles at the very top of the political order have been savage, treacherous and inhuman. The treatment of the defeated Newars at Nayakot by Prithvi Narayan Shah, the deposition and exile of the Kala Pandes in early nineteenth century by Bhim Sen Thapa, the arrest and suicide by Bhim Sen, the Prime Minister for 35 years; the assassination of Matabar Singh in 1845, and the massacre of the Kot in 1846 when nearly all the top-most Sardars were extirpated amply prove the ferocity of the power struggle. Fortunately this orgy of violence was limited to the wielders of power at the top only. A recent example is the patronage of the Newars by the King in the post 1960 years in place of the Brahmins and Thakurs particularly the Ranas. However, even this patronage has mellowed down and heads do not roll now when power changes hands.

Below the top echelons come the senior civil and military officers and the Subbas or heads of government offices. Power and prestige come from the office one holds in the government apparatus. With the advent of competitive examinations for government offices an expanding middle class has emerged. Their numbers are added to by modern businessmen and professionals, doctors, teachers, journalists, lawyers etc. The influence of the middle classes, however, is not great and Nepal will have to witness a democratic revolution before the mass of the people apart from government officers, will influence policies and their implementation.

Notes

1 See Landon's Nepal, Vol. II; Appendix xvii; The Races sof Nepal, pp. 239-46; also Sylvain Levi: Le Nepal Les Novars at Les Gurkhas, pp. 219-78; also Eden Vansittart; Notes on Nepal, pp. 56-187.

2 See Crooke, Castes and Tribes of North-Western Provinces and Oudh, Vol. IV, pp. 380-406; also Census of India 1931, United Provinces of Agra and Oudh, Part I. The Tharus in the UP allege that they originally lived in the hills of Nepal. The powerful Panchayat of the UP Tharus and Boksas is a typically Nepalese institution.

3 Hodgson, J.A.S.B. (1840), p. 1121.

4 J.A.S.B., Vollume II, (1839), p. 623.
The following account of the Mechis in this article is true in its essentials to the present day: "They are addicted to trade, are averse to military service, have no artisans among them, are truly in a very primitive state of society. They are, however, very cheerful, have no jealousy or prejudice towards strangers, are industrious and honest and crimes of violence, are of rare occurrence among them."

5 See "Newars-An Eassay on the history of Newar Culure" by K.P. Chattopadhyay in J.A.S.B. (1923), p. 465. An exhaustive bibliography will be found in the footnotes to this essay. His conclusions, however, suffer from the defect of his never having visited the Nepal Valley. The best account of the Newars, however, still remains the classical description of these people by Sylvain Levi.

6 J.A.S.B. (1842), p.4.

7 Ibid., pp. 4-5.

8 J.A.S.B., XVL, pp. 1238-1389.
"Selections, from the Records of the Government of Bengal", No. XXVII, Papers relative to the colonization, commerce, physical geography, etc. of the Himalaya Mountains and Nepal by B.H. Hodgson. The following papers may particularly be seen: (i) On the Aborigines of the Sub-Himalayas; (ii) Comparative vocabulary of the several languages, dialects of the Eastern Sub-Himalayas; (iii) Origin and classification of the military tribes of Nepal; (iv) On the Chepang and Kusunda ribes of Nepal; (v) Note on Nayakote and the remarkable tribes inhabiting it.

Three

Society and Religion

Nepal is said to be a country with a static structure of society. This is the result of the acceptance by the vast majority of people of "Sanatan Dharma" or the ancient customs and social norms; or in other words of the Hindu view of life. The traditional mode of life includes the cultural heritage from pre-Vedic ancestors and permeates most of their observations, customs and celebrations. It also forms the mental background for the attitudes and spiritual ideals that have held undisturbed sway over the minds of the peoples inhabiting the entire territory of Nepal. A conservative attitude towards all aspects of human activities and a genuine respect for a spirit of toleration are the two main characteristics of this popular mode of life in Nepal and in South and South-East Asia. Only in recent years has a revolutionary tendency inspired the minds of their people educated into western systems of thought and behaviour which has led them to challenge the accepted norms and build a new society. Of such persons there is still great dearth in Nepal. This is why the Government of Nepal itself and the British Indian Government as her ally had been able to preserve the status quo in Nepalese society till the end of British rule in India. Peace time governments dislike violent or revolutionary breaks from the past because any great change would certainly undermine the strength of the people in power especially when these men have the monopoly of power. In Nepal an equilibrium had been achieved in society which could be preserved only upon the solid foundations of Hindu tenets of thought and action. Some would call this a stagnant structure of society and would like to blame the people in power for having kept modern civilisation and outlook towards life away from the millions of human beings in Nepal. However, one might be excused if one presumes that at present there is an industrial and materialist civilisation obtaining in most parts of the world and that inspite of many of its faults, this civilisation is more adapted towards industrial development and modernisation than the civilisation of former times dominated by an autocratic class and an exclusive church. In that sense Nepal has started to change in recent years.

In Nepal social classes are quite distinct. From 1850 to 1950 at the top was the Rana family. Practically all power and the highest offices of state were monopolised by members of this family. Then somewhat lower down e.g. for the rank of colonels in the army or district executives or bara hakims etc. the cadre was chosen from the less fortunate members of this family or from associated families. Next came another important class of officials. These were the Kazis, Subbas etc. who were recruited mostly from the Newars and sometimes from the Brahmins. They acted as superintendents and head clerks of offices and a great deal of official routine was in their exclusive charge. These three classes viz. the Ranas, the higher executive officials and the clerical officials formed the privileged classes. Since 1950, however, the royal family and its relations have assumed the highest privileges and social esteem. After the royal family now come the royal advisers e.g. ministers of State and higher officials and the new cadre of senior army officers, and administrators. Engineers, doctors and academics are still rare and more so outside Kathmandu.

Among the unprivileged classes would come the shopkeepers, some of them now fairly rich, the agriculturists, craftsmen, labourers and the ordinary soldiers.

Apart from this division some sort of superiority is still asserted by the Gorkhas and allied races who think the Bhotia, the Newar and even some newly assimilated tribes namely the Gurungs and the Magars as being inferior to themselves.

The main characteristic of society in Nepal is its division into innumerable groups. It is interesting to study how lack of communications segregates human beings into small tribal or caste entities, and how such an economically self-contained village, as a unit of social organisation, contributes to the strengthening of the Hindu caste system and the sanctions behind it. The world in which such a peasant works, lives and dies is hardly a day's journey to his East or West, North or South. In other words, his entire world lies within a radius of about twenty kilometres from his village. The world of his actions and emotional, social, cultural and economic existence is self sufficient and independent of similar units lying in the farther localities of the country and with his mind circumscribed within these narrow limits, he is bound to establish inside this tiny world various gradations and differentiations as between different members of society. His first attachment is to his family and then to the caste or sub-caste in which he was born. There is hardly anything else beyond these two concrete social ties which claims or inspires his intelligence or loyalty. The words "race" and "country" so fashionable in the modern world are quite unknown to him and but for a few decades had been non-existent in his vocabulary. Perhaps in his native dialect the word "race" or its equivalent meant his caste or family and the word "country" the area around his own village.

Thus in Nepal we find society divided horizontally into innumerable sections which owe their origin primarily to their localities or the mixture of different races, and are magnified by the analytical niceties of Hindu philosophy and popular religion. The process of rising up or going down the social scale is easier for whole groups like the Gurungs and the Magars than for individuals. Generally, the whole caste or at least some families in it rise or fall in social estimation together. This social process is in complete contrast to what usually happens in a Western country e.g. England. There the individual goes up or down the social scale by himself. The upper classes usually absorb talent from the lower strata of society, marry it into their own group and give it at least some of the facilities which they had reserved for themselves. In Nepal, this process is coming gradually and such instances have occurred only in quite recent times.

There is little difference in the life-style of the people in a village or a small town. The towns are few and far between and consist mostly of a few official buildings and a certain number of shops. The houses in the towns are slightly better than in the villages and the shops contain slightly more and varied articles for sale than those in isolated villages. The people about town are a little more polished in their manners and speech and are more familiar with the officers and their official duties than their totally ignorant brethren in the villages. But there are hardly any industries in the towns except at Biratnagar and Birganj and only Kathmandu can boast of a couple of modern technical schools and a university. There are hardly any amenities such as cinema houses, hotels etc. or exchange centres for culture and knowledge such as higher schools, clubs, theatres etc. in most of the towns except Kathmandu.

Nepal is a Hindu Kingdom, and her inhabitants are mostly classified as Hindus. But Hinduism is a word lacking in precision and embraces within its fold the philosophical Brahmin as well as the primitive Kusunda who has by now learnt to have a tiny stone emblem representing some god or an evil spirit whom he worships in his own way. But religion is as important in Nepal as it is in the rest of South Asia. The main reason for this is lack of any substitute for religion. The majority, therefore, take to religion as the only outlet for their emotions, and deeper mental activities.

The main elements of Hinduism in Nepal, to a modern analyst, seem to be toleration; a self imposed isolation from the ideas, customs and manners of outsiders; an emphasis on renunciation and a placid attitude towards life. In Nepal Hinduism, however, has been in an expansive mood. It does not proselytise; it simply absorbs. In Nepal within the Hindu fold are to be found learned Brahmins who are quite conversant with Vedic and Puranic literature, the military tribes collectively called Kshatriyas which include the Surya and Chandra Vanshi Rajputs, the Gorkhas, the Khas, the Gurung, and the Magars, part of the Newar population, some Bhotias and even some animist tribes living in jungles and marshes. But a benevolent spirit of toleration pervades the entire country. Both Hinduism and Buddhism are tolerated and respected almost equally by the rulers and the leaders of society .There are, however, differences between the Buddhists and the Hindus in their rituals, sacraments, religious celebrations, birth, death and marriage rites etc. The prevalent form of Buddhism is akin to the Tibetan type although a couple of Hinayana "Bihars" or monasteries are found even near Kathmandu itself.[1]

Hinduism in Nepal is afraid of everything that lacks Sanskritic authority. The laws of Manu still form the mainsprings of the laws of the land. The ideas which brought into existence Sikhism, Brahmo Samaj and Arya Samaj in India got their first stimulating drive from the impact of Hinduism with Islam and Christianity. But Islam and Christianity never entered Nepal and hence the traditional authority of Hinduism continued unchallenged and undisturbed till recent times when modern Indian culture with its discovery of the conflicts and contradictions in old established values began to penetrate into Nepal through innumerable channels of intercommunication. The belief in pre-determined fate and futility of human endeavours against it has been challenged and a positive outlook towards life has been placed before the masses by the reformists both in India and Nepal. The demand for constitutional and responsible Government is only a part of the general questioning of established values by those who have witnessed mighty changes being wrought about in India and elsewhere after the Second World War.

The prevailing form of Hinduism in Nepal will, however, be found to include:-

(i) some aspects of Brahmanism e.g. Vedic hymns and passages from the Smritis are often quoted, honoured, and enforced;

(ii) some aspects of Buddhism,
(iii) some aspects of Buddhist Tantras and Hindu worships of Shiva and his consort Shakti, and
(iv) some remnants of devil worship.

Brahmanism is still a great force. Cows are held in great esteem and cow slaughter is unthinkable. Killing the holy cow is one of the most heinous offences and entails the severest punishment. The rules of marriage prescribed by Manu are honoured and the Shudras still suffer from the disabilities fastened on them by the ancient Hindu lawgivers. The great durbars during festivals are held with Puranic rites and large numbers of Brahmin attendants. It could be mentioned here that both in Nepal and Thailand royal ceremonies are started with Brahmanical rites though the Buddhist monks dominate the later ceremonies in Thailand. In Nepal, the Brahmins especially the Raj Gurus hold pride of place exclusively and continuously.

Buddhism has also influenced the common man irrespective of the fact of his being a Buddhist. Buddha has become a Hindu God-one of the ten incarnations. Practically all the Hindus of the Kathmandu valley take part in Buddhist festivals and offer prayers and offerings in Buddhist temples.

Buddhist Tantras and Hindu Shaiva practices have much in common. It is sometimes very difficult to distinguish between the two. These practices are the hertiage of the occult form of Hindu-cum-Buddhist religion which prevailed in large parts of South and Central Asia between the 8th and the 12th century A.D. They manifest similar human fancies as we witness in the praying wheels of the Tibetans, and the rosaries of other religions. Tantras are supposed to be short cuts to religious grace and occult power. In order to draw the ignorant and the slothful towards religion, the priests proclaim that particular religious practices bestow miraculous powers. Then gradually religious values are lost sight of by the multitude as well as the elite and supernatural powers become the only objectives for religious observances. Paths have to be discovered to obtain these powers and elaborate designs, sounds and rites are prescribed to satisfy individual fancies. Sometimes this hankering after weird designs, sounds and practices degenerates into ritualistic satisfaction of animal desires but such extremes are not as common as some authors would like us to believe.

It is very difficult, however, to appraise the popular Shaivism of the people. They are fond of good food and are greatly addicted to sacrificing fowl, goats and buffaloes to their innumerable gods and goddesses who in some form or other, are supposed to be connected with Shiva or the destructive symbol of supernatural power. There are many temples of Shiva in Nepal, the most important being the great temple of Pashupatinath in Kathmandu and the shrine of Muktinath. The most favoured temple of the Tantriks is that of Guhyeshwari near that of Pashupatinath in Kathmandu.

It would not be out of place here to refer to the sect of Kanfata jogis in Nepal. They claim themselves to be the followers of Gorakhnath about whom legend and history are not wanting either in Nepal or in India. What exactly are the tenets of their creed is not yet definitely known. Sometimes "Aughars" or Kapaliks are also included amongst them. These Kapaliks live near burning ghats and find themselves at home amongst corpses, half-burnt human skulls etc. But usually the Gorakhnaths or the Naths have families and are agriculturists by profession. They are distinguished from their fellow villagers only in that they hang large rings made of bones or horns of animals from their ears in the centres of which holes about the size of peas are cut through.[2]

Gorakhnath is supposed to be the special protector of the Gorkhas and the coinage of Nepal bears his name on one side and of the ruling king on the other.

The social customs in Nepal are much the same as in other parts of India. Except in the case of high caste Brahmins and Rajputs, "marriage has little religious significance. It is merely an institution to regulate sexual relationship and an arrangement for bringing up childern."[3] Usually the bride-price is paid before marriage and marriages by proxy e.g. Kumbha biyah or Pratima biyah are not unknown. Widows can remarry and girls are sometimes known to give up one man and live with another. Sexual relationships are established merely by consent of the partners and their guardians. No elaborate ceremonies are essential. Also the custom of a brother taking his deceased brother's widow is found in some places in Nepal. But among the Brahmins and the Rajputs marriage laws are as strict as among the high caste people in India.[4]

At the present time, it is difficult to ascertain the religion of the ordinary inhabitants of the Kathmandu Valley. There are some who are unmistakably Buddhists and there are others who are definitely Hindus, but in between come a very large class of people who might be Buddhist Shaivas or Shaivite Buddhists. In other words, the popular forms of Shaivism and Buddhism are so much alike that it becomes extremely difficult to differentiate between them. In 1880, H.A. Oldfield thought that Hindus formed only about one-third of the Newar population; [5] but in 1939 less than one quarter of the population was officially reported to be Buddhist. Buddhism appears to have been assimilated by Hinduism and Hindus regard the Buddhists as some of their own castes.

The "Banhras" or priests amongst the Buddhists have the highest social standing as the Brahmins have among the Hindus. The "Udas" are a mercantile community like the "Vaisyas". The third and largest class is that of "Jaffus"; who correspond to the "Shudras" and are agriculturists and craftsmen.

"Banhra" is a corrupt form of the Sanskrit word Bandya *i.e.* respected. They are divided into nine different classes, each following some hereditary following. "Socially, all nine classes of Banhras are on terms of perfect equality; they eat together and intermarry among one another promiscuously, but they will neither eat nor intermarry with any other Newars who are not Banhras.[6]

"The 'Udas' consist of seven different classes, the first of which is Udas; but this name has been applied collectively to the whole order, this one class being the most extensive and important in it".[7] In fact the Udas are the descendants of the Buddhist laymen, as the Banhras are of the Buddhist monks. The Udas also eat together and intermarry amongst themselves only.

The next lower group of Buddhists mainly follows agriculture and handicrafts. The agriculturists are called Jaffus and have six classes. Below them are several castes of handicraftsmen. And lowest come butchers; certain classes of musicians; charcoal makers; workers in leather; fish-catchers; sweepers; and washermen.

However, on all subjects relating to the laws of caste and Dharma, the Buddhist Newars are under the jurisdiction of the Raj Guru, who always consults Hindu as well as Buddhist scriptures when deciding cases involving Buddhists. This has contributed towards the assimilation of Buddhism into Hinduism although sometimes assemblies of Vajra-Acharyas (the highest order of Buddhist priests) are convened to lay down the meaning of disputed texts in the scriptures, but they have not been numerous during the last many years.

Another institution which is bringing together Hindu and Buddhist Newars is the "gatti". It is the assembly of all the members of a particular caste, and its decisions are binding upon all irrespective of religion. The main concern of the "gattis" is to assign to every family in each class certain hereditary duties connected with the national festivals, and with the celebration of public ceremonies of a religious character. The ultimate sanction behind all these laws of the gatti is loss of caste, which is dreaded equally by the Buddhist and the Hindu Newars.

In Nepal, the highest object of Buddhist worship is Adi Buddha or Adi Prajna *i.e.* the Supreme Being. He is the origin and First cause of All. All the principal temples in Nepal are dedicated to Adi Buddha and his spirit is believed to pervade and sanctify these edifices; but the person of the supreme deity is never represented either in sculpture or in painting. Homage is paid to Adi Buddha under the form of a flame of fire, which, drawn direct from the rays of the sun, is regarded as the only legitimate emblem of the Supreme Being, and of the divine light with which He illumines the world. His all-seeing power is typified in the pair of eyes which are always figured on each of the four sides of the capital or toran of every chaitya. The 'Tri-Ratna' *s*, Buddha, Dharma and Sangha are the next most sacred and commonest objects of worship. Then come the five (or, according to some, six) Divine Buddhas with their respective Shaktis or consorts, and Bodhisatvas. And after the 'divine' rank the 'mortal' Buddhas with their Shaktis and Bodhisatvas, forming an innumerable host; of whom, however, only the last seven-ending with Sakya Singh or Gautama Buddha-possess any practical interest.

Of all these divine and mortal Buddhas only four are worshipped commonly. These are the divine Buddha, Amitabha, the father of Padma Pani; the divine Bodhisatva, Padma Pani, the creator of the existing universe; the mortal Buddha, Sakya Singh, the founder of the Buddhist religion; and the mortal Bodhisatva Manjushri, who introduced Buddhism in Nepal.

The Newars, who had introduced the Hindu system of caste amongst themselves, were gradually led at first to tolerate, then to respect and finally even to worship many of the gods of the Hindus. At last the images of Hindu gods were admitted into Buddhist temples and they received from the people their proper share of worship and homage. The Hindu deities whose images are most frequently met with in Buddhist temples are Bhairava, Mahakal, Devi Bhairavi, Ganesha, Indra and Garur.

Sometimes the complicated designs and formulae of the Tantriks are also seen about the precincts of Buddhist temples. The Buddhist temples in Nepal may be divided in the same three classes as Cunningham divides the Buddhist monuments of Central India, namely:-

(1) The dedicatory, which are sacred to the supreme deity;

(2) The memorial, which were built upon celebrated spots; and

(3) The strictly funeral, which contain the ashes of the dead.

Of these the most important and peculiarly Buddhist are the dedicatory temples. They are generally dedicated to the supreme deity or Adi Buddha and are always chaityas or mound-temples. They are usually of considerable size and have a more or less lofty spire; and there is, in most cases, a monastery or Vihar attached to them.

The most essential and characteristic feature of the chaitya is the simple and massive hemisphere or solid dome of masonry which forms its lower part, and which in some cases, rises abruptly, without any intervening plinth, from the basement on which it stands; while in other cases it is connected with its basement, by a narrow cylindrical plinth of stone or of brick.

The nature and form of the basement vary considerably, in different temples. In some the plinth itself constitutes the only basement; in others a raised and narrow step runs like a pathway round the base of the temple; while more commonly, the basement is formed by a range of three terraces, of greater or lesser height and width, rising one above another, and on the uppermost of which the hemisphere rests. This hemisphere or dome is called the "garbh". The top of the hemisphere or "garbh" is somewhat flattened and is crowned by a square capital, the upper and lower edges of which are ornamented by a cornice. This capital is called the 'toran' and on each of its four sides are always painted or sculptured, a pair of long, obliquely placed and half closed eyes. These organs, as sources of light, are regarded as typical of the all-seeing omniscience of Adi Buddha.

The "toran" forms the basement to a more or less acutely conical or pyramidal spire, which invariably consists of thirteen segments or divisions, typical of the thirteen Buddhist heavens. The spire itself which is called "churamani", may be either circular or square, and may be constructed either of stone, of brick or of wood. It is built round, and supported by, a long and upright beam as its axis, the upper end of which forms the top of the spire, and has resting upon it a copper-gilt bell-shaped ornament called the 'Kalas' or 'Kalsa'. Sometimes over or round the base of this bell-shaped 'Kalas' an ornamental "chhatra" or cylindrical canopy is erected, which rests, by long and light supports, upon the uppermost of the thirteen segments of the spire.

There is hardly a Newar festival in the valley which can be said to be purely Hindu or purely Buddhist. In many Hindu festivals, as at the Indra Jatra, Banhras officiate as priests, and crowds of Buddhist Newars are seen assisting at their celebrations and joining in the worship of the Hindu deities.

On the other hand, the Hindus regard the Buddhist deities as eminent saints; they visit their temples and join in the festivities in their honour, even those of the most exclusively Buddhist character, as the Machendra Jatra. This is partly due to the fact that these religios ceremonies are observed in Nepal much as Christmas is kept in Europe as a season of feasting and festivity, rather than as one of prayer and religion.

The festival in honour of Machendranath is the most important Buddhist festival in Nepal. The Nepalese (Gorkhas and Newars alike) say that rain invariably falls at the time when the Machendra Jatra takes place. It is held in the month of "Chait", the first month of the Hindu-cum-Buddhist calender, and the image is washed and dragged in a triumphal car through the principal streets of Patan and it ends by exhibiting Machendranath's shirt to the people. The festival extends over a period of about two months. The Gorkhas, including the king and the Prime Minister take part in the procession, and this is one of the reasons why this festival is so important.

Of the other festivals the most important are Shivratri, Holi, Indra Jatra and Dashara or Durga Puja the last being almost the national festival. Thousands of male buffaloes are publicly sacrificed during the DASHARA. There is great rejoicing and the entire court, the gentry and the populace at Kathmandu puts a gay appearance. Men, women, and children put on their best clothes; shops and houses are decorated and temples and public places are filled with crowds. For the entire period of ten days a wave of gaiety sweeps over the country and the people forget their poverty and personal sorrows. Another celebrated festival is that of Shivratri in early spring when large crowds from all over India visit the sacred shrine of Pashupatinath at Kathmandu. Yogis and devout Hindus attach particular importance to this temple of Shiva where he is worshipped as the lord of the animal kingdom. The temple is surrounded by the pilgrims and it is after three or four days that the last of the pilgrims gets a chance to throw his offerings into the enclosure of the deity.

Notes

1 For further details about Buddhism in Nepal, see Sylvain Levi, Le Nepal. Paris. (3 volumes).
2 See Atkinson. Volume II. pages 771 et seq.
3 India Census, XVIII, U.P., part I, page 566.
4 See Dr. L.D. Joshi, The Khas Laws of Kumaon.
5 H.A. Oldfield, Sketches from Nepal, Volume 2, page 131.
6 H.A. Oldfield, Sketches from Nepal, Volume 2, page 139.
7 Ibid., p. 145 et. seq. The rest of this Chapter generally follows Oldfield's description of Buddhism as found in the valley of Kathmandu.

Four

The Nepalese Personality

A few years back it was difficult for an outsider to find a sizeable number of men of strong character and determined personalities among the elite of Nepal. The educated and the intelligent in general were not prepared to make sacrifices for freedom of expression and association which breeds and nurses sturdiness of character. The whole social atmosphere of Nepal was overcast by the superiority and the legal powers assumed by a hereditary aristocracy. In Nepal, there were till recent years no constitutional rights of the citizen guaranteed by the laws of the State. In the last resort, sovereign law was the will of the King. Irrespective of his own goodness, the King represented a system of government which was run for a family and which could not tolerate, by the very nature of its hereditary composition, any talent outside the circle of its own hand-picked men. The irremovable government run by the King's nominees did not desire to be embarrassed by the criticism of its own citizens and the best way it found to keep them silent was to be wary and jealous of their achievements. The people in Nepal were made extremely suspicious of one another and that suspicion increased as you tried to mix with the higher circles. People, therefore, did not express themselves freely and frankly; every one that counted seemed to be putting on a mask or a dumb face when you asked him about the social and political problems of his country. Again the punishments one was liable to undergo for any political offence were heavy and ruthless and the people were constrained to bear a lot at the hands of the officials and keep the tribulations of the misuse of official powers to their own hearts. It was difficult under such a social environment to bring up men and women of character as are to be found in the democratic and more advanced countries of the world. On the whole, it would not have been fair in Nepal to expect scores of men of strong character and fully integrated personalities emancipated to a great extent from the bonds and restrictions of their surroundings. Nepal, however, unlike most other autocracies did produce men of character on a large enough scale in the last few years, thanks to its proximity to Gandhi's India and Mao's China.

But, in a slightly different cannotation, the character of the Gorkhas may be said to possess strong and unbending characteristics. The Gorkhas are a fine type of humanity. If discipline and efficiency be the only qualities of civilised man, then the Gorkhas are perhaps more civilised than any other race on earth.. Discipline and efficiency have almost become a mania with these people. From early childhood, the Gorkha boys delight in marching in columns, turning left and right at the words of their leaders and doing the jobs entrusted to them with machine like precision. The Gorkhas are known throughout the world to be the best guards and pretorian guardsmen. There is a certain military smartness and hardihood in them which differentiates them from the rest of the Asian people. They share many qualities with the Pathans but bear more unquestioned loyalty to their employers than- them.[1] In most respects they stand on par with the Sikhs as a military people.

But the great weakness with the Gorkhas is their illiteracy and consequent narrow and cramped outlook. The standard of living is very low and there are few avenues to success, fame and wealth open to the common people. Those who are born in the dominant families monopolise most of the posts at the disposal of the government. The traders have no social standing or prestige and their earnings are never quite fabulous. The common people were destined by the laws of the state to be either peasants or soldiers. There was hardly any socially profitable outlet for the genius of individuals and there were hardly any opportunities for them to achieve anything great in art, literature, industry or commercial enterprise. "As their ancestors have been in the past, so must they be at present"- was the social and administrative rule.

Amongst the common people one may discern three types. Firstly, one forcibly comes into contact with the martial Gorkhas. In an interesting passage B.H. Hodgson one of the first British Residents in the country gives us a summary of their military qualities:

> These highland soldiers, who despatch their meals in half an hour and satisfy the ceremonial law by merely washing their hands and face and taking off their turbans before cooking, laugh at the pharisaical rigour of our sipahis, who must bathe from head to foot, and make pooja, ere they begin to dress their dinner, must eat nearly naked in the coldest weather and cannot be in marching trim again in less than three hours.

> In war the former readily carry several days provisions on their backs; the latter would deem such an act intolerably degrading. The former see in foreign service nothing but the prospect of glory and spoil: the latter can discover in it nothing but pollution and peril from unclean men and terrible wizards, goblins and evil spirits. In masses, the former have all that indomitable confidence each in all, which grows out of national integrity and success: the latter can have no idea of this sentiment which maintains the union and resolution of multitudes in peril, better than all other human bonds whatever.[2]

The second type one comes across in Nepal is typified by the Newars. In contrast to the pugnacious Gorkhas, the Newars are a mild and submissive people. It is well known that the Newars especially those of Kirtipur fought magnificently against the Gorkha army of Prithvi Narayan Shah, but seven generations of political servitude have now cowed down the spirits of these people considerably. The Newars are essentially husbandsmen. They cultivate the fields, engage in business and furnish clerks in the various departments of the state. They like luxuries and a luxurious life and the hard life of a soldier is not to their liking. They are not admitted to the army, as a matter of state policy, and that might explain their non-martial propensities of character, which however, make them on the whole a loveable people. Most of the foreigners who have visited Nepal, had nothing but kind words to say of them, especially so Sylvain Levi who still remains our classical authority on the character and civilisation of the Newars.

The Newars are a people that loves beauty and all beautiful things that abound in life. In dress they are a colourful people and their women know hundreds of ways of decorating the hair and making themselves look lovelier and more attractive. They take meat, eggs and fish and a lot of wine. In their personal habits, too, they are fond of the pleasures that this world can provide and community dancing and merry making are common occurrences of Newar social life. They have a natural inclination towards art but at present their abilities are seldom utilised by the officials or the wealthy. The Newars, in short, are a romantically minded people and will progress greatly in all the various arts of peace once they are given encouragement and opportunities.

Thirdly, we come to the Brahmins, the Buddhist monks and the Nath panthi Sadhus. All these are necessary components of Eastern civilisation where religion always finds a position of great eminence. They guide the religious life of the population into traditional paths and society pays them for doing so. They are mostly harmless men themselves, but a young man with modern economic outlook would readily question their social utility, economic or otherwise.

About the character of the fourth type namely the upper most circles of society, it is rather difficult to generalise. This social group which has produced administrators and high officers for the state service for more than a couple of hundred years, stands at the apex of society and politics in Nepal. It monopolises power, prestige and wealth, and the fairest ladies in Nepal are to be seen within its fold. Huge palaces with high walls enclosing huge compounds point to the splendour and luxury that roll within them. This class till a few years back possessed almost the entire wealth of the nation and occupied all the important offices of State. There is being voiced a strong protest by the newly educated youngmen against the monopoly of power by these families. Education on western lines in Nepal has increased unemployment and has given the educated people the wine of Western thought. "Power corrupts people and absolute power corrupts absolutely", re-echo these youngmen. Some of the most vociferous of these rebels had been put into prison but a few made good their escape into India, from where they directed their crusades against the ruling circles.

It is highly probable that in an aristocratic and exclusive class some irregularities of conduct and even some cases of oppression might occur. It is also probable that the educated unemployed should cast aspersion for all evils on those who are in sole charge of affairs to the exclusion of their own class the intellectual middle class.

However, the royal and the Rana families and others related to them have produced, generation after generation, men of great ability and character. Families which have produced Maharaja Prithvi Narayan Shah, Kings Tribhuwan and Mahendra and Ranas Jung Bahadur, Chandra and Padma Shamshers and others are families that can claim the highest honour and respect. The aristocracy in Nepal, as in other countries, is self-confident, proud and keeps itself aloof from the common folk. They realize the responsibilities of their unique heritage and from early childhood are introduced to the intricacies of the job of governing people. Some of the old members of these families have had little modern education, but the younger generations have been given the best education available. The strength of these families lies in the fact that they know that they are born to rule and that the whole of Nepal, in accordance with traditional family laws, is the common inheritance of their families. This breeds in them that self confidence which is the one great secret of preserving and asserting power. Also the avoidance of social, marital or other intercourse with the common people preserves in the ordinary mind the latters' inherent superiority and right to positions of authority.

In a way recent Nepalese history is a record of the doings and failings of these great families. The eras of efficient administration are interspersed with periods of bloodshed in which rival parties from these very families have cut one another's throats. These blood baths have marred the achievements and the greatness of these families. They point to the fact that behind their administrative ability and strength lie the formidable drawbacks of intrigue, suspicion, cruelty and other dark passions of powerful aristocracy. However, it is very likely that such incidents will become matters of past history in the days to come. On the whole, the aristocracy in Nepal, inspite of its failings, has provided Nepal with an efficient administration and peace for the ordinary men, benefits not to be lightly disparaged. This is the claim made by the supporters of the present aristocracy and it will be difficult to refute it. But the question, however, remains: "Have not the people of Nepal paid too dearly for these benefits and have not national wealth, the educational and cultural progress of the common people and development of their character and personality suffered terribly because of the all powerful aristocracy?"

Notes

1 There is a story about a Pathan orderly of an English Army Officer who was travelling in the Frontier area guarded by this Orderly. It so happened that while the officer was taking some movies of the landscape, a few Pathan women passed across the range of his camera. The orderly, who was in other respects a faithful servant of his employer, could not bear this sight and stabbed the Englishman dead.

However, such things can never be imagined in the cas of a Gorkha. He is always sincere, once and for all and under all circumstances. The story of the Gorkha Company under the U.N. in Lebanon comes readily to mind. The invalding Israili army with massive tanks, guns, helicopters and fighter bombers was refused passage across the bridge-head which the Gorkhas had to guard. The Israili afraid to kill the Gorkhas to the last man, withdrew and crossed the river at a different point after making temporary bridge.

2 B.H. Hodgson on "Original Classification of the military tribes of Nepal" J.A.S.B., II, pages 217-224. See also Capt. E. Vansittant (J.A.S.B. 1895) & Major L.A. Waddall (Among the Himalayas-pages 309-4) for instances of the valour and military virtues of the Gorkhas.

Five

Art and Literature

It used to be said that in Nepal the arts of peace were monopolised by the Newars and the arts of war by the Gorkhas. This, however, is not the whole truth. In the valley of the Baghmati the Gorkhas came and have remained as the conquering race and naturally they have become the consumers of the finest products of art and craftmanship of the Newar people. In and around this valley the Newars are in a preponderating majority and hence most of the occupations are filled by them. Also the best craftsmen of the country are found in this valley because of its having been the centre of government of the Newar Rajas, then of the Gorkhas and also because it is the residence of most of the rich members of the ruling families. Other places in the Kingdom could not and cannot afford to keep craftsmen of outstanding brilliance. The Newars as a whole, are a people with a delicate sense of beauty, and they have long standing traditions of art. The old Newar princes used to encourage, foster and favour works of art in stone, wood and metal; and thousands of sculptural monuments in this valley testify to their patronage and superb taste. Some of these artistic traditions have been lost for want of sympathy and encouragement from the men in power. However, a few artists of outstanding ability continue to work in neglectful isolation. Their out-put will not be found inferior even if one put their works side by side before the ancient great works for the critical eye of the connoisseur to compare, to appreciate and to judge.

But there are craftsmen and ancient cultural traditions beyond the habitat of the Newars as well. We must not suppose that artists and craftsmen are to be found only in the Kathmandu region and that the rest of the Kingdom of Nepal in this respect is quite unimportant. As a matter of fact, the same civilisation obtains with minor variations from the Simla hill states to Darjeeling and Eastern Nepal. It might be called in certain respects to be essentially the civilisation of the Khas or the Prabatiya people. In some particulars, this civilisation seems to have had a parallel development with the civilisation obtaining throughout South Asia from 2000 B.C. onwards. The predominance of sex as the main motif in all art seems to point to a pre-Vedic civilisation. Some people even think that the Khas may be the descendents of the Dasyus of the Vedas which further points to a pre-Vedic origin of the main cultural traditions of most of Nepal.[1]

In Nepal, the mixture of the races has also led to a mixing of cultures and civilisations. The Khas-a simple, hardy people-have the simpler variation of the sex theme in their temples, books, paintings etc.; while the more artistic Newar, with a mixture of Tibetan blood, indulges in greater profanity and elaboration of design and converts almost everything into the sex episode. The Limbu to the east is again a very much less artistic variation of his Newar cousin. But art flourishes only in big valleys where nomadic people settle down for their lives and the lives of their children and of their children's children. Thus we find the richest monuments of art in the valleys of the Baghmati and the Vishnumati; of the Karnali; of the Rapti and of the Kosi.

The arts in Nepal, as in all countries in medieval times, are closely linked to religion. In other words, religion has been the chief outlet for the artistic energy of these people. Architecture, sculpture, wood and metal carving, painting and writing and copying of books have all owed their inspiration, and consummation to the aesthetic tendencies in the religious outlook of the rulers and the leaders of the people of the country. Roughly there are two distinct types of religious art. First the Buddhist, second the Hindu-cum-Tantric. Of these the Buddhist artists have been much more dignified. Their output has seldom that open sex appeal as that of the Shiva margi Hindu artists. In general the main artistic designs and elaborations of the Buddhists, are the simplified variations of what one finds in the Buddhist temples of Tibet, Mongolia, Sri Lanka, Burma, and Thailand. From the point of view of pure art their output comes nearer the accepted standards and specimens of Great Art. Of Buddhist Art we might take the temple of Swayambhu Nath as a fine example and the temple of Pashupati Nath as that of Shaiva Art.

The first difference one notices between the two temples lies in the very architecture itself. Swayambhu is like a towering pagoda on top of a hill. The long stairs and the great stone figures of Buddha and some of the animals whose forms he took in his previous births line the steps and remind one of the great Buddhist temples in Burma, Thailand and Sri

Lanka. The round form of the temple also points to Tibetan influence in its structure. On the other hand, the temple of Pashupati Nath is situated on the banks of the Baghmati and has a typically Hindu form in its square base and square roof. It might be said that roughly Buddhist art is fond of the round form, and curves, while Hindu art, is not exclusively addicted to but delights in and emphasizes straight lines, sharp angles and tapering cones.

Before the temple of Pashupati Nath is the huge copper figure of the Bull or the "Nandi" and a number of wooden brackets with exquisitely coloured figures on them stand in marked contrast to the innumerable prayer bells hung all round the Swayambhu temple. Also the Buddhist temple has no interior and there are only a few pockets in the body of the stone structure where some images of the Buddha are kept while the Pashupati Nath temple has a square baradari under its roof and the god Shiva is placed in the centre of the floor area, to enable the devotees to walk round the seat of Pashupati Nath.

Good stone work is found mainly in the Buddhist temples. The main themes are mostly the same. The commonest of all, found at almost every main cross-road, is the Buddha sitting in meditation and touching the earth with his fingers. On solid pieces of rock, big and small, are carved the figures of the Buddha on all the four sides and artistic designs are introduced to harmonise with the figures and the general designs of the temples. What is the special significance of the Buddha looking out on all the four sides is not difficult to appreciate. It is simply an effort to portray his omniscience. In most cases the craftsmanship is excellent and can be favourably compared with the four-faced lion heads of the famous column of Ashoka.

Stone figures of curious mythological animals are quite common. Generally, one finds them in pairs and at the gates of both Hindu and Buddhist temples. The figure on the right side of the temple is generally the male and that on the left side the female. In one temple at Patan a pair of elephants with dwarpals or door-keepers on them do the work while two quaint beasts watch the 'Kal Bhairava' in the heart of the city of Kathmandu.

But it is in wood that the Newar craftsmen have excelled. In most temples one finds two or more roofs coming out one over the other from the main buildings. The inclined wooden props that support these roofs are masterpieces of wood carving. The best examples of such wood work are to be found in the Pashupati Nath temple.

These wood figures are usually painted with different colours. The scheme of colours is usually bright with sharp contrasts but even then their effect is quite pleasant and smoothing to the eye. The corner pieces usually represent demons or mythological beasts with wings, horns, etc. The other pieces usually represent different gods and goddesses of the Hindu pantheon or the various persons mentioned in the Buddhist religious texts. Sometimes the main figures are of individuals only. But equally frequently they are of some god with his wife to his left as well.

There is however one point which needs special mention in connection with wood engraving, and that is the theme of the incidents portrayed below the main figures. These are mostly love scenes and purport to represent the various incidents of the theme. The audacity with which these are left for the public to gaze at is really astonishing. Young and old may all come and watch these intimate scenes though few Nepalese are actually fond of casting more than casual glances at them.

In metal work also the Newars have several fine achievements to their credit. Brass seems to have been the metal they liked best. Perhaps the nearness of copper mines to the Capital influenced their choice, as also the ease with which gilding or goldplating can be done over brass. Fine examples of metal work in Hindu temples are to be found in the temple of Ganesh near the gorge where the Baghmati forces its way out of the Valley and in the temple of Pashupati Nath itself. Both these represent the conveyances used by the respective gods-a huge mouse for Ganesh and a huge bull for Pashupati Nath. And both are masterpieces of simple and dignified execution.

But the most charming examples of metal work are to be found in the Buddhist monasteries. The different figures of the Buddha in these monasteries are usually of the same design and represent the great Master in one of his well known "Mudras' or postures. Images of the Buddha were in great demand in the Valley and the craftsmen copied the standard works of the masters as best as they could although the quality of the output varied greatly. The face of the Buddha in most of these works has that gracious serenity, composure and essential humanity that distinguishes him from the elaborate images of the Hindu gods and goddesses. The dignity and the serene characteristics of his facial expression had become the accepted cannons of Buddhist art even as early as the beginning of the Christian era.

In painting also the best examples are to be found in the monasteries of the Buddhists. In some of them can be found a close resemblance to the paintings of the Kangra school, although Tibetan influence is more marked in almost all these paintings. These paintings belong to the Tibetan school and were made by Nepalese monks who had obtained their training in painting in the monasteries of Tibet. But in many manuscripts are to be found examples of a similar though of an essentially Newar school of painting. The Nepal Museum has some exquisite Newar paintings on cloth and parchment. These consist of old paintings both of the Newar and the Tibetan schools and of potraits of the various members of the Rana and the Shahi families

Early Gorkhali or Nepali literature started in the twentieth century itself. Some of the important early authors were Rudra Raj Panda, Balkrishna Shamsher, and Lekhnath Sharma. Rudraraj Panda is an M.A. from the University of Allahabad and was the principal of the Trichandra College, Kathmandu. His best known work is "Rupmati", a novel of Nepali family life. This was the first book of its kind in Nepali literature. In this novel, the author exquisitely depicts the character of Rupmati who has to bear the hardships of a daughter-in-law's life in a Hindu family and has to come out triumphant in the end through patience and suffering .

Balkrishna Shamsher is one of the best dramatists in Nepal. His famous dramas are 'Andhabeg' and 'Prahlad'. "Andhabeg'is a social drama on modern lines. The main characters are Gururadhwaj an ordinary householder living in the heart of Kathmandu-and Pampha, his wife. In the tragedy we find Gururadhwaj killing his cousin Jaibir because he suspected him to be in love with Pampha and later poisoning himself when he found that his cousin was innocent. Prahlad is a Puranic drama that has been written for the stage times out of number in almost every language in South and South-East Asia. But Shamsher's efforts at blank verse have been a great success in Prahlad which incidentally is one of his earlier works.

Bhimnidhi Tiwari as a young man achieved great success with the production of his first play "Sahansheela Susheela" in Kathmandu. He has followed in the footsteps of Shamsher and has written a short society drama in "Susheela". This play gives us a picture of the life inside the great durbars or households of the members of the Rana family in Kathmandu. Susheela is the submissive wife who bears innumerable insults from her husband and yet loves, honours and obeys him. She represents the old type of Hindu wife who is honoured but is fast disappearing all over Nepal. This play is also remarkable for some simple songs (jhyaure), an example of which is:

> Say not, my darling, that you have to leave
> We shall take off our clothes and cross the waist deep
> waters of the Trisuli Ganga to the opposite bank;
> I have missed you greatly and may swoon if you leave,
> We shall retreat into the lonely forest and spend the entire day
> there;

It takes a year to fall in love but a moment to get stranged;
Say not, my darling, that you have to leave.

Among other authors mention must be made of Adhikari who edited a book on the folklore of Nepal and 'Jigar' who tried to introduce the ghazal form into Nepali versification. Similarly, Pondhalaya's Ritu Bichar is a khand Kavya describing the six seasons on the lines of Kalidas's Ritu Samhar. It is a work comprising about 600 couplets. It was first published in 1916 A.D. and is considered to be a classic now. We shall, however, leave the post 1950 literature, which is too recent for proper evaluation.

The historical literature in Nepal which has been published so far, comprises of few books. For example, there are historical accounts by Ambika Prasad and Ramji Upadhyaya. Another excellent book is the history of the reign of Prithvi Narayan Shah by Surya Bikram Jnawali. Of these the last is a work of great importance to the student of history, and is the result of painstaking research and thoughtful appreciation. More recently Baburam Acharya has published a 4 volume history of Shri 5 Bada Maharaj Prithvi Narayan Shah, from the Royal Palace, and Chittaranjan Nepali has written on Bhimsen Thapa's reign. In English, D.R. Regmi and Rishikesh Shaha have produced authoritative histories of Nepal and won international recognition.

But the gems of Nepali language are hidden in her folk songs. These are the songs that a young Nepali girl, sitting with her sickle at the side of the village stream or up in the alpine meadows, sings and which her mothers have sung in their youth.

One of the best known of these jhyaures is:
I have little hope from such a man who transgresses the moral law;
I wish I would go away to my mother's village;
The man has sold my necklace and squandered the proceeds,
I wish I would go away to my mother's village.

Now lastly a word about the Newari language. The Newari language is quite different from that of the Gorkhas. We have not enough material to pinpoint the relationship of the language of the Newars to the other languages around it. This is mainly due to the fact that the Newari manuscripts are rarely found in libraries outside Nepal and the printing and publishing of books in Newari has been actively discouraged in the past to the point of prohibition.

There are, however, certain aspects which come out prominently even after a short acquaintance with spoken Newari. Firstly, that it is not an Indo-European language. The verb forms and the names of every day things in Newari are quite different from those found in Sanskrit, Prakrit or other modern North Indian languages. Secondly that Newari has been and is being influenced considerably by Tibetan, Sanskrit, Hindi and Bengali.

It has been suggested by some that Newari is a Tibeto-Burman language brought by early Tibetan immigrants into the valley of the Baghmati; others dispute this and assert that Newari is a collateral of the pre-Vedic languages that were spoken by the aboriginal races in most of the valleys and the plains of South Asia. They claim to have found resemblances between early Tamil and Newari. These points, however, need careful study by philologists versed well in all three of the languages-Tibetan, Newari and early Tamil. However, the resemblance between Newari and Tibetan is too obvious to escape notice. Thus the word mother becomes 'ama' in Tibetan and 'ma' in Newari. Similarly, one becomes 'chik' and 'chhaku',-two becomes 'ni and 'niku'; 'three' becomes 'sum' and 'suku'; and so on. The word 'eye' which is 'mika' in Newari becomes 'mikha' in Tibetan, and nose is 'nhaya and 'nhe' in Newari and Tibetan. A more detailed study of the vocabularies in Newari and Tibetan made by the author showed that a majority of words resembled each other in these two languages, but not in Newari and early Tamil. In fact Newari is nearer to the language in the Limbu and Kirati region than to Gorkhali or Parbatiya languages of Gorkha, Palpa and other regions to the west of the valley of Kathmandu.

Nepali developed as a colateral language with Khari-boli in North India early in the thirteenth century. We have copper plate inscriptions of local rajas in Nepali from that period. Nepali, Gorkhali or Khas Kura became the lingua franca of the entire Himalayan Kingdom. The language had royal patronage and was used by the Gorkha rulers in their correspondence with their officials. Dibyopadesh (The Great Testament or Counsel) by Prithvi Narayan Shah was in Nepali and all government work, including case work, was done in Nepali. The Shrestha or Common Law of Nepal did much to standardise the language. The translation of the Ramayana in Nepali verse by Bhanu Bhakta Acharya (1814-64) brought literary glory to the language.

King Mahendra, after taking over power in 1960 took several step to patronise Nepali writers and poets. He himself was a lyric poet and his verses in Nepali have been translated into English and published under the name of M.B.B. Shah *i.e.*, Mahendra Bir Bikram Shah. The prominent writers were given royal patronage, but they were constrained not to criticise the regime or the system. However, dissent was present and was applauded by the public. In Nepal, as in other societies where opposition to a ruling elite is restrained, literature is one of the chief outlets for expression of dissent. In this respect Koirala's novels come ready to mind. There are also scores of literary and other books in Nepali which are published in Darjeeling and easily available in Nepal.

There are few newspapers and periodicals, published in Nepali, Hindi and English. King Mahendra required the press to get clearance from government officials for all reports on political activities and programmes. However, with the media revolution, most Nepalese have easy access to broadcasts in Nepali from China, India, the BBC and Moscow. The radio station in Darjeeling broadcasts most of its programmes in Nepali. These include Nepali folk songs, literary and political discourses in Nepali and the whole range of Indian perception of world events and trends. The transistor radio has brought all the people of the world together and state boundaries are no longer able to prevent dissemination of information from different capitals of the great powers. State govemments have, therefore, now to take into consideration that the information available to their people is not confined to hand-outs from their own radio-stations and newspapers and that any one anywhere in any part of the world has now available to him perceptions of events as broadcast from different radio-stations round the world. Music and dance are favourite pastimes of all castes and classes in Nepal. Folk dances and accompanying music have caught the imagination of the Nepalese. In one respect, this emphasizes the national character of the Nepalese, from the Khas to the Limbu regions and exhibits their identity as distinct from the dominant classical and film music of South Asia which is broadcast by most radio stations in Pakistan, India and Bangladesh.

Music and dance are prominent activities at all religious and family celebrations. Both Hindu and Buddhist religious ceremonies are accompanied by traditional dance forms and music on drums, cymbals and wind instruments. Quite often festivities incorporate processions to and from temples and river sides and these allow the general populace to take part in them by forming part of the processions for part of the way they traverse. In other words, music and dance are intimately interwoven in the lives of all people in Nepal from the King down to the poorest Nepali citizen. This makes the hard and dreary lives of the people not only bearable but also pleasant and carefree.

Note

1 For Khas. See Atkinson: Gazetteer of the Himalayan Districts.

Six

Communications

Perhaps the main reason why Nepal does not share in the modern civilisation or whatever there is of it to her South in India is her lack of internal communications. There are few roads fit for vehicular traffic in the country. The lack of communications is painfully brought to one's notice when one has to go any distance east or west of the Capital. For example, the best and quickest way to reach Doti or Sallyana from Kathmandu is not to proceed inside Nepalese territory in an east to west direction, but to come down from Kathmandu to Raxaul, continue the journey in an Indian railway train and proceed to one's destination through Tanakpur or Nepalganj.

As a matter of fact, Nepal is a country where wheeled traffic is at a discount. In the first place, the Himalaya mountains do not permit an unindustrialised state like Nepal to develop its communications in the interior hills because a macadamised road going over hills and mountains requires a lot of engineering enterprise which one, under the present circumstances, cannot expect in Nepal. Secondly, wheeled traffic implies a great deal of goods and human traffic which unfortunately is not forthcoming in Nepal. Thirdly, wheeled traffic means bicycles, mopeds, motor-cycles, cars, motor-buses, railway trains etc. which have now become part and parcel of our industrial civilisation and are inseparable from it. In other words, wheeled traffic and modern civilisation go together and in whichever country we miss the one we might as well expect to miss the other.

The most important factor about communications in Nepal, then, is her lack of wheeled traffic. We should, therefore, expect to get only animal and human transport facilities in Nepal. Rich men may provide themselves with horses, 'dandies' or 'dokas'. The 'dandy' is generally used for ladies of high rank and is carried by four to six men. The 'doka' is a curious contrivance in which one man carries on his back another seated inside a deep straw basket with his feet dangling comfortably outside the basket. For carrying luggage etc. the Nepalese usually employ mules or stout coolies. The Bhotiyas, inhabiting the upper regions of the Himalayas, generally use sheep for carrying their goods to and fro from the market towns of Nepal and India to their homes.

It was perhaps to remedy these drawbacks that the Nepalese government, in the twenties erected an electric ropeway to carry goods from Bheempheri to Kathmandu. It was a refreshing sight to see big packages move up and down the ropeway while one had to struggle hard in footing one's way on the very inadequately kept roadway to the capital city.

The ropeway was run by electricity and had considerably improved the export and import of goods into the Baghmati Valley. In earlier days, all goods to the Nepal Valley had to be transported on human backs from Bheempheri. This was hard both on the porters and the consumers of goods. The porters dwarfed themselves by almost breaking their backs with loads of nearly one hundred kilograms each carried over most inadequate road surface across two mountain ridges. The merchants in Kathmandu and the other towns had to pay handsome amounts for the carriage of their goods, which they charged to their customers. The ropeway had, however, solved and effected economies in the carrying of goods to the capital. But there was one sight which few visitors to Nepal would forget. The ropeway carried most goods but could not carry a deluxe motor saloon bodily to Nepal. And there were a good number of cars in Kathmandu even before the Tribhuwan Rajpath was built. These cars had been brought by making elaborate and curious arrangements for their transport.

The saloon cars were taken to Bheempheri by railway and the macadamised road. At Bheempheri the motor road ended and a bridle path began. Here the wheels of the car were removed to be carried separately to Nepal. The main body of the car was then fastened to two long poles so that four men could put their shoulders to the projected parts in front and behind the car on each side of the pole, thus making 16 people in all; two more poles were fastened transversely and two to three men lifted each pole from each side of the car, making in all 8 to 12 men on the sides. Thus about 25 men were required to move the saloon car. This, however, was not the end of the trouble. The bridges on the bridle road were narrow suspension bridges, too narrow to allow the body of the car to pass through them and too frail to stand the load of a car and 25 men at one time. This difficulty was overcome by making detours from the road at river sides. The streams were divided into two or three smaller channels by throwing huge stones in between and these channels were bridged by throwing across them logs of wood which made temporary crossings possible. On the whole, carrying a saloon car to the Nepal valley was an arduous and expensive task.

Symbolically, however, Nepal claimed, even before 1940, to have her own railway line and her own tarred roads. Within the boundaries of Nepal ran a short gauge railway line from Raxaul, on the frontier, through Birganj to Amlekhganj-a distance of about 30 kilometres. The railway runs through a stretch of dense Tarai forest where tigers and leopards are not unknown to have been seen near the railway lines. Before the railway was started, this part of the Tarai formed the most unhealthy portion of the journey to Kathmandu. The water in this area was thought to be the cause of 'awl' and other fevers and the whole of this area was supposed to be most unhealthy to spend even a night in . For the convenience of the travellers, a system of water supply had been organised, the water being carried from the foot of the hills in good channels to a number of watering and resting places on the way. These places with fountains of water and open pipes can be seen to this day from the railway carriages as the line winds through the sloping Tarai.

The railway is a state-sector establishment of the government of Nepal. There are hardly a dozen engines in all. The trains are slow and as overcrowded as those in India. We could describe here the road system from the railway terminus to Kathmandu as it was before the revolution of 1950. Amlekhganj, the terminus of the railway line, was at the foot of the hills. From here a bus service took passengers and goods along two river valleys joined by a tunnel to Bheempheri. The motor road was a good macadamised road and was kept in good condition. Its total length was about 40 kilometres. At Bheempheri one had to change from modern to medieval modes of transport. There were nine rest houses and 'dharamshalas' maintained by the State at Bheempheri, as well as on the way to Kathmandu. From Bheempheri a bridle path led to the Garhi where passports and permits were checked and examined. This was also the place where taxable goods had to pay import and export dues. Both Bheempheri and Garhi had small military establishments as well. At Bheempheri barracks had been constructed which accommodated up to a thousand soldiers. The bridle path degenerated into ravines and gullies at places where the slope was very steep. The journey was tedious and even well to-do people, engaging hill ponies or "jhampans"[1] or 'dandies' found it wearisome.

It was not difficult to surmise why the road was maintained in such a wretched condition. It was not due to lack of funds or organisational ability or zeal. There was a Public Works Department at Kathmandu and Nepalese engineers could very well improve the road to stand comparison with any other mountain road in Tibet or in India. The British-Indian Government had made excellent roads in several hill stations particularly in Simla, Nainital and Darjeeling. The Nepalese Government could not be expected to rival the skill and resources at the disposal of the British-Indian Government, but they could very easily and economically improve the main road that led to their capital city. It was due to the deliberate policy of excluding all foreign contact that had led Nepal to keep the road as a bridle road. The Nepalese government did not encourage visitors, especially curious journalists and the ruling Ranas were averse to displaying their wealth and resources to critical observation. One recalls to mind the saying of Jung Bahadur, the Nepalese Prime Minister, when some one drew his attention to the bad condition of the Kathmandu road. He is said to have replied that a good road would facilitate British penetration into Nepal and in case any conflict took place between the two powers, a good road would speedily bring British Indian troops to Kathmandu. He had, therefore, decided, he said, not to bear the calumny for having been the man responsible for constructing the road that opened the country defenceless before British troops.

However, in the valley of Nepal several motor roads joined at Kathmandu. Thankot lay at the end of the bridle road from Bheempheri to Garhi, Kulikhani, Chitlang and the ascent of Chandragiri. From Thankot buses and cars plied to Kathmandu, which was connected with Bhatgaon and Patan also by motorable roads.

There were hardly any other motor roads before 1950 in Nepal except fair weather roads developed by conractors for the cartage of timber across the Tarai. In other words, Nepal, was the land of bridle roads and footpaths. Pack-horses and men walked along precipices and across rope bridges. The scenery was picturesque and the climate warm and pleasant. One would only like to go and remain in these out-of-the way places when one got tired with the efficiency and speed of modern civilisation. However, so far as economic condition of the people was concerned medieval means of communication meant a low standard of living and a parochial outlook on life.

In most parts of Nepal, especially the drainage areas of big rivers, timber is usually sent to plains down the streams. Trees are cut down in the forests, and hewn into sleepers. These sleepers, mostly used by consumers in India, are sent down the rivers in hundreds of thousands. On reaching level ground some way down the Tarai, a sort of barage is made at an incline to the width of the river and the sleepers are collected on the river bank to be forwarded by bullock carts or goods trains to their destinations.

Since the year 1937, the Nepalese postal system has been closely linked with that in India. Letters, postcards and ordinary book-post articles can be sent from Nepal to any place in India and outside and vice-versa. The Nepalese sometimes even employed the Indian postal facilities for forwarding their mail from one part of the country to another. Thus it took less time to send a letter from Kathmandu to Nautanwa in India from where it could be carried to Butwal by hand or per Nepalese post than to send it direct along the mountains to Butwal. In the case of a Gorkha soldier or officer in India, who wanted to send a letter to his family in Nepal, he had to give the name of the exchange office of the Indian Postal Department nearest to his village or town in the address. Thus if a letter was sent to Pokhra, it was necessary to give the name of Nautanwa Bazar, Indian Post Office on the frontier, for prompt delivery; otherwise if the letter was simply addressed to Pokhra, Nepal, it might be sent to Kathmandu from where it would be taken by inland mail to Pokhra. This might easily lead to a delay of one to two weeks.

The Nepalese have also developed short lines of telephonic communication between different towns in Kathmandu valley and Raxaul, covering something like 400 kilometres. Messages, which in other places would be sent telegraphically, were often despatched in Nepal through the telephone. But now telecommunications are receiving high priority but laying of telegraph and telephone lines and organising postal services in a country of bridle roads and footpaths is costly and time-consuming. The transistor radio, however, gets news and government orders from Kathmandu instantaneously and at little cost. It also works as a great force for national integration and identity.

Note

1. A jhampan or dandi is a carriage or wooden couch carried over the hills on the shoulders of four men.

Seven

Trade and Commerce

Nepal is a land-locked country. She has no port of her own and all her imports and exports have to pass through India or Tibet.

Calcutta is the nearest port for Nepal. And the facilities afforded by the Indian Government for Nepalese trade in and via India have made Calcutta the greatest buying centre for Nepal.

All goods destined for Nepal pay no customs dues on disembarkation at any Indian port. They pass through Indian territory duty free. This, however, applies only to goods imported from outside India. Cotton goods, sugar and hundreds of other articles partly or wholly manufactured in India have to pay excise as well as customs-duties at the Nepalese frontier. The Nepalese are strict in enforcing their customs regulations, and all goods and luggage that pass through the frontier posts are examined carefully for any articles on which duty is payable to the Nepal Government.

Nepal is an agricultural and pastoral country. She exports most of her surplus products to India, which, however, does not amount to any significant share of the Indian market. Nepal also buys the major portion of her imports from India, and her economy is dependent to a large extent on Indian trade policies. There was significant trade between Tibet and Nepal in the past. Mostly Nepalese traders worked as brokers for the produce of Central Tibet which they sold again in the Indian market. In the same way they sold manufactured goods imported from India to the Tibetans. However, the Tibetans were not very friendly with the Nepalese, and did not mind coming down themselves to the Indian outposts with their goods before the India-China conflict. In this way, Simla in the West, Almora in the middle and Darjeeling in the East had become the centres for Indo-Tibetan trade and commerce. At present, however, all trade between India and Chinese occupied Tibet is banned. Therefore, Nepal-Tibet trade is booming.

The Nepalese possess great buying capacity in Indian currency. There are in all, over two to four hundred thousand Gorkhas who are employed in India, some of them are in the army while the majority are employed privately as watchmen or personal attendants. Then there are thousands of retired Gorkha soldiers in Nepal who get their pensions from the Indian Government. It would be difficult to assess correctly the amount of Indian currency that is available to Nepalese citizens from the Government of India and private Indian employers per year. On an average every Gorkha in India would be getting about Rs. 900.00 per month or Rs. 108,00.00 per year. This would work out to about Rs. 300.00 crores per year. If we add to this, the amount of the pensions and the indirect subsidy in the form of exemption from Indian customs duties, the amount of Indian currency available to Nepal would be between Rs. 1,000 and 1,200 crores per year. This means great buying power for a poor mountainous country like Nepal.

The political and military forecasters have to ponder over the question whether such huge sums of money from India will be available to Nepal from year to year in future also. Perhaps these amounts will be reduced considerably as the Nepalese working in India settle down there permanently.

The Nepalese buy mainly clothing apparel from India. The fabrics turned out by the Indian textile mills, and even imported Japanese cloth is much cheaper than the cottage spun cloth of Nepal. The Nepalese, however, produce very fine designs and cloth of great durability and silken surface. Its dearness, however, compels the poor to buy cheap imported cloth.

Then with the westernization of the upper classes, the demand for luxury goods has increased greatly in recent years. Most of the money that is paid by India to the Gorkha soldiers and the common Nepalese folk finds its way in the shape of taxes and levies into the hands of the government and the state officials. The aristocracy, however, spends it in buying motor cars, radios, gramophones, photographic goods, gorgeous sarees, finest scents, and hair oils and hundreds of other articles of personal luxury from England, the U.S.A., Japan and other foreign countries.

From Nepal the export of timber to India is the main item of her foreign trade. In the thirties, the Nepalese embarked on a policy of industrialisation. A small department of government at Kathmandu called 'The Association for Enterprises' or the Udyoga Parishad was established.

Later a small match factory was established at Birganj and a jute mill at Biratnagar. Plans were made for rice-mills, sugar mills, cement, steel-re-rolling and cigarette factories. Even the private sector is not very energetic inspite of heavy subsidies. There are only a couple of small sugar mills but several small sector, rice, oil and timber mills are run by the people in the Tarai.

After the 1950 revolution a number of units were established for stainless steel utensils and synthetic textiles, mainly for the Indian market. In May 1969, the government of India, following international practice, ordered total stoppage of imports of Nepalese manufactures unless excise duty was paid as in the case of Indian units. This was in accordance with the Trade protocol concluded at the instance of Nepal in November 1968.

The Birlas in the sixties obtained a licence for setting up a cotton textile unit with 12,500 spindles, but the project was later given up.

In the State sector, however, the USSR set up a sugar mill of 1000 ton capacity at Birganj and a cigarette factory with annual capacity of 200 million sticks at Janakpur. An agricultural tools and equipment factory at Birganj was also set up. China set up a tannery in 1965 (capacity 21,000 pieces of tanned hide and 30,000 pairs of shoes) near Kathmandu but withdrew its projects for paper and cement. The USA helped set up a saw-mill at Hetanda in 1965 with an annual capacity of 7,00,000 cubic feet.

Nepal has approached several foreign countries to set up new industries in Nepal. Private investors after visits to Nepal declare that the Nepalese domestic market is too small for earning profits and there has been hardly any private foreign investment. The industries in the State Sector have also not been success stories. Several of these factories are not running at full capacity and few are earning profits.

India has offered several times since 1965 to help Nepal in setting up industries with Nepalese or Indian raw materials but Nepal is unwilling to set up joint-industrial ventures. Nepal favours private sector people to set up industries, fearing government to government approach with India. Foreigners, however, do not want to put their money in Nepal without guarantees that nationalization will not be enforced and law and order will be effectively maintained.

The result is that there has been little progress in industrialisation and Nepal remains a poor agricultural and pastoral country inspite of the great efforts and promised subsidies by the Nepal Industrial Development Corporation.

Nepal is supposed to be rich in minerals, although no scientific survey in detail has yet been undertaken. The exploitation of these natural resources, however, is bound up with the problem of cheap and efficient power supply. In other words, the future industrialisation of Nepal is a question of her electrification. Unless the numerous water falls scattered in almost every part of the kingdom are harnessed to provide cheap lighting arrangements for the people and cheap power for the factories, there can be hardly any question of industrialising the country. In this respect, therefore, Nepal's future is linked with that of India. Nepal cannot make dynamoes and motors for herself. Therefore, Nepal will get the means of cheap power supply only when Indian factories turn out motors and dynamoes by the thousands and consequently at cheap prices. Nepal cannot afford to install power stations by buying costly installations from abroad. She has thus to wait till Indian industrialisation makes it possible and worthwhile for her to utilize her hydro-electric potential and industrialise herself.

Nepal has a silver currency. The Nepalese rupee is about 165 to 100 Indian rupees. The rupee always carried the name of the ruling prince (not of the Prime Minister). Thus the coin minted in the year 1927 A.D. bears the legend, " Shree Shree Tribhuwan Bir Bikram Shah Deva 1884". The year refers to the Vikram era. On the same side are engraved the sun and the moon, the symbols of the Nepal State-the Trisul or trident indicating the emblem of the God Shiva and the four emblems of Vishnu namely a wheel, a counch-shell, a lotus flower and a club. On the other side is a legend "Shree Shree Gorakhnath" and "Shree Bhawani Ek Rupiya Nepal". This shows the influence of religion in Nepal, the patron saint of whose ruling dynasty from Gorkha is Gorakhnath. The rupee in Nepal is divided into 100 paisas. There are coins for 1, 2, and 5 paisas. The money in Nepal was on decimal system even when the Indian rupee consisted of 64 paisas and 16 annas.

Eight

The Army and the Government

In Nepal, the mainstay of all political power has been the army and all executive officers of the government, till recently, have held army ranks as well. To appreciate this important factor in the polity of Nepal, we shall have to go back to the times of the Ranas. During the period of the rule of the Ranas, the Prime Minister was styled "Maharaja Prime Minister and Marshal". Thus the same man was the supreme head of the entire civil administration and the army. He was responsible to none, not even the king of Nepal, but everyone else in Nepal owed him due allegiance and proper obedience. Next to the Prime Minister was the Commander in Chief of the Nepalese army. Then came the senior commanding General-Western Command who was followed in rank and succession table by the Commanding Generals of the Eastern, Southern and Northern commands respectively in that order. Then came a number of Generals, Lieutenant Generals and Major Generals, all of whom belonged to the family of the Ranas *i.e.* the Prime Minister's family. The other officers' ranks were bestowed on members of families related to the Rana family *i.e.* practically every one holding an executive post in Nepal also held a military appointment and was somehow or the other related to the Ranas.

The soldiers in the army were recruited mainly from the Gorkha elements in the population and junior officers' cadres were mostly filled by men who rose from the ranks. This meant that with the exception of the Newars, who were considered deficient in military virtue, men of all other tribes and castes were admitted into the Nepalese army. These men were at first enlisted in the various regiments without reference to religious prejudices. General Jung Bahadur, however, introduced the system of forming distinct corps of Rajputs, Magars, Gurungs and Limbus. In this way clan and caste feelings which existed amongst the different groups, although not fostered, were also not actively discouraged by the government. This practice led to two distinct advantages. Firstly, in case of mutiny, of which one hears very seldom in Nepal, one regiment would be suitably used to crush the erring soldiers of another unit. Secondly, regional and clan regiments foster esprit de corps internally and spirit of healthy emulation with respect to other regiments.

The organisation of the army in Nepal was similar to that of the British Indian Army. Commands were distributed in exactly the same manner. The pay of the soldiers, however, was much less and often quotas were levied for the army from the villages on more or less a selective conscription basis. Leave was generally granted to the majority of the troops during harvest and sowing seasons to enable them to assist in the cultivation of their lands.

The army was kept under strict discipline and its manoeuvres were steadily and regularly performed. But the Gorkhas have not learnt the science of war systematically. They prove to be good soldiers because they have military virtues in their blood. Their officers were, however, quite out of touch with modern developments and were not keen on following the progress of other armies. This had necessarily to be so because promotions depended solely on succession rights in a particular family. But, it must be conceded that the Rana family has produced and has to its credit even today a number of very able military commanders.

There is a gun foundry at Kathmandu and a large manufactory of fire arms and ammunition is situated not far from the capital. The Nepal army has hardly any field artillery or cavalry or armour. Modernisation of the army, of course, has never been thought about. In a mountainous country, lack of communications is the best defence and the Gorkha leaders have shown military acumen in refusing to follow modernisation which would mean that they will have to depend for all their equipment on foreign sources. Even to this day their army is self-sufficient, and this instrument of self-defence they can use under all circumstances. There is hardly any commissariate-attached to their army. When on march each soldier carries his own provisions for the number of days he expects himself to be away from the next market place. The simplicity of the Nepal army is also marked in their want of camp equipage. They have hardly sufficient number of tents for their officers. It is this very hardi-hood of the soldiers that has earned military renown for the Gorkhas wherever they have made their appearance.

These days the King is the Supreme Commander of the Nepalese Army and the soldiers are paid and equipped better, and have more barracks to live in when they are not on active service. Their equipment, however, is restricted to mountain artillery and field mortars and even electronic communication systems are mostly absent. The Nepalese think that they have not to be prepared to fight an all-out war with either of their neighbours. They also think that in case of any aggression from one of their neighbours, they will be helped by the other. Jawaharlal Nehru had made a public commitment on these lines. As regards the Chinese, the Nepalese monarchy counts on their help to come to its rescue in an emergency. Therefore, the army still remains mainly a peace-keeping force for internal security.

The executive head of the government used to be the Prime Minister. In him also rested the powers of granting pardons to criminals and of sanctioning capital punishment. He was also the supreme law making authority. In fact, his word and his will was law. His orders could not be questioned by any other authority in Nepal executive or judicial. He was also in charge of the treasury. The accounts of the treasury were never placed before the people, as all the revenues collected in Nepal were deposited with the Maharaja Prime Minister and all disbursements were made with his authority. It was held by all who knew even a little of Nepal that the post of the Prime Minister was a very lucrative one; the net gains of the office varying from five to ten crores of rupees a year before World War II.

The Prime Minister was assisted by two Chief Secretaries called Qazis. Their functions were similar to the Foreign and the Home Secretaries of the Government of India. There were also a number of other Subbas or superintendents of offices at Kathmandu in charge of the various departments of the government. Local matters of the various parts of the country, however, were primarily dealt with in the private offices of the Commanding Generals' each of whom had a number of Subbas and Khardars or junior superintendents to assist him.

The whole country was divided into 'ilakas' or districts each in charge of a 'bara hakim', who was always someone related to the Rana family. He also held some military rank usually that of a Colonel. He was in sole charge of his district and his position was analogous to that of the Collector or Deputy Commissioner in British Indian districts. He represented the government in his part of the country, and was the head of the entire governmental machinery there. He heard appeals in certain criminal, revenue and civil matters also. He collected the revenues due to the government and he looked after the police administration of his 'ilaka' as well. He was, in other words a Collector of revenues, superintendent of Police and district judge of India combined into one. He was helped in turn by a number of subbas and khardars, who functioned as the heads of the various departments under his charge.

The administration of justice was based on the dharamshastras, and mainly on the cannons of Manu. In general there were two types of courts-one religious and the other secular. In the religious tribunals men were on trial for transgressions of the Hindu moral Code *i.e.* the rules governing castes, inter-caste marriages, inter-dining, the inflicting of pain or death on the cow and the want of respect for the gods and goddesses of the different localities. These courts were presided over by 'dharamadhikaris', who were all appointed by and were sub-ordinate to the 'dharamadhikari' at Kathmandu. In the secular courts were tried infractions of the laws of the secular state of Nepal. These laws have now been codified and are obtainable from Kathmandu. Usually these courts consisted of 'bicharis' who worked in pairs. Sometimes a 'dittha' presided over these tribunals. He did not take any part in the proceedings and functioned mainly as an arbiter. This is rather difficult to appreciate at first. The legal system in Nepal was entirely different from that of India or a European country. There were no legal practitioners in Nepal. The courts were there to bring justice to any one who applied to them. They followed the traditional precepts of Hindu jurisprudence namely that it was the duty of the ruler to bring justice to each and every one of his subjects. The subject had not to pay court fees before filing a petition nor had he to engage the services of shrewd lawyers in order to put his case before the judges. Once the 'bichari' or 'dharamadhikari' came to know of any breach of the secular or religious laws of the country, it became his duty to investigate the matter, bring the culprit to justice and restore any person injured by the breach of the laws to his former position. In petty cases a single judge could deliver judgement. But in complicated cases, usually two judges took part in the proceedings. One judge took the part of the appellant and the other of the defendant, and in this way they tried to elucidate the facts before them. Evidence was taken before the court, generally, without an oath, but the men were supposed to be in honour bound to disclose the true facts to the best of their knowledge. In the end one judge might convince the other of right being on his side, when judgement was given accordingly. In cases where the judges could not agree between themselves, an umpire or 'dittha' presided over the court and the judgement of the 'dittha' as to the facts and the application of law to them was final. Appeals from district courts, however, could be taken to the supreme court in Kathmandu, where the proceedings were much the same. Finally every one had the right to approach the Prime Minister and lay his case before him personally, provided he could get access to the Prime Minister's presence.

One could dwell at length on the main characteristics of the legal system of Nepal but it would be sufficient here to say that the main elements of the organisation of the state in Nepal were rule by the Rana family, the military character of the administration and the absolute and unquestioned authority of the Maharaja Prime Minister and Marshal in all executive, legislative, judicial and military matters. The rule of the Rana family lent to Nepal the characteristics of a hereditary oligarchy; the military character of the administration made the executive machinery a sort of military aristocracy and the rule by the Prime Minister made Nepal an absolute dictatorship.

The basic nature of the system did not undergo any fundamental changes when the king took over. Instead of the Maharaja Prime Minister, all authority then vested in the King, and all administrative rules and laws followed his wisdom and benevolence. Nepal has experimented with several constitutions since the revolution of 1950-51 brought about by King Tribhuwan, but the fundamental law in Nepal till the enactment of the new contitution in 1990 was that all executive, legislative, judicial and military power vested in the King as the ruler of a Hindu Kingdom and the administration was carried on under his direction, guidance and superintendence. The King of Nepal was the supreme Sovereign and it was the duty of all his subjects to obey him sincerely and faithfully. Disaffection towards and disobedience of the King amounted to treason in Nepal and those guilty of such behaviour were liable to be kept in prison as a matter of State policy. Within these parameters subjects of the King in their individual capacity could petition him for redress of grievances or for alteration in the rules of business for the administration.

But even in a Hindu Kingdom, changes take place. There has been in recent years a Supreme Court in Nepal and certain fundamental rights are enumerated.

There is provision for counsel to appear for their clients and a professional class of lawyers is coming up in the capital and the bigger towns. The trend is definitely towards Rule of Law.

Similarly, steps have already been taken to recruit the permanent administrative services from the general public through merit tests. It will, however, take several years before the new entrants reach senior positions to influence policy-making and its implementation. The trend towards evolving an administrative system similar to the ones obtaining in Great Britain and India is evident. This is a welcome sign and a significant milestone on the road to modernisation.

Nine

Land Administration

Throughout Nepal, the inhabited village is the unit of social organisation and land administration. The villages or permanent settlements of cultivators are inter-mixed with grazing grounds, dense forests, river beds, waste lands and cultivated fields. These are grouped into clusters or villages-large or small.

The population in Nepal villages has been sparse and the forests have never been far-off. The produce of the forest including wild game was free to every villager like water, rain and sunshine. By and large, every villager had some land near his hutment, some near the source of water and the rest in the uplands. The village community was governed by a council of elders with one or more spokesmen or headmen. It was a "sabha", or "soviet" or "panchayat". The villagers allotted specific fields to the officials, as remuneration for their work. Specific plots were earmarked for the headman or pradhan, the priest of the local deity and for the share of the raja or authority superior to that of the village headman. The village 'sabha' or council had to see that all able bodied persons in the village worked hard to get the best crops. It was the duty of the village headman or headman to take the produce of the raja's fields to him or his representative at the next higher seat of administrative authority. It was generally assumed by everyone that the village council headed by the headmen or group of elders would be very fair and strict in its obligations to the deity or deities and the raja. Land disputes between the villagers were settled by the village elders themselves and they did not have to wait on the representative of the raja to come to the village and settle local disputes.

The land in these villages belonged to the families that first cleared the forest or plant growth and established the first fields in the villages.

The village people, as a group, had started clearing forestland and the division of fields between the different families was by consensus. The work-schedules of the workers on land would be directed by the heads of the families and in case of disputes by a general consensus of the family or the village council, if necessary. It was assumed that everyone knew what was the right thing to do and the disputes were settled in the family or in the village council by general consensus which would emerge because of instinctive acknowledgement of Dharma or right conduct by every one in the village. The opinion and advice of the village elders and the village priests would be welcome and would be given great weight. Ultimately, it was the overwhelming majority of opinion that prevailed as the consensus.

The conception of breaking new land or expanding existing cultivation seems to have been as old as the first village settlement. The family which cleared the first portion of these forests would naturally claim the forest land near its holdings. It was also natural that additions to one's land would be adjacent to one's existing holdings. A person was expected to extend his holdings into the forest near the boundaries of his own holdings so as not to come into conflict with similar rights of his neighbours on either side of his fields. It was for the neighbours to extend their cultivation towards the forest, if they so desired, and, therefore, each one had to be left with the option to extend or not to extend his cultivation into the forest nearest to his plots of land.

The basic feature of land administration in units of villages has come to us from the earliest times when man first started cultivating land in the river valleys for production of foodgrains. The village has remained as an administrative unit because it was a separate and distinct unit even in the earliest times, when all around, it was surrounded by thick tropical forest. As the centuries rolled on, the village encroached on the forest surrounding it. The result was that all culturable land was brought under the plough in the villages and also in level patches of land higher up in the hills.

The first villages in Nepal appeared on the banks of the rivers wherever the valleys widened and open fields were available. With the pressure of increasing population, less fertile lands were also brought under cultivation and the hill sides were cut into terraces. Further, in summer months when no grass was available in the low-lands, the villagers moved with their cattle to the higher mountains. Generally old men stayed behind and younger people went up with the cattle and sheep and goats. In the lower hills, called the Mahabharat hills, the problem of grazing would come in winter and the villagers would have to move down into the Tarai forests along with their cattle. Thus the typical Himalayan village came to be established in Nepal with a three-fold division of land; namely, some land near the source of water, some dry land at the higher terraces and pasture land in the upper ranges or the Tarai for grazing cattle in summer and winter months respectively. In all these villages the basic rule of conduct was that land belonged to the person who first cleared the forest and made it culturable. And the basic structure of administration was democratic and republican with a council of elderly people for general land management which represented the village as a unitary whole as against the outsiders and which negotiated with the raja's representative or whoever came with authority to enforce his orders.

When a large number of villages come up in an area, there is natural exchange of views and visits and barter of goods. This natural requirement is met by a large village which is at a convenient point of inter-communication between the different villages. Generally the large village will be the village of the dominant group in the entire community with its headman or the raja himself residing there. It may be the other way round also. The raja or leader of the dominant group might select a suitable village for controlling the rest of the group from the point of view of communications, defence, natural wealth, nearness to water etc. On the other hand, the nomadic people seem to have always had a republican type of land administration primarily because their attachment to particular fields was not great. The nomadic group is republican whereas the permanently settled cultivators are monarchical. A strong man naturally becomes the raja of permanently settled land. Monarchical control is difficult to achieve when the people can shift from one place to another with their cattle and other belongings. There are mainly three groups of such nomadic tribes in Nepal, the Sherpas of Arun Kosi, the Bhotias of Buri Gandaki around Mustang and the Bhotias of Jumla region. These nomadic peoples paid nominal land tax collected by the headmen and paid to the "jammawals" or "subbas" appointed by the different rajas of the different regions. They were, however, prosperous people from the Nepalese standards and their main income was from trade with Tibet. This dependence on trade has diminished with the Chinese occupation of Tibet and these people are now more dependent on tourism and permanent cultivation.

In all these villages the most important aspect of land management was the fact that land was not considered to be the property of any single person or family. The rights over land, whatever they were, were subject to overall control of the village community and no transfer of any particular field could take place without tacit or particular appproval of the village community and the headman who was also responsible to the raja or overlord.

Secondly, the village was required to safeguard the share of the raja in the crops grown and to deliver the same to the nominees of the raja. This was the duty of the village elders or headmen towards the raja. They were known as the 'pradhanas or 'panch janah' and they were the intermediaries between the village and all outsiders. In other words, the village community was a closely knit and compact society where the rights of the individuals, the families and the community as a whole were well recognised and accepted by every one. In such a society theft, oppression or forcible possession of another man's fields were extremely rare. However, when some fields were abandoned, the village council asked some other member of the community, generally the nearest heir to cultivate the fields and appropriate the crops grown. But when the owner returned, he claimed back his fields after the crops grown by some one else had been harvested.

With the authority of the raja increasing, the responsibility of the headmen to deliver the raja's share increased. The raja now nominated one of the headmen, generally a member of the most important family in the village as the village 'pradhan' or 'gramani'. The office of the 'pradhan' or 'gramani' was ordinarily hereditary and for his services to the raja and the village community he was granted land which paid no taxes for the raja and at the same time ensured enough remuneration for his labours. On the one hand, he was responsible for the collection of land tax and on the other hand, he was required to make an equitable and generally acceptable distribution of the land-tax on the different families of the village. This, however, was subject to the general control of the village council over all aspects of village life.

The village, from the earliest times, had been a permanent centre of activity. With houses built of stone, fields fenced and water channels dug for irrigation, it was not easy to abandon these in the hope of getting a better place for sustaining a livelihood. This led to an increase in the authority and the responsibilities of the raja. He was required to protect his subjects, punish thieves, honour the rules of social conduct humself, provide munificent charity to Brahmins and monks and punish all those who violated the rules of human conduct as laid down in the ancient books. Thus the raja besides being a protector of his subjects was also an administrator of justice. He appointed his officers from the higher castes to supervise the administration of towns and villages and they in their turn appointed officials for their own help. One of the most important duties of these officials was to collect taxes and render detailed accounts to the raja. The incidence of taxation of agricultural produce was generally one sixth of the gross produce. Irrigated fields, however, paid a little more and marginal lands somewhat less than this generally accepted share of the raja. In times of war or other emergency, the incidence of taxation was raised by the raja to provide for the extra expenditure which his treasury had to bear. In years of surplus production, too, the raja's share was raised to keep a buffer stock for lean years as it was the raja's duty to provide food for his subjects in years of drought or other agricultural calamity. The dues from land were paid in kind. Other items of taxation were sale of gold, cattle, merchandise, fruits, flowers, herbs, honey, meat, firewood etc. Besides, the artisans and manual labourers were required to put in a few days free labour for the raja. Although all the commodities of gain or enjoyment were taxable, several persons were exempted from taxes. They were the Brahmins, the widows and dependents of soldiers killed in war, minors, unmarried girls, the raja's servants and the village and other deities.

As land became a valuable possession of the family a set of rules were evolved for the inheritance of landed property which could be summed up as follows. In the absence of a son or near relation of the head of the family, the sapinda males-males within six degrees-could succeed to the property of the deceased. The widow was not entitled to succession in the landed property, but she could claim her ornaments and gifts, and maintenance from the family of her deceased husband. In the absence of any heir, the property passed to the raja. Such cases were, however, extremely rare as adoption of male heir was the general practice. These general principles were not mandatory and the local customs of inheritance etc. were honoured and enforced by the raja.

In Nepalese villages the raja had only a share in the produce of land. He had no ownership rights on the land which was cultivated by his subjects. So long as the raja received his share of the produce, he was not to interfere in the customary rights of the cultivators. Vacant land, barren land, forests, not being the raja's forests, meadows and pastures were the property of the village community which alone could let out unoccupied arable land to any cultivator and thus create new rights. The raja, however, was entitled to his share of the produce. The raja's property rights were restricted to the lands under his personal cultivation and the forest areas reserved for his game. The proprietory right in land, thus, vested in the village community, and this was so recognised. But from times immemorial land could be donated to the village and other deities, Brahmins and Buddhist monks for their maintenance.

The early village societies were classless and there was no appreciable difference between rich and poor. But by the time of Asoka's visit to the Nepal valley the difference between the two classes of society had widened and a rich and a poor class had come into being. Simultaneously about this same time, a new class of sharecroppers had sprung up. The monks and the priests of the different religious codes of the time forbade the monks and the priests from carrying out cultivation with their own physical labour. Most of the Brahmin orders as also the Buddhist monks consider ploughing and other agricultural activities as a stigma to their social status and carry out these operations on their holdings with the help of hired labourers or servants. The monks and priests required the help of labourers and servants to manage and operate their farms, and if they were too engrossed in their own priestly work and could not even undertake the burden of cultivation, the land was let out to them for a share of the produce at the time of the harvests. This system was well established in the time of the Buddha and its origin can be traced to the time when land was gifted for the maintenance of the worship of local deities and to Brahminical priests by the raja. The Buddhist canon laid down that a monk shall have no personal property and even if he had any he was required to renounce it before entering the monastic order. However, a monastery could have its own buildings, other properties and valuables. Large farms, orchards, and other land was donated to the monasteries for their maintenance. Cultivation of gifted land was carried through hired farm labour or sharecroppers. The former involved organisation of a system for management of farm labour, payment of wages and supervision of the various agricultural operations, which was cumbersome and against the precepts of a monastic life. Therefore, the latter system of cultivating land through sharecroppers was preferred. This did not involve the monasteries or the Brahmin households in direct cultivation and yet it assured them of a regular share in the produce. The harvest was divided at the threshing fields. One-sixth portion was given to the monastery or the Brahmin priests and another one-sixth was reserved for the raja. This share was generally donated by the raja to the monastery or the priest concerned. But some times when the monks or priests were avaricious, they gave out the work themselves to the servants, male and female, and supervised the cultivation. In such cases the monks or priests appropriated the produce after alloting a small share to the servants for their sustenance.[1]

The raja at times made gift of his share of the village produce to a religious or charitable institution or to any of his distinguished officers. In the event of such an assignment of the raja's share, the collections were made by the normal machinery of the raja and thereafter the amount pertaining to the gifts of land was transferred to the individual or the institution from the raja's funds. But grant of land by a raja only meant that the share of the produce of such land which should have gone to the raja was now given to the assignee. In course of time the use of copper, silver and gold coins developed first in the river valley areas and then became widespread. The silver coinage of the Mallas in the Kathmandu valley became the usual coinage not only of neighbouring rajas but of Tibet also. Rajas like the raja of Gorkha and Palpa struck their own coins and after Prithvi Narayan Shah, the Gorkha coins became the monetary units of the entire Gorkha Kingdom. Along with the development of money the share of the raja from the produce was calculated in money terms and generally levied as such. This was because it was easier to send money to Kathmandu than the raja's share of the produce. The village 'pradhan' or the spokesman of a trans-Himalayan village recognised by the raja as such were helped by professional record-keeper families. The accountants and tax collectors of the raja came to be known as patwaris or keepers of land records. Although these offices were not strictly hereditary yet the claims of the near relatives were considered for filling the vacancies. In other words, the raja or his representative was not bound to appoint the heir of the deceased person for collecting his share of the produce but generally this was done as it was the most convenient arrangement.

Note

1. I-tsing—A record of the Buddhist religion, p. 61.

Ten

Women in Nepal

We shall discuss the role and the position of women in Nepal from two perspectives. One is the influence of geographical or environmental conditions and the other is that of social and economic factors.

Nepal is the pre-eminent Central Himalayan country. To its east are Sikkim, Bhutan and Arunachal and to its west Kumaon and Garhwal in Uttar Pradesh, Himachal Pradesh and Jammu and Kashmir in India and Chitral in Pakistan. The geographical conditions, with minor variations, are the same throughout this Himalayan region. The variations also come because of geographical factors. The high valleys between the main Himalayan and the Karakoram ranges are quite different from lands in the Tibetan plateau and have more in common with the sub-Himalayan regions. Then come the middle mountain ranges south of the Himalayas. Then come the thick forests of the Tarai which have been de-forested and populated in very recent times. We shall notice the influence of these factors on the lives of women in Nepal as we take up the broader aspects of social life in detail.

Firstly, we find that the life of women in Nepal is life-long hard work. They run the households because most of the time the men, except the children and the elderly males, work outside the house and quite often in distant lands. In the house the husbands are treated as treasured and welcome guests as they are the bread-winners. The men join the British and the Indian armies, work as house guards and personal attendants in India, Hongkong and most other countries where the British and the Indians are to be found. This is because Nepal is a very poor country and for their very sustenance the Nepalese have to seek worthwhile incomes outside their country. Most of the Nepalese abroad, however, keep their homesteads intact and the custodians there are the wives and the joint family. The greatest chunk of Nepal's national income comes to the households via the post offices and in the form of money orders. So men work outside the house, mostly in distant places and the wives look after the infertile fields, the farm animals and the joint family. Even when the menfolk return to the villages, all household chores are performed by women except ploughing. Even when the wife goes to the road side stop where her husband would get down from a transport bus, the husband would walk in front and his personal baggage and parcels of gifts for the household would generally be carried by the wife and daughter.

The women are the first to get up in the morning and the last to retire in the evening. They attend to the children and prepare tea and light food for the family. Then the young girls in the family will have to fetch water for the household. Water is scarce throughout Nepal except where the habitation is near a river. In the trans-Himalayas the houses are together and water is near at hand. So also in the Tarai where the village is next to a water point. But in the middle mountains level land is scattered far and wide and the Nepalese build their individual houses in their own lands which may be a couple or more kilometres from the village. In the middle mountains arable land and human habitation is generally located between altitudes of 3000 to 4500 feet above sea level. At these heights the springs and rivulets may be at some distance and the time consumed in fetching water could be considerable. This is always the work assigned to women in Nepal. The cows and sheep, if any, have to be taken to the forests in the highlands which could be from 5500 to 8000 feet above the village households. This is the task for the young boys and girls once they are about ten years old. In the rainy season the women would also go to the forest to bring back stacks of grass to be turned into hay for winter months. They have also to collect fire-wood from the forest to cook food. All this takes several hours and is sometimes quite risky. In summer months, when there is hardly any grass to be found, the women have to climb oak and other broad leaf trees to cut down branches so that the animals could be fed with the leaves. If the woman falls down, and has a fracture she cannot get any surgical assistance except near district headquarters where trained surgeons are available.

In the trans-Himalayan region of Bhote women have to work equally hard. There the men and the boys take the sheep and goats to the pastures from sunrise to sundown. So the women have to get up quite early and deliver meals to the menfolk before they leave for the meadows. And after the wool is collected, its processing, carding, spinning and weaving is done by the women. Every woman in Bhote, from childhood, learns how to work with wool. She makes woollen cloth, carpets and scarfs for the household and for sale. Their menfolk also are absent from the household for most part of the year. The women have to look after the houses at about 9000 feet in summer months and at about 7000 feet in winter months. In summer months, the young boys often go to the higher altitudes in search of fresh grass but in winter the men folk and a few women leave for warmer valleys along with their flocks. This may easily take six to nine months. So in these high altitude villages also the women have to take complete responsibility to run the households for most parts of the year.

In the Tarai, however, things are a little different. Because of historical reasons the Tharus and similar other castes carry most of the burden of agriculture and the women look after the households where they are real masters. It is said that when the ladies of the higher caste soldiers fled to the forest sanctuaries in the Himalayas to escape falling into the hands of the conquering Muslim armies, they could not escape to the hills as their menfolk had been killed or were missing and the routes to the higher ranges were not known to the ladies. So they look shelter in the thick forests of the Tarai. The only menfolk with them were their palanquin bearers. The Tharus are their progeny and to this day the women are greatly respected amongst them.

Women in another tribal group could also be noticed here. When one travels in Central Nepal especially between Kathmandu and Pokhra one finds several inns on the road side. They are called "Bhattis' or "Thakalis'. These are run by women folk who call themselves "Thakalis' or residents of the village of Thak in upper Kali river. These inns or Thakalis are neatly kept and provide excellent food. The Thakali inns also serve home brewed beer and liquor. It is possible that the Thakalis learnt the art of brewing beer from the Bhotes who excel in this and who also run this type of inns on their trade routes. East of Nepal, it is common to find women sitting in shops and doing business and Khasi women selling home made brews around Shillong; but the Thakali inns are a speciality of Central Nepal only.

Nepalese society, however, has been unkind to women. Although, they run the households, the master in the eyes of law and society is the male. The social unit is invariably the joint family and the representative of the family is the eldest male member living in the household. In the eyes of law, women live throughout their lives in tutelage, first to their fathers, then to their husbands and in old age to their sons. It is for this reason that the birth of a son has always been deemed essential. If a wife could not give birth to a male child, the husband was expected to marry again. The position of women amongst Hindus was thus always subordinated to the nearest male agnates. Because of this Hindu society took recourse to the doctrine of "Stridhan' or Women's property. All gifts of jewellery etc. to the women by their parents, husbands, sons and other relations were their absolute property and in general the women carried their jewellery on their own persons in the form of gold or silver ornaments. Thus they served as human banks for their 'stridhan' and as theft is practically unknown in Nepal, the women feel quite safe.

Apart from "Stridhan" social customs enjoined proper care and reverence for the women. Often the mothers received more reverence than the male heads of the households. This was partly due to the fact that in any household the grand-parents would be old and infirm, the fathers would be away and the mothers would be in charge. However, the condition of a Hindu widow has been sad to say the least. But quite often the younger brother marries his elder brother's widow and amongst several communities like the Newars, Bhotes and Tamang widow remarriage is quite prevalent.

Nepalese women run the households, will work on their fields and even run shops and inns but they do not work individually as maids or servants in other people's households. The poor Bengali or Kerala girl will travel to distant places to work as housemaid but not the Nepali. This appears to be the custom in the entire Himalayan region. But now things are changing and these days Nepali women living in India will take up any work that Indian women do. Even in Kathmandu and the district headquarters the spirit of equality has spread to Nepalese women belonging to the middle classes. There are now several women lawyers, doctors, and writers. Nepalese women give dance performances and music recitals in Kathmandu, Darjeeling, Gangtok and other cities. This process of modernisation started with King Tribhuwan's proclamation of 18th February 1951 inaugurating a democratic form of government. And in 1990, Sahana Pradhan took part on behalf of the left parties at the highest level meetings of government and political parties.

Before we conclude, we would like to mention a few women who have shaped Nepal's history. Maya Devi was a Nepalese Raja's daughter. She was married to Shuddodan Raja of Kapilvastu who belonged to the Sakya clan of Kshatriyas. It was customary in those days for the first child to be born in the mother's parental home. So Maya Devi with her attendants was on her way to her father's house in Nepal when Siddarth Gautam was born to her at Lumbini in Nepal. She was resting there in a grove of trees when the pains came and she stood up holding to a branch of the tree above her. The child was delivered while she was standing. Maya Devi retired to her parent's house and died shortly afterwards. The child was reared by one of her sisters who was also married to Raja Shuddodan.

Maya Devi was a Nepalese princess who married an Indian Raja. Three hundred years later the compliment was returned by Charumati, a daughter of Ashoka who came from Patna or Pataliputra to Nepal, married a Nepalese Kshatriya Prince Devapal and made Nepal her permanent home. Ashoka came to Kathmandu, erected five stupas in Patan, and gave her daughter Charumati in marriage to a Nepalese prince. Like his other daughter Sanghmitra in Sri Lanka Charumati did a lot to spread Buddhism in Nepal. Because of her residence, Patan which had been a small town became the most important and popular town in the Baghmati valley. Her husband established a monastery for Buddhist monks. Shortly afterwards Charumati established a nunnery for Buddhist nuns. Buddhism flourished in the entire Himalayan ranges and constant contact was maintained with the great centres of Buddhism in Patna and Nalanda. This helped to make the Kathmandu valley the cultural centre for all Nepal.

We now come to a third Nepalese princess who helped shape the history of the region. In the case of the above two princesses, Maya Devi and Charumati, the interaction was between Nepal and India. In the 7th century A.D. Tibet produced a great warrior king, Sangtsen Gampo (c. 605-650). In those days, respectability was won by having marriage ties with old and well established royal families. The Tibetan king had the Tang Emperor Tai Zong as his neighbour to the North and Ansu Varman in Kathmandu. He married a Nepalese royal princess, called in Tibetan chronicles Princess Bri-Btsan. Later he married a Chinese royal Princess Wencheng and King Songtran Gampo received the title of Imperial son-in-law (fu-ma-du-wei) from the Tang emperor Tai Zong. The two princesses were accompanied by several Buddhist priests, scholars, architects and wood-workers, masons, stone carvers and painters. They brought with them new techniques and new ideas and the receptive Tibetan King embraced the Buddhist faith and prodded his people to assimilate the new precepts and learnings. He sent his best scholars to Nepal and India to bring the learning of these countries for the good of his people. The King then asked them to evolve a suitable alphabet for Tibetan and to translate all the great books into Tibetan. The Tibetan alphabet is based on the Brahmi of ancient India and some of the rare books of the Buddhists have been available in their Tibetan translation even when they had been destroyed in India. Princess Bri-Btsan, which appears to be Tibetan form of Priya Devi endeared herself to the Tibetans and they called her the Green Tara, Tara being the highest female divinity in Mahayan Buddhism.

Another Nepalese lady deserves mention here. She was Queen Tripur Sundari Devi. She was daughter of the Raja of Gulmi in western Nepal and she was married to Ran Bahadur Shah. As the queen bore him no children, Ran Bahadur neglected her and married a Brahmin girl. This was not approved of by the people in general but the offspring of the marriage Girvan Judha Bikram was accepted as the heir to the throne as the other son of Ran Bahadur was from a maid servant, a Keti. In 1800 A.D., Ran Bahadur was forced to abdicate and he retired to Benares, leaving Girwan Judha Bikram in the charge of the Keti. In Nepal durbar, conditions rapidly deteriorated under the Keti. Things were no better in Ran Bahadur's household in Benares. Queen Tripur Sundari Devi had come to Benares with her profligate husband as a devout Hindu wife. But Ran Bahadur took to a Benares beauty and, forcibly collecting her jewellery from Queen Tripur Sundari Devi, gave them to his new mistress. The Queen now felt greatly distressed and decided to return to Nepal. Queen Tripur Sundari Devi was accompanied by her maid servants only. When the Keti who was the Regent learnt that the Queen was approaching the fortress of Chirapani, she sent orders to the commander not to admit the Queen to the fort. The commander obeyed his orders and the Queen skirting the fortress walls proceeded on the road to Kathmandu. The Keti was in panic and hurriedly sent a company of soldiers with specific orders not to allow the Queen to move further towards the capital. The officer met the Queen and her female attendants at Chitlang a few miles from the valley and stopping the procession conveyed to the Queen the orders he had received. Queen Tripur Sundari Devi got down from her palanquin and is reported to have said: "I am the daughter of a Gorkhali Raja and the lawful wife of a Gorkhali Raja. Do you think you are doing the right thing by preventing me, who am in distress, from going to my own lawful house?" On hearing this, the officer bowed his head in shame and moved out of the way along with his men. That morning the Queen stopped about five miles from the capital. Kathmandu was in tumult and by the evening most of the senior officers and the common people had come to the queen for welcome and the Keti had fled from the capital to the sanctuary of a temple along with her own son and the heir-apparent.

Queen Tripur Sundari Devi then assumed the Regency and gave amnesty to all who had opposed her. She now started her benevolent and kind rule and Nepal rapidly returned to peaceful conditions. Learning of this episode in Benares, Ran Bahadur, whose stipend had been stopped by the East India Company by this time, decided to return to his country. He was accepted by the Queen and the populace as the rightful Regent. But he was a cruel prince and for two years the Nepal Court witnessed several murders, executions and painful deeds. In 1804, Ran Bahadur was murdered in Court and after a blood-bath the Nepal durbar settled down to the Regency of Queen Tripur Sundari Devi and the Prime Ministership of Bhim Sen Thapa. The Queen left the affairs of state in the hands of the Prime Minister and the elders at court. In 1816, Girvan Judha Bikram Shah died of smallpox leaving behind an infant son Rajendra Bikram Shah. Queen Tripur Sundari Devi continued as Regent for the infant prince. She gave full support to the Prime Minister in war and in peace and seldom interfered in the affairs of state except to see that good faith, compassion and fair play was observed in all matters concerning the state. This was insured by the Prime Minister Bhim Sen Thapa, whose one concern was the safeguarding of the interests of his country and preventing the East India Company from making Nepal a subsidiary state to the Company's government. Queen Tripur Sundari Devi had stopped the murderous enmity between the Pandes and the Thapas ever since the murder of Ran Bahadur in Court and consequent execution of several noblemen and officers as conspirators. The Queen, however, died in 1832 and Nepal witnessed another spell of murders, and revolts inspired by the court till Jung Bahadur came on the scene in 1846. The Nepalese remembered the Queen, a devout Hindu wife inspite of all transgressions of the husband, a queen mother and queen grand-mother lovingly looking after a stepson and a step grand-son who were heirs to the throne and a noble queen who brought justice and fair-play to a realm full of murders, squabbles, family feuds and conspiracies. She was remembered as a great and worthy woman and a benevolent queen by all her subjects for decades after her death.

Eleven

Rituals, Family Life, Food Habits and Dress

The ceremonial forms and observances of the majority of the population of Nepal derive from Vedic rituals, sometimes forgotten and sometimes ignored but always held in esteem and awe. While the synthetic influence of the Vedas and Hindu religious scriptures, as interpreted by the Brahmin priests, is all-pervading; some ceremonies go back to immemorial antiquity and can be traced to other groups inhabiting the Himalayan regions side by side with the main 'parbatiya' or hills group of peoples. In course of time spans of centuries the Vedic gods and ceremonies are ousted and new gods and goddesses are brought into the Hindu pantheon by the priests. Variations are adapted to suit local customs and diversity is accepted. But the cultural pattern persists and is strengthened by the adaptation.

Birth-A corner of the house is set apart for the mother during child birth. The midwife is generally in attendance and cuts the child's chord. The time of birth is recorded by the elders so that the priest may cast the correct horoscope. A fire is lit near the mother's corner and rock-salt, butter, grains and mustard seeds are thrown into the fire to purify the air. This is repeated morning, afternoon and evening for eleven days. The child and the mother are considered ceremoniously unclean. They take a regular bath on the twelfth day when after a short puja or ceremony by the priest, the mother and child join the family. The separate corner for the mother and child is washed with cowdung paste and urine of the cow is sprinkled in the house and its surroundings with stalks of grass. The custom is suited to the hills as the mother and child get compulsory rest and protection from infection. The fire with the smoke from burning mixture of grains, salt, butter etc., the pasting of the floor with cowdung and sprinkling of cow-urine are hygienic steps for the protection of the environment. Cow dung and cow urine are antiseptic household utilities easily and uniformly available. This first ceremony is called the "nam karan" ceremony and the duty of the priest is to announce the "rashi nam" or the name of the child as determined by the horoscope. However, the child can be given a name by his mother or father, which will be used in the school, the village and civil life.

But every woman in Nepal is not so fortunate. The majority of them are poor and have to take part in the household work after just two or three days. The Nepalese women are healthy because of life-long hard work and take child birth in their stride. In most households these days the sixth day after the birth of the child, the near relatives are invited to a formal feast. These are the relatives who are also considered unclean till the twelfth day, and on that very day the priest holds the purification and name giving ceremonies.

First giving of solid food

The child is fed on mother's milk till this ceremony is performed. It is called "anna-prasan" and is generally held in the sixth month. Relatives and friends are invited to a feast. The priest performs a little "puja" and the parents, for the first time, feed the child with rice, pulses, meat or fish.

Chuda Karma or Cutting of hair

This ceremony takes place in the third year or later and the barber, where available, is called to cut the virgin hair with a razor. The priest may or may not be called and there is generally a feast for the relatives.

Upanayan or thread ceremony

This is for the three higher "varnas" of Hindu society only. Initially it was the occasion when the boy was given the sacred cord worn over the left shoulder and across the body. On this day, the boy was sent to a preceptor's home to learn the Vedas and the useful arts pertaining to his 'varna' *i.e.* being a Brahmin, a Kshatriya or a Vaishya. The Parsees also wear a cord but round their waist and the Buddhists of the Hinayan regions retire to a monastery whenever they feel like doing so for a short or a longer period. This ceremony has in recent years been neglected and quite often is combined with the marriage ceremony. Of course, the Gorkhas, Magars etc. *i.e.* the majority do not observe this ceremony.

Marriage

We have already discussed the legal and customary aspects of Hindu and Newar marriages in the chapter on religion. We propose to take up the ritual aspects here. Generally, the parents arrange the marriage. Most marriages take place amongst known kinship families and the horoscopes are tallied by the family priests. In most cases a betrothal ceremony is held. It is called "magai" or "tilak", where small presents are exchanged between the parents.

The marriage ceremony itself is held later after consulting the priests who determine the auspicious dates for happy marriages and the parents select the date that suits both parties. On the date fixed the bridegroom and his party arrive at the bride's house sometime in the evening. In the families of soldiers a mock battle is enacted with balls of rice or vegetables till the priest of the bridegroom explains that the groom and his party have come for honourable marriage and not forcibly carrying away the bride. The throwing of the balls by the bride's party now stops and the bridegroom, who comes on a pony or palanquin, gets down, comes forward and the bride's parents welcome him with an "arati". In this ceremony a small lamp with cotton wick and ghee is lighted in a special kind of vessel which is swayed from right to left in front of the bridegroom. The bridegroom puts his palms in front of the lighted wick which is at once his show of respect for the light and his acceptance of the welcome. He is then taken towards the house where the bride's parents wash his feet before taking him inside. This is more of a token now than actual performance. In olden days travellers washed their feet before entering a household. Now-a-days with shoes on every one's feet a little sprinkling with water over the feet is enough. A new custom is gradually spreading amongst the well-to-do and that is "jai-mal" or garlanding of the groom by the bride. This has come from Northern India and is an innovation.

The actual marriage ceremony is performed, generally at night, before a ceremonial fire and with the bride, bridegroom and the parents. The exact time of the "yagya" is decided by the priests after consulting the almanac. Then starts the formal 'kanya-dan' or act of giving away the girl by her father or guardian. The father places the hand of the bride into the hand of the bridegroom. This is called 'pani-grahan' or acceptance of the hand and symbolises the promise of the groom to accept the bride. He also puts red "sindur" along the hair parting of the bride indicating that she is now a married woman. Then the bride is made to put her foot on the mill stone while her brother or mother puts some roasted grain in her hands which she sprinkles over the fire. The next ceremony is the "sapt-padi" or taking of seven steps jointly by the bride and the bridegroom. Then the couple come out in the open and are asked to look at the Pole Star. The idea is that they should be firm and bound to each other for life. This completes the ceremonies. All this time, however, the bride's younger sisters or relatives play tricks on the bridegroom and extract token favours from him. Generally his shoes are hidden and delivered to him only after he pays small change for the same. As the groom's party stays at the bride's place for the night, festivities continue till late at night and the women of the house take part in dancing and singing, celebrating the occasion.

Next morning the groom's party returns with the bride and the presents given to her by her parents and relatives. On arrival at the groom's house, the sisters of the groom prevent the entry of the bride at the door and allow her to enter only after receiving presents from their brother. Generally on the third day the husband and wife return to the house of the bride where she remains for the night.

Marriage customs differ widely in Nepal. While the above rituals are generally respected, many tribes manage without the Brahmins. The Gurungs of Kaski and Lamjung more often call the local Buddhist "Lama" for their rituals. The Bhotes and the Tamangs prefer the "Lama". The tribes in eastern Nepal are more liberal in matters of courtship marriage and divorce. The boys and girls are allowed to meet frequently and the decision about marriage is settled between themselves. The age of marriage is about 20 for boys and 16 for girls. But the marriage bond is as permanent and binding as in the rest of the country and the people seem to be happier and more carefree and social in the bargain.

Divorce and widows

Divorce and widow remarriage are permitted by most communities in Nepal. Marrying the widow of an elder brother is the right thing to do. So also is the custom of a widow or abandoned woman to live with a kinsman and become a part of the household. In such cases, a formal marriage ceremony is not performed.

Divorce, itself, though uncommon is a simple affair. The husband or the wife can ask the "panchayat" or the "elders of the community" for it. The elders hold a meeting, hear the parties and finally settle the matter. A fine is generally imposed on the party found to be at fault, and either party is allowed to remarry. In higher castes, Thakurs, Chhetris and Brahmins divorce is not practised, widows are not remarried but a man may have more than one wife. A soldier can not afford more than one wife, but a non-commissioned officer may go in for a second marriage because of his having bought more land in his native village than could be looked after by one wife.

We could also allude to the customs of polyandry, and celibacy for monks and nuns in the higher Himalayas and trans-Himalayas. These customs have been very helpful for society as they have kept population constant for umpteen centuries in these most unproductive regions of the world.

Death

Death is attended with numerous ceremonies, some of which go back to pre-historical times. Death is preferred on the bare ground rather than on a bed. When the relatives think that the end has almost come, they take the body down from the bed and place it on the ground. Ganga jal or water from one of the sacred rivers or "sun-pani" or gold water is put to the person's mouth and also sprinkled over him after death. "Sun-pani" is water in a pot in which some piece of gold is dipped and some sacred leaves like "tulsi" or "doob" grass is also kept. This is considered good enough if water from one of the sacred rivers is not at hand.

The corpse is then washed and wrapped in plain white cloth for men and red cloth for women. Sometimes the relatives wait for a few hours in case a son or a near relative can arrive in time for the funeral. It is assumed that the spirit of the dead person haunts the neighbourhood of his house after death. It follows the corpse to the burning ghat and unless the prescribed ceremonies are performed it turns into a malevolent ghost. Therefore all relatives, friends and neighbours who learn of the death throng to the dead man's house to accompany the corpse. The dead body is tied to a bamboo frame and the solemn procession, consisting of only men, starts with a leader or Brahmin who carries a forked twig in one hand and a cloth piece with grain and sesame seeds in the other. The leader drops grain and sesame seeds on the ground to indicate to the procession exactly to follow his foot steps. When the procession reaches the burning ghat, which is generally on a river side, a funeral pyre is made near the flowing waters. The corpse is laid on the ground, the Brahmin utters some prayers and the son or nearest male relative lights the fire. After the corpse is burnt, the ashes and pieces of bones left unburnt are washed into the river. In case the relatives want the ashes to be thrown into a more sacred river they are collected in an earthen pot and taken home. Only the well-to-do can afford this. After this, all take a bath in the river or sprinkle river water over their heads.

The funeral procession takes exactly the same route on its return journey as it had taken on its journey to the burning ghat and at the first cross roads, the leader collects a thorny branch from any tree or bush nearby and puts it under a stone at the cross road. The fork is also placed there. The intention is that, in case the dead man has turned into a malevolent ghost, the latter should follow the other road and not return with the crowd. All the men in the procession then go to a nearby "dharamshala" or pilgrims' hut and are fed by the son of the deceased. The procession returns to the house of the deceased, is met by the relatives who sprinkle cow's urine over them and, in some cases, after warming themselves over a ceremonial purifying fire each man returns to his own home.

In the house the son-who had his head shaven clean at the burning ghat-performs ceremonies for the peace of the dead man's spirit for thirteen days. The spirit is supposed to be wandering around the house and the son is expected to look after it. He keeps aloof from others, sleeps on the ground and has only one simple meal a day. This he shares with his father's spirit by first putting a portion of it wrapped up in leaves outside in the open where the spirit is supposed to partake of it. Actually it is eaten up by birds. The son offers prayers for the dead man's spirit three times every day—sun-rise, mid-day and sun-set. This continues for twelve days and the final ceremony for the dead takes place on the thirteenth day and is performed by a Brahmin. The household prepares a feast for the day and all relatives are called. At the ceremony small portions of all the food articles are placed in a plate made of leaves and left in the open. This is the final offering to the dead man's spirit. After this ceremony the spirit is expected to join the universal spirit and rest in peace. The relatives partake of the feast and make small presents to the Brahmin or priest. The male cousins up to five generations share the twelve days of mourning, are supposed to be unclean during this period and do not visit temples or friends. Male cousins after five generations mourn for only three days.

Bhotes, Gurungs and Tamangs employ Lamas for the funeral ceremonies and quite often bury the corpse. This is mainly because of the dearth of fire wood in the localities inhabited by them. Instead of the thirteenth day purification ceremony, they perform what is called "arghun" between the third and the thirteenth day after death. It can also be postponed if the son is not present or the resources of the family do not permit the celebrations. In this ceremony a sheep and a fowl are sacrificed and distributed to the guests and the ceremony is presided over by the 'Lama'.

Connected with these rituals are shraddhas, pilgrimages, recitation of sacred books and household prayers. At the end of the rainy season a fortnight is set apart to remember the ancestors. A deceased mother is remembered on the ninth day and the father on the lunar day of his death. On that day balls of boiled rice are offered to the departed ancestors. These two days are observed in every household and special meals are prepared to which relatives are called and feasted.

Pilgrimages are undertaken for pleasure or as atonements for some moral lapses which continue to afflict one's conscience. These are also advised after mental depression, shock or ailment. These take the people in their thousands to sacred temples or spots mostly in secluded places where ardous journeys have to be undertaken to reach them. From times immemorial Kailas Mansarowar, Mukti Nath, Varanasi, Pashupati Nath and several other spots have called pilgrims to themselves. To this day most people in Nepal consider a pilgrimage as a very pious act, and people save for months and years to undertake such pilgrimages and earn religious benefits.

Recitation of sacred books is also common. The Buddhist Lama does it as a routine. For the Hindus the 'Bhagwat' with stories of Krishna was a favourite text but for the last couple of centuries the "Sat Narain Katha" or the story of Truth has been gaining in favour. It is generally recited on a full moon night but it can be held on any other day also if so desired. The recitation in Sanskrit is followed by a simple "puja" or ceremony and distribution of sweets. The sweets can be sugared fried flour and bananas, which can be afforded by every one, or princely feasts. The "Sat Narain Katha" is held when a wish has been fulfilled or an auspicious event has taken place and is a thanksgiving ceremony.

Household prayers are distinguishing features of the Himalayas. In these mountains, the forces of Nature cannot be ignored. Thunder, lightning, losing one's way in the forest, meeting wild animals etc. are facts of daily life. So there are as many gods in heaven and as many spirits on land and water as the forces of Nature one encounters. For the protection of the village, there is a "gram devata", for the family a "kuldevata" and for oneself an "isht devata". Every forest has a "Van devata", every prominent peak has a "devata" or "devi" and every burning ghat a "maha kal" or "pishach"-the god of death or a malevolent spirit. In the mountains you are overwhelmed by Nature. Human habitations are few and far apart and modern means of mass communication have not yet penetrated to all areas to inculcate a common mass culture based on TV and Radio broadcasts. Therefore, the majority of the Nepalese who are away from the towns and modern highways have to make peace with all the elemental forces they have to face in their lives. The best way is to try to please all the gods and goddesses who protect and to keep at bay all the evil spirits which try to harm. Therefore one will find small temples in all villages, forests and river sides. If there is no temple, there may be a small raised platform or even a simple collection of rough-hewn stones to indicate the sacred spots dedicated to the relevant god or goddess. It is part of the heritage of the ancient inhabitants of the Himalayan regions. The Vedic sages meditated on these forces of Nature and called them Indra, Agni, Varuna etc. Only the Raja could obtain the services of the learned for his ceremonies to please the gods with sophisticated names but the common people had to be content with their own understanding of these forces of Nature. These traditions continue to the present times. The wise men from all over the East come to the Himalayas for meditation. They believe in the Supreme Buddha or the Upanishads of the Hindus. But both Buddhists and Hindus are very tolerant in matters of belief and rituals. These wise-men, when they see these local temples, and local icons, simply nod their heads and walk on, holding that the people who are not yet enlightened have to follow what their ancestors followed and that their beliefs and rituals should neither be shunned nor condemned. Even shamans and simple tricksters are tolerated so long as they merely prescribe worship of local gods and feasts to the community. In every society there are men and women who can work themselves into trances and in that state possess some extra sensory perceptions. It is easy to ridicule these men but in the remote villages of Nepal they perform a social function. They diagnose spirits and ghosts possessing men and women and devise ways and means of frightening them away. Their services are useful in cases of mental illness, hysteria and depression. These ailments are generally attributed to evil spirits or ghosts getting possession of the ailing person. And in many cases the exhortations of the shaman are successful.

The people also believe in the evil eye or jealousy of the people visiting them; harm predicted in the horoscopes and spells and counterspells. The evil eye is averted by simply burning red-chillies and ghee in a spoon and passing it over the head of the person, generally a child. It is more likely that the smoke thus produced destroys the viruses common in these areas and helps cure the affliction of the suffering child. To avert the disaster predicted in horoscopes, the Brahmin priest or the Lama is asked to repeat appropriate mantras from the scriptures hundred, thousand or lakh times. Spells and counterspells are more like witchcraft in other primitive societies. They are cast to win over a person's love or remove his or her infatuation over another person. It is sometimes resorted to destroy someone or his progeny but in all undeserved cases the spell is supposed to revert and destroy the spellthrower himself. However, cases are known where evil-minded people have persuaded others to drink some potions which have partially or totally destroyed their mental faculties.

But these variations from organised religion are not more common in Nepal than in say Indian or any European society. There will always be some unconventional men and women, rituals and ceremonies in all societies and it is no good to emphasize them. On the whole Nepalese society, with several diverse cultural traits, is a well regulated and friendly society. People are satisfied with their lot and family life is happy and peaceful. The family in Nepal, amongst all the tribes, polyandrous or polygamous, is the anchor of the society. It is one solid unit and the grand parents and the grand children are loved and well cared for. It is unthinkable that a son or daughter-in-law will not look after his parents. Similarly, the women in a common household will look after all the children of their husbands and their brethren if they live together. This family bond is illustrated by the use of words intended for the father and his brothers. The elder brother of a person is called by his children 'bara bap' or elder father. The younger brothers may take liberties with the elder brother's wife but for the elder brother a younger brother's wife is like a daughter and he may never even touch her clothes while passing nearby.

The wife comes to her husband's house at an early age. Since her childhood she has been taught that she does not belong to her father's house and her real home and house is her husband's house. The mother-in-law and the other women in the house again inculcate the same tradition. The wife has no existence apart from the family of her husband and throughout her life she is a daughter, a wife or a mother. She is repeatedly told that she comes to a new household in a wedding 'doli' a palanquin and leaves it only on a funeral 'doli'. The traditions of the household and the family are in her custody and the continuity of the common family traditions is her contribution to national stability. Throughout history she has shared her husband's fortunes in prosperity and distress and that too without a murmur. She accepts the occasional waywardness of her husband and even accepts a second wife or other woman in the house. All the offspring of her husband are dear to her and she is expected to look after all of them as her own children. This, however, does not mean that the family is never disrupted. Divorces are uncommon but are simply arranged with the approval of the elders in a family or larger community group. The Nepalese wife carries out all household chores as the husband does all business with the world outside the house. In most cases the husband is away from the house, in his youthful days for long periods, earning the bread for the household. So when he comes to the house, say for about a month in a year, he is very well looked after by the wife. She would willingly press his legs, arrange hot bath for him and prepare her best cooking dishes for him. The man just accepts all this as routine. Similarly the wife, whose husband is at home, likes him to go to the nearest tea shop, spend the day gossiping, smoking or drinking tea with his friends and leave the wife alone to look after the hundred and one daily chores of the household. On the whole family life is quiet, familiar and nothing to speak about but steady and tolerant. Of course, there are cases where wives are harassed by the in-laws to distraction necessitating the services of an exorcist or Brahmin. In extreme cases wives and widows in particular may have to secure salvation by joining a Buddhist nunnery or leave for Varanasi or Mathura where Hindu religious institutions offer food and shelter. But on the whole, family life is a stable and vigorous institution in Nepal and to this day there are no signs of the family breaking up into exclusive individual units. Even in legal matters it holds good. Land in a village is owned in a broader sense by the different communities and the rights of preemption allow kinsmen to stop persons outside the kinship from buying land in their village. The right allows a kinsman to regain the land sold by a person to an outsider by paying him the price paid by the latter. Sharing of wives by the brothers also preserves land for the family and polyandry by limiting births helps the same purpose.

Food habits

In Nepal, because of the climate, all men and women, of all castes and tribes, eat meat. If one is a pure vegetarian, he is so because of his personal preferences. However, the cow is a sacred animal and killing a cow is totally banned by law. Custom provides that all Nepali citizens, even when abroad, must abstain scrupulously from partaking of beef or any beef extract. A Nepali will never order beef and will refuse it if he is told of its being part of a dish. But now-a-days he willingly never orders a beef dish and at the same time asks no searching questions when in a western home or restaurant.

As early as the Nepal Tibet War of 1850s, Jung Bahadur obtained a ruling from the Raj Guru *i.e.*, the religious preceptor to the king and the state that yak was not cow and, in later years, that Gorkha battalions when on duty overseas will have no restrictions on food except for beef.

The Nepali enjoys a meat dish especially of wild pig or goat. He relishes fowl, eggs and fish and in most martial tribes and even with Bhotes and Tharus, a ceremony is seldom complete without plenty of meat dishes. His staple diet, however, is coarse rice in the day and coarse millet or buck wheat chapatis or bread at night. In other words, he has rice in the day and chapatis at night. Potatoes and onions are common vegetables and tomatoes, peas, cauliflower and cabbage are recently being propagated to the remotest villages by the soldiers returning from duty outside the country.

Cows are difficult to feed in the mountains. They are small animals and their yield is hardly a litre or two per day. This must have been the reason why the cow was declared a sacred animal. There is no legal prohibition, but the longtailed sheep, used as a beast of burden is also seldom killed for meat. In certain Gurung areas the household pig is avoided and Ghales do not eat chicken or eggs. The Bhotes and most tribes in Eastern Nepal eat buffalo meat and on ceremonial occasions it is killed in most parts of Nepal.

A Nepali household will generally start the day with a glass of tea. Porcelain cups are rare and steel glasses and plates are in common use. The children get a couple of "chapaties" kept from the previous evening with some vegetables or chutney left over. The main meal of the day will be early in the morning before work starts for the family. Coarse rice with dal and some vegetable is generally served and the working day starts a couple of hours after sun-rise. In the day one or more intervals with glasses of tea may be expected and sometimes some fried dish of potatoes may be produced. The evening meal is ready soon after sun-set consisting of chapaties, and one or more vegetables, with potato as an ingredient, and chillies or onion pieces. This is over a couple of hours after sun-set. On special occasions sweetened flour-balls or cakes are made. These can be kept for a week or so.

The Nepalese make very good wines and brews and both men and women enjoy drinks and smoking. The Thakalis who run inns on the Pokhra Kathmandu road make excellent hard drinks and the Bhotes and the eastern tribes in the higher altitudes offer exquisite beer type drink made of fermented barley. They also make some drinks like the Tibetan "chhang" which is both light and refreshing. In Nepal, people enjoy the good things of life and good food and drinks add to the openness of their character and cheerfulness. They are good mixers and will join in singing and dancing when they are in a social party. They are welcome guests in any European group and any Army Mess in India or abroad.

Dress and Jewellery

In the mountains the dress is made from home spun and woven pieces of woollen cloth. The Bhotes copy the Tibetan styles as these are more suited to their arid and cold climate. In Central Nepal, a rough home spun sheet covers the upper part of the body down to the waist. It is wrapped in such a way that it leaves both the arms free and sports a sag at the back in such a fashion that small articles can safely be put in it. It is called a "khadim". In higher mountains tight trousers are worn made of home-spun woollen cloth. In the lower mountains only a kilt suffices.

The typical Nepali formal dress is a double-breasted waistcoat called "chaubandi" fixed with tapes instead of buttons. This keeps the breast warm in the cold climate. Loose trousers of the same material are worn and a loose piece of cloth is wound round the waist. This serves as a wide belt and is said to prevent backache. Quite often a coat of modern design is worn over the waist coat or "chaubandi".

The Nepali, however, is best recognised by his cap. It is a simple affair made of white or coloured cloth, high on one side and low on the other. In recent years the "chaubandi" and the Nepali cap have gained in popularity, and emphasize the Nepali identity.

The women put on a many-plaited skirt. This gives them greater freedom compared to an Indian "sari" while carrying firewood or grass from the forest. They put on a bodice above the waist and cover their bodies with a cotton or woollen shawl depending on the weather. They do not cover their faces and the shawl makes do as a pad for the protection of the head while carrying a head load.

As theft is practically unknown, jewellery on the bodies of women carries the savings of the family. Necklaces made from different coloured beads from India are cheap and universal. But generally jewellery consists of gold or silver articles. It starts with ear rings, and nose rings. The Gurung women, however, do not like nose rings. Bracelets and bangles of gold are common. For the feet anklets and toe-rings are generally made of silver. Richer families sport gold necklaces with single or more strings. The "Sat-lari" or the necklace with seven strings is a sure sign of riches. The Bhotes and some tribes in the east obtain turquoise jewellery from Tibet and are proud owners of the same. The Newars in Kathmandu make the best jewellery and set the pattern for all the goldsmiths in Nepal.

Twelve

Music, Dance and Drama

In Nepal, songs and music are inseparable. The bamboo reed grows everywhere in the Himalayas and is the commonest musical instrument. The shepherd boy plays on his flute whenever he sits by his flock in the meadows or the hill tops. The girls when they are out in the forest, collecting fuel wood or cutting grass often start humming musical tunes to arrest the drudgery of their work. Even the Brahmins and the Buddhist monks say their prayers and scriptures with musical intonation. The folk songs change from valley to valley, but by and large, they are sung with an intonation and rhythm peculiar to the Himalayas. Then there are songs for different occasions; *e.g.* to celebrate births or weddings of special festivals connected with sowing, harvesting, reaping or threshing of grain. Religious music is reserved for temples and monasteries and primitive extravaganza for the devil or the Mahakali dances *i.e.* the destructive elements in nature.

But first let us have a look at the musical instruments. The flute made from bamboo or other reeds is found all over the Himalayas. It is easily made with the help of any small knife and is easy to tune. In the high mountains, the horn is equally common. It is easily made from Yak or buffalo horn. In monasteries and temples, however, horns are larger and are made from copper which is found almost in every district of Nepal. Sometimes these horns are of enormous size and their sound can be heard at great distances. They are blown like trumpets and sturdy monks are deputed to blow them on special occasions. The flute and the horn are almost readymade by nature. The drum, however, needs more human handiwork. There are dozens of varieties of drums in Nepal. The "Damru" has two surfaces and a thin middle portion. It has two strings striking the two sides when the "Damru" is moved from side to side. In

India, the man with a dancing monkey carries a typical "Damru". Then there is the "Dholak" which is placed on the legs when the player sits down or is hung from the shoulders, when the player is standing or dancing. This type of drum is elongated when it is used in a temple and is called "Mridanga". There are also large kettle drums in temples and monasteries called by various names in different regions which are derived from the Sanskrit words "Bheri" and "Dundhubhi".

For keeping time, Nepalese have varieties of cymbals, large and small. Every household will probably have a few pairs of brass cymbals while princely durbars, temples and monasteries will have much larger versions of the same, alongwith some gongs and prayer bells.

The "Vina" or the harp shaped "Vina" is found only in princely houses and seems to have been imported from China and India. The indigenous stringed instrument is a simple contrivance made with dried gourd or pumpkin shell and a single metallic string. It is called an "Ek-tara" and is used by peripetatic mendicants.

The musical instruments of Nepal confirm the simple agrarian background of the general public. They are pastoral or agrarian and even their local chieftains or "Pradhans" are locals whose contacts with the far more fastidious civilisations of China and India were limited to importing of luxury items, but all the people loved their songs and they had them for all occasions.

Music has always gone with dancing. The Nepalese-Gorkhas and Newars alike love dancing. Shiva-the Mahadeo, the great Lord of the mountains loved dancing with his damru. He is said to have been the first deity who taught dancing to his devotees. And a popular myth with the Buddhists has been Buddha's "Mar Vijay" or victory over temptation by the daughters of Mar or the god of Love. Later another legend gained ground, namely, that the Buddha was entertained in Sukhawati or the Western Paradise by "apsaras" or celestial maidens,"gandharvas" or singers and "Kinnaras" or musicians. The recent discoveries in Danhuang (on the old silk Road and at the Western end of the Hexi Corridor) of several grottos with depiction of Buddhist themes from Tibet, Mongolia, Nepal and Western India testify to an ancient tradition of dancing and music. Some of these "apsaras" play musical instruments such as the flute and the harp and the "Kinnaras" have drums and cymbals. In the Sanskrit classics all these celestial beings are said to be inhabitants of the Himalayas. The "apsaras" dance gracefully. Some have rather solid figures, are gorgeously dressed and richly ornamented, while others have slender, wispy bodies and are simply clothed.[1]

Even to this day both these types are found in Nepal. The main route from India to join the old Silk Road through Central Asia was from Varanasi via Muktinath and Taklakot and from Hardwar via Niti, Mana and Jad Ganga passes to Kailash. These routes joined the Silk Road at Khotan, and Tibetan, Nepalese and Indian goods merchandise and cultural traditions were preserved in the travellers inns, grottos and monasteries on the main highways.

The tradition of dance comes from very ancient times in Nepal. What we call as folk-music, folklore and folk-drama are components of Nepalese tradition of music, dance and drama. These merge one into the other art form. Nepalese dances include household dances for all special family occasions. Almost everywhere in Nepal the women in the bridegroom's house join in the "Ratoli" which is an exclusively women's affair. In it every woman in the household and amongst the guests is expected to take part, each one giving an exposition of her mastery of the art. Men and boys are strictly forbidden to watch or take part in "Ratoli". Another exclusively women's dance is the "Jora" held after the evening puja on Tij which comes eleven days after the birthday of Krishna, which falls on the eighth day of the month of Bhadon. It symbolises the ceremonial cleansing of Krishna's mother after his birth.

Then there are village dances where both men and women take part. Generally, the unmarried girls join the dance while the boys play the "Dholak". The dancers in a long row gracefully move forwards and backwards with rhythmic movements of the hands, head and the waist. The Magars and the Gurungs patronise this type of dance which they call "Ghanto". For watching the "Ghanto", the men have to bring some contribution which may be a small sum of money or some other present. However, for several other dances men and women link their arms and dance in a closed circle. With each dance movement, the dancers advance one or one-half step in the circle. This allows the dance to continue till the actors get tired. Such community dances take place on special festive occasions before the pradhan's house, the open courtyard in front of a temple or in a monastery or on the meeting ground of a festival or "Mela".

In Nepal, sowing, transplanting, and harvesting of rice are community programmes. All the able-bodied women of the village take part in these operations.

The village drummer moves in front with beats of his drum and the appropriate songs and the monotonous agricultural work is done at a fast pace by the women. The sound of the drum-beats and of the music works as a hypnotic and fields after fields are covered in a single day. The productivity of human labour is certainly increased manifold by this accompaniment of music and rhythmic movement of the women, especially in transplanting and harvesting. There are also several dances in Nepal, where men and women dance and sing in pairs. Such are the : "Juwari" in Western Nepal and the "Dhan Nach" in Limbu and Rai areas.

A visit to the temple or the monastery was a thanks-giving occasion, both for individuals and the community as a whole. The journey as well as the festivity at the religious centre was accompanied by music, dance and drama. In the temples, the dance procession was itself a sort of folk-drama. It celebrated a famous victory of the local Chieftain or the call to prayer on auspicious occasions. The folklores narrated on such occasions acquainted the populace with the myths and the legends of its cultural heritage and assumed the form of a moving drama. The Devi Dance with masks in the Himalayan monasteries is even now a mixture of music, dance, drama and religion. In the end, the Good wins and the Evil is vanquished. Similarly, in Hindu villages the Ramlila is performed by local actors in the ten days of Dashera ending with the victory of Ram over Ravan *i.e.* Good over Evil. It fulfils the spontaneous expression of the individual's desire to take part in the drama as a witness or as an actor and as the story is well known to every one, the occasion is quite disorderly and more like a festivity than a dramatic performance. Such is also the celebration in the Buddhist villages on a Full Moon in early spring for the birthday of the Buddha.

The theatre as such and classical music hardly developed in Nepal, not because the people had no such talent but because the country was divided into very petty principalities, where the Chief was hardly any better-off than the rest of his people except for the Kathmandu Valley with the three towns of Kathmandu, Patan and Bhatgaon. The Malla rulers there were great patrons of all artistic activities. Some were themselves masters of music, some composed songs and several wrote dramas or had them acted in their palaces. The traditions of Maithili literature and drama greatly influenced the local Newari plays. The Rath-Yatra type of drama had been part of Kathmandu's heritage. In this, the ruler and all his subjects, Buddhists and Hindus joined in the procession and the ceremonies at the beginning and the end of the celebrations. The classical Sanskrit tradition was also popular. The play was introduced by the Nandi, the Sutradhar and the Nati-the director, the prompter and the principal actress who introduced the writer of the play, the subject matter and the occasion. They also utilised the occasion to praise their benefactor namely the ruler and his reign and his achievements. The local tradition was most important as most of the plays were in Newari-the local language. The theatre consisted of a special platform in a spacious part of the palace where the common people could also attend the performances. The plays were enacted in daytime and had to cater to all tastes, sophisticated and profane alike. There were classical and light dances thrown in between the dialogues and romantic Newari songs were popular. There were no curtains, so the background of scenes were described by songs, poems and prose descriptions. The actors were identified by their dresses, regal robes, warriors' swords, mendicants' yellow robes etc. Women's parts were enacted by young boys dressed in women's clothes. Sometimes masks were also used as in the Buddhist dances in monastaries especially to depict gods, goddesses and demons. The orchestra consisted of one or more drums, harps and flutes and occasionally a trumpet. This was necessary for the songs and dances in the play.

The Malla rulers were great patrons of the theatre. Pratap Malla ruled in Kathmandu from 1641 to 1674. He was keen to be known as a great poet, musician and artist. He loved to watch plays in Newari, Maithili and Bengali. The rulers of Patan and Bhatgaon did not want to lag behind and the palaces in all the three capitals soon had auditoriums where plays were enacted. The rulers of Patan were often good writers of dramatic pieces. The themes were invariably from the Sanskrit epics and dramas. The love story of Shiva and Parvati, the wanderings of Nala and Damyanti, the story of Usha and Pradymna, legends of Gopi Chand, Vikramaditya, Padmavati etc. were the commonest themes.[2]

The dramatic tradition ceases with the coming of Prithvi Narayan Shah. We do not hear of poets, musicians, actors and singers. The durbar is concerned only with political and military developments. The rulers, the prominent people and the Gorkha soldiers are seen absorbed in drills and war games on the parade grounds to the exclusion of all other entertainment. Great scholars like Shakti Ballabh, Vanivilas and Lalita Ballabh received recognition in the Gorkha Durbar but little was done to encourage painting, music and drama. Late in 1957, however, King Tribhuwan established the Royal Nepal Academy to study and encourage the development of literature, art and culture in the Kingdom. The king is the chancellor of the Academy. The study of the literary tradition is one of the main activities of the literary divisions. The art section deals with music, theatre, sculpture and architecture-both in the classical and folk dimensions. The culture department deals with the political, economic, social, religious and artistic history and tradition of the multi-national and polyglot country. It is too early to assess the impact of modern ideas and idioms on Nepalese literature, art and culture, but Nepal is definitely having a renaissance in all these fields-more from the people themselves than from State patronage. But a distinctive development of the Nepali, the Hindu-cum-Buddhist and Himalayan influence in these arts is still to come. The rich tradition is there and in the years to come we will be justified in expecting memorable contributions.

Notes

1 Duan Werjie, President of Dun Huang, Art Research Institute in "China Today", May, 1990.

2 For details of other dramatic works see D.R. Regmi: Medieval Nepal, Part-II, pages 844 et seq.

Appendix - I

Descriptive Account of the Main Tribes and Races of Nepal

The Thakurs and the Chhatries have the highest standing in the social hierarchy of Nepal. The King of Nepal is himself a Thakur and hencc all Thakurs consider themselves to be the highest Chhatries. The Thakurs are the descendants of erstwhile rulers of the numerous principalities into which Nepal was divided befoe the Gorkha conquest. Most of these families claim descent from rulers of solar and lunar races in India and claim that their forefathers had migrated from India at different times in the past. The Nepalese historic traditions refer to several rulers of principalities in India coming with their retinues to Nepal and settling down in the country with the consent of the previous rulers and the people.

The Chhatries claim descent from leading noble men who accompanied the Indian rulers when they came to Nepal. This happened particularly after the conquest of northern India by the Turkic armies in the twelfth century. The Chhatries rank next to the Thakurs in Nepal. They follow Orthodox Brahminism and are particular about their religious observances.

Sometimes the word Khas is applied to these higher castes but it is now accepted that the Khas were the original races inhabiting most of Nepal. Khas are said to have occupied mountainous regions from the Caucasus, Kashmir, Kumaon, Nepal, Kham and Kampuchea. The tribe inhabiting the lands north of Gorakhpur where Gautam Buddha was born, was probably one of the Khas tribes. So also the earlier rulers of Nepal, to one of whom Devapal by name Ashok gave his daughter in marriage.

The Newars are the people living in the valley of Kathmandu and its neighbourhood. They are the business community of Nepal and are found as small shopkeepers, money-lenders and craftsmen throughout Nepal.

The Newars developed the arts of Nepal which are the typical specimen of its civilisation. The temple architecture of Kathmandu as also its sculpture, both on wood and stone are superb examples of Newari genius. The Newars are a people devoted to the arts of peace and are either orthodox Buddhists or orthodox Hindus. Newars, however, have several sub-castes. Sometimes, the girls while still young are ceremonially married to a fruit. The later marriage tie rests lightly on the Newar women. Divorce is easy and remarriage is allowed. Because of the first marriage to a Bel fruit the women are never considered widows even after the death of their husbands. This is an adaptation of the rigid Hindu marriage ties to local custom. The Newars are almost equally divided into Buddha-margis and Shiva-margis *i.e.* as Buddhists and Hindus.

The Magars are nearly 30 per cent of the population of Nepal and form the bulk of the population to the west of the Kathmandu valley. The Gurungs are nearly 20 per cent of the population and are mostly found in the Sapt Gandaki area. Limbus and the Rais live in the country east of the Arunkosi and form about 5 per cent of the total population of Nepal.

These racial groups have adopted Hinduism although many tribal customs persist specially among the eastern Limbus and Rais. Some of the people belonging to these groups, however, are Buddhists. These communities live in areas of higher altitudes. They believe in Buddhism but the same people in the middle and lower valleys have adopted Hinduism. There has been little education amongst these groups and the Jhankari or the Ghost Healer is very much the man in demand for curing diseases and for religious ceremonies. The Gurungs in the west are subdivided into the charjat and the sora jat castes, that is the four and the sixteen castes. The first four are Ghale, Ghotane, Lamchhane and Lama. The so called 16 castes are the larger group which is sub-divided into numerous family groups but is supposed to be inferior in social status to the first four castes.

The Gurungs have preserved several Tibetan traditions. They keep the bargha or time cycle of twelve years and each bargha is given the name of an animal or a bird. From this one can easily verify the age of the Gurungs. The other custom that the Gurungs have preserved from their Tibetan ancestors is the arghun or death ceremony. The ceremony is conducted after death and may be for one or more persons. Effigies of the deceased are made which may be very life like in the case of rich persons. They are dressed in the best clothes of the deceased and a great celebration is held where a sheep or a buffalo is slaughtered to provide a rich feast. There is a lot of drinking, feasting and rejoicing throughout the day and the night. The next day the clothing is removed and the effigies are broken up and thrown over a cliff.

The Magars are the more Hinduised people. This was probably due to the coming of the Rajput rulers and Brahmin priests to their home lands when most of Northern India and Bihar was overrun by Turkic armies in the 13th and 14th centuries. The Magars are divided into seven castes which include Burathoki, Gharti, Pun, Rana and Thapa. They have separate habitats but intermarriage is common. They claim themselves to be the desendents from Suryavanshi and Raghuvansi (descendents of the Sun-god and of Raghu) Hindu rajas. Brahmins attend to the religious cermonies in all Magar homes. Amongst them Thapas are the largest group followed by the Puns and the Gharties.

The Limbu and Rai groups claim to have descended from two sets of ancestors, the Lhasa gotra and the Kashi (or Varanasi) gotra *i.e.* one claiming to be the descendents of the settlers from Lhasa and the other claiming to be the descendants of settlers from Kashi or Varanasi. The Limbus and the Rais do not marry any girl who is related by birth but otherwise the marriages are arranged without the prior consent of the parents. The Rai Limbus generally bury their dead but now they follow the Hindu custom of burning the dead body and consigning the ashes to the waters in the nearest rivers. Both Limbus and Rais call themselves Hindus but they do not always require the services of Brahmins for their religious ceremonies.

The Tamangs are found north of the Kathmandu valley and include several Lamaist tribes. They are divided into several clans who are akin to the Gurungs in their language, customs and religious ceremonies. The Tamangs, however, call themselves Lamaists and Lamas officiate at their religious ceremonies. Buddhist tablets are common for protection against evil spirits. They display prayer flags on their temples and collect mane walls and chortans at the crossroads.

The Sunwars are a small agricultural community mainly found to the east of the Kathmandu valley. The Sunwars say that they originally came from Western Nepal but now they have established their identity independently from Magars and Gurungs. They ask the Brahmins to officiate at their ceremonies and they generally follow Hindu rites. They keep away from the Rais and Limbus even if they have settlements in the Rai and Limbu districts.

The Kiratis are said to be the descendents of the Kirati rulers of the Kathmandu valley. The Kiratis call themselves Hindus but men of their own tribe officiate in their religious celebrations and Brahmins are not very welcome. They give special importance to the worship of Parbhang whom they call their Ghar Deota or household deity and whom they like to propitiate with the sacrifice of fowls, goats or buffaloes.

The Bhotia tribes include several tribes that are of Tibetan origin and who keep their distinct identities. The largest in number are the Lepchas who are a recent arrival from Sikkim, and live mostly in the eastern Rai Limbu districts adjacent to Sikkim. The Lepchas have their own language which is a dialect of Tibetan. They follow Tibetan Buddhism and Lamas officiate at their religious ceremonies.

The Sherpas are people of Tibetan origin who live south of the Everest mountain group. They follow Tibetan Buddhism of the Red Hat sect. They do not follow any Hindu customs. They live in valleys at very high altitudes where only barley, maize and potato grow. They are sturdy mountaineers and can carry loads on their heads over long distances and at great heights.

The Bhotias called as such in Nepal are tribes of Tibetan origin who live in the Trans-Himalayan regions of Nepal. They live in the upper basins of the Mugu Karnali in Humla district which is called Magan Bhot. There are also other Bhotia settlements in the upper reaches of the Marsyandi, the Kali Gandak, the Bhari and the Trisuli rivers as also in the upper reaches of the Tamar river in the extreme east.

To sum up, the Chepang, the Kusunda and the Hayu tribes may be described as fragments of people similar to the Kolarian races in India who are known as the earliest inhabitants of Nepal. Their numbers are insignificant and they are now anthropological rarities. The Tharus and the people of the lower castes which are found in different places in Nepal such as the doms, the barbers or nais and the shoemakers or chamars etc. are the representatives of proto-australoid races. These have been least influenced by admixture with fresh racial stocks common to the country. The Tharus escaped admixture because they live in forest-clearances which were inhospitable and unwelcome to foreigners. The other lower castes, however, got mixed up with fresh racial blood coming from outside and the offspring not being acknowledged by the higher castes.

The Khas is the main racial group in the greater part of Nepal between the low hills and the higher mountainous terrains. The Khas is the basic stock of the higher castes of Brahmins and Rajputs. They include the Nepali Brahmins, the Chhatries and the Thakurs, and the Gorkhas.

Races of the highest social standing from South Asia often migrated to Nepal to establish new principalities. When the Kushans were overthrown in India several of their chieftains migrated to Nepal. So also the Rajput princes when they were pressed by Mohammadan and other conquerors from the 12th century onwards even as late as 1857-58 when the leaders of the Indian revolt against the British migrated to Nepal with their followers. All these newcomers have now been absorbed in the population of Nepal.

So also constant streams of people of Tibetan and Khampa origin have been coming to Nepal. The early Kiratis are one such tribe known to Sanskrit literature. They are spread over the foothills of the Himalayas from Nepal, through Sikkim to Bhutan. These Kiratis established their rule in the Kathmandu valley for a short time from whence they were pushed north-eastwards by the subsequent rulers of the valley. The Yuchi also appear to have pushed several streams of Khampas and other Tibetans during the first four centuries of the Christian era into Bhutan, Sikkim and eastern Nepal. It is the admixture of these Tibetan immigrants with the Khas that has given rise to Gurungs, Rai and Limbu tribes. Lastly, we have the pure Tibetan tribes in trans-Himalayan Nepal, who occupy arid valleys at heights of 3,000 metres and above.

In Nepal, different tribes professing Hinduism and Buddhism have been living side by side for countless generations. There has been little racial or religious prejudice or conflict between the different communities as they have all been gradually assimilated into the social fabric of the country.

Appendix - II

The Gorkhas of the Indian Army

The problem of the Gorkhas in the Indian army is whether it is better to recruit a professional army from the citizens of the country or from outsiders as happened in the case of the Swiss Guard of the Bourbons and the Foreign Legion of Colonial France.

Gardner one of the first Residents at Kathmandu believed that "even on entering the company's service the Gorkhas would not separate themselves entirely from their native country, as they could not remove their families from Nepal", and he thought "that however faithfully they might conduct themselves on general occasions, in the event of any future rupture with Nepal they possessed that feeling of patriotism which would induce the greater part of them to adhere decidedly to their natural allegiance". [1]

On the other hand Hodgson advocated their enlistment in the Company's armies. He observed "I calculate that there are at this time in Nepal no less than 30000 Dhakeriahs or soldiers off the roll by rotation, belonging to the Khas, Muggurs and Gurung tribes. I am not sure that there exists any inseparable obstacle to our obtaining in one form or other the services of a large body of these men; and such are their energy of character, love of enterprise and freedom from the shackles of caste, that I am well assured their services, if obtained, would soon come to be most highly prized. In my humble opinion they are by far the best soldiers in India, and if they are made participators of our renown in arms, I conceive that their gallant spirit and unadulterated military habits might be relied on for fidelity; and that our good and regular pay, and noble pension establishment, would serve to counter poise the influence of nationality".

In May 1857 Jung Bahadur, on hearing of the outbreak of the Mutiny placed the whole military resources of Nepal at the disposal of the British

Government. Lord Canning, after some hesitation accepted a contingent of 3,000 Gorkhas in June but his acceptance was a half-hearted one and left a feeling of disappointment on Jung Bahadur's mind.[3]

From Hodgson's private papers quoted by Sir W.W. Hunter (page 257) we get "I urged the great value, negative and positive of the proferred aid of Nepal for putting down the Mutiny. I said that I was not unaware of the suspicions generally entertained of the Nepalese durbar, but that I nevertheless felt convinced, if the Jung were fairly trusted and put into the hands of a representative of his Lordship having tact, experience, and a liking for the Gorkhas, good faith would be kept with us, some useful military service done for us and above all in importance at such a moment, the spectacle exhibited of the Hindu state par excellence in alliance and cooperation with us."

"I then pointed to the great ability of the Jung, as demonstrated by that wonderful career which had made him the virtual ruler of his country, and to the opportunities for rightly estimating our power which the Jung had enjoyed during his visit to England. Such ability concurring with such opportunity, I continued, could hardly be at fault, and the exigencies of the Jung's position must make a personal connection with us of value to him. That, further, a man of the Jung's talents could not have noted in vain the risks his country had run in times past from collision with a power which again and again he had seen rise superior to every difficulty. Lastly, I pointed out to Lord Canning that Nepal most eagerly coveted the restoration of the western Tarai. Recent events had placed it at our disposal; and the prospect of the grant of it to Nepal, while it might form a tie on the Jung, would offer to us the means of most, conveniently rewarding the Durbar for faithful service."

Even then the Gorkhas were not accepted well by the Company's Government.

"You praise these Gorkhas like your husband," said Lady Canning to Mrs Hodgson, "but I can assure you that they are looked on here as being little better than the rebels".[4]

However, Sir George MacGregor, a personal friend of Hodgson was appointed as the British Officer to be attached to Jung Bahadur during the joint military operations against the Sepoys in Oudh. Finally, Jung Bahadur himself took part in the operations with a force which totalled 17,000 men.[5]

We can now turn to the employment of the Gorkhas in the Indian army. The old local battalions constructed out of the conquered or disbanded Nepalese troops after the war of 1815 had been embodied into three Gorkha regiments by Lord Dalhousie in 1850. Hodgson's representations backed by the opinions of Lord Canning's military advisers led to the formation of the 4th Gorkha Regiment in 1857. The battalion which afterwards became the 5th Gorkha Regiment was raised in the following year. The whole Gorkha force was reorganised on a permanent regimental basis in 1861 as a result of the lessons learned in 1857.[6]

Next let us turn to the various Gorkha Regiments:

"1st Gurkha Regiment- The Nusseree battalion was raised on April 24th, 1815 and was in 1850 designated the 66th Gurkha Regiment of Bengal Light Infantry, taking the place of the 66th Bengal Infantry, which was disbanded for mutiny. This became the 1st Gurkha Regiment in 1861, and a second battalion was added in 1886. A new Nusseree battalion was formed in 1850, and disbanded on the reduction of the army in 1861.

2nd Gurkha Regiment-The Sirmoor Rifle Regiment was raised on April 24th, 1815 and was made a Gurkha regiment in 1850. It was called the 2nd Gurkha Regiment in 1861, and a second battalion was added in 1886.

3rd Gurkha Regiment-The Kemaoon Regiment which was raised on April 24th, 1815, was reserved for Gurkhas in 1850. It was designated the 3rd Gurkha Regiment in 1861, and a 2nd Battalion was added in 1887.

4th Gurkha Regiment-This regiment was raised in 1857. It became the 4th Gurkha Regiment in 1861, and a second Battalion was added in 1886.

5th Gurkha Regiment-The Huzara Gurkha Battalion was raised in 1858 and was designated the 5th Gurkha Regiment in 1861. A second Battalion was added in 1886. These two battalions of the 5th Gorkhas belonged to the Punjab Frontier Force.

In addition to these were the three Regiments in the Assam Corps, later called the 42nd, 43rd, and 44th Gurkha (Rifle) Regiments of Bengal Infantry, the 9th Gurkha (Rifle) Regiment of Bengal Infantry, and the 39th (The Garhwal Rifle) Regiment of Bengal Infantry making altogether fifteen regiments of Gorkhas and hillmen in 1895.

In round numbers there were nearly 14,000 Gorkhas in the Indian army in 1895 as each regiment was 912, strong.

The early record of some of the famous Gurkha regiments is added to show how the Gurkhas have served in the Indian Army.

HISTORICAL RECORD OF THE 6TH GURKHA RIFLES (1817-1919)

During the Khurda rebellion in Cuttock, the Cuttock Legion was raised by Captain Simon Fraser. In 1822, this Cuttock Legion took part in operations against Kols in Singhbhum. In 1823, they were taken to Bengal and the regiment was renamed as the 8th Rangpur Light Infantry. In 1827, the regiment was localised in Assam; and its name was changed to Assam Light Infantry after they had taken part in operations against the Singphos and Kamptis in Northern Assam in 1826.

It was in 1828 that the Gurkhas were for the first time enlisted in the regiment. In the Second Burma War and afterwards, the regiment took part in operations against the Abors. On reorganisation consequent to 1857 troubles, the regiment "was taken on the strength of the Line and designated the 46th Bengal Native Infantry". In 1871, class companies were introduced and muskets were replaced by rifles. The regiment took part in numerous operations against the Nagas (1875-1885); the Chins (1889) and the Chin-Lushais (1890).

In 1891 this regiment, from which the Hindustani element was removed in 1885 and whose designation had been changed to 42nd Gurkha Light Infantry, was used in the measures taken against the Senapati in Manipur. The name was changed to 42nd Gurkha Rifles in 1902, when Lee-Enfield rifles were also issued. In 1903 the name was again changed to 6th Gurkha Rifles and in 1904 machine guns were issued to the Regiment and the 2nd battalion was also formed.

During the First World War, the 1st battalion of the regiment had to do outpost duty at Port Said, was sent to Gallipoli where they took part in some of the severest fighting, were withdrawn to Anzac and later to Alexandria, were mobilised again after return to India and sent to Mesopotamia and were used in Persia in 1919. The 2nd battalion was sent to Mesopotamia in 1917, later to Salonica, Samsun, Batum and Constantinople after which they returned to India. The 3rd battalion was formed in Rawalpindi on February 5th, 1917 by drafts from other regiments. It was mostly used for convoy purposes in the Waziristan Valley.

Field-Marshal Birdwood wrote about this Regiment's part in Gallipoli:-

Having arrived at Anzac the 1/6th Gurkhas were in time to take a leading part in the very heavy fighting which took place in the attempt to cut across the waist of the peninsula, and it was no fault of theirs that success was not attained. Of all the troops who took part in that fighting I think I am right in saying that only the 6th Gurkhas, under Major Allanson, reached the summit of Sari Baír, and actually looked down on the Dardanelles, as the regimental history says, "the Keys of the whole peninsula was in the hands of the Battalion". Never shall I be able to forget my own feelings when I received the report that the 6th Gurkhas were on the summit. It looked as if real success was now in our hands, and that the Gurkhas had opened the road to Constantinople; but we all have to remember the old saying that mortals can only deserve success, and if troops ever deserved it on a day which was momentous for the British Empire than surely the 6th Gurkhas deserved it on that day.

Notes

1 Report dated 29th July 1837, Kathmandu, by Dr. A. Compbell and recorded as Principal Transactions in the India Office M.E.S.

2 Quoted from the report drawn up by Hodgson in October, 1832, as finally reporduced in the report for the Government of India drawn up under Hodgson's instructions when resident in 1837. See Sir W.W. Hunter-Life of Brain Houghton, Hodgson page 109.

3 Sir W.W. Hunter-Life of B.H. Hodgson, 256.

4 Ibid., page 256. Lady Canning's Journal.

5 See Malleson-History of the Indian Mutiny. 321 et seq. Volume II.

6 Page, 258-9, Sir W.W. Hunger.

A return supplied to Sir W.W. Hunter by General Sir Oliver Newmarch K.C.S.I., Military Secretary at the India Office, gave the exact total of the Gurkha regiments at 13,734 in February 1895 including 1895 including about 2000 hillmen from neighbouring tribes.

"Note on the Growth of the Gurkha Regiments in the British-Indian Army" quoted from Sir W.W. Hunter pages 259-260.

Thirteen

Early History of Nepal

Few historical facts have been definitely established about Nepal prior to the period of Gautam Buddha. The only sources of our knowledge of the earlier periods are the local traditions preserved in the different chronicles of the rulers; some of which were written by Hindu pundits and the others by the Buddhist monks. The Vanśavalies are compilations of similar traditions mixed with legends mainly pertaining to the Kathmandu valley.

The early history of Nepal, therefore, is more a social history than a history of kings. The country is divided into numerous valleys by the Himalayas and lack of easy communications often made one river valley inaccessible to the others.

The high mountain valleys, therefore, have hardly been affected by the political happenings in the rest of South Asia and have carried on undisturbed by the passage of time, with their ancient social organisation because of economic and geographical segregation. These high mountain valleys are populated by people of mixed Tibetan origin. There is hardly any culturable land and even at the height of about 4000 metres above sea level there is no vegetation except for the high altitude rhododendrons. These are followed by Alpine meadows ending in Himalayan glaciers and the permanent snowline. Winters are severe and prolonged. The houses are built for protection against the snow. The lower storey is meant for yaks, the intermediate one for sheep and goats and the upper storey for the inhabitants. The yaks, the sheep and the goats keep the upper storey warm. Old men and women stay at home spinning wool and making it into rough woollen cloth, carpets etc. The young persons at a very early age take the sheep, yaks and goats to the Alpine meadows in early spring and return with their flocks in early winter. The women collect grass and leaves from trees from the neighbouring forests for the animals kept at home and for firewood for the hearth.

The animals kept are the yak, sheep, goats and fowl. The people are generally polyandrous and divorces and remarriages are common. Many men and women also remain unmarried.

The people are extremely poor. Their possessions are mostly the clothes and the ornaments they wear and sheep, yaks and goats they look after.

The pastures are shared in common and so also the making of houses. The elders in the village community decide most disputes which are enforced by general consensus. Most of their ceremonies are performed by magic men who have learnt something of Lamaistic Buddhism. There is an old saying that disputes arise because of wealth, women and land. In these high altitude valleys there is little personal wealth; women are generally free to leave their partners at will, remarriage is common and the pastures are common ground for all animals to graze in. Therefore, there is no need for magistrates or local rajas and the village elders command respect to ensure adherence to traditions and customs.

Such has been the history of high altitude Valleys from times immemorial such as Humla, Jumla, Mustang and Salang in the west and the Sherpa Valleys of Lobang and the Wallong area in the east.

To the south of these high altitude valleys lie the river basins in the inner Himalayas. Because of the terrain, the local principalities were small and their chieftains often were at war with each other for possession of the level basins or fair maidens. These principalities included those of Baitadi, Doti and Silgarhi in the west which were greatly influenced by the richer valleys of Askot, Champawat and Pithoragarh in Kumaon which lay on the west bank of the Kali river. To their east lay principalities like Salyana, Pokhra and Gorkha. Further east lay the rich Valley of Kathmandu, Patan and Bhatgaon which was rich, prosperous and in constant contact with both Tibet and India. In the extreme east there have been local principalities at Dhankuta and Ilam. These were greatly influenced by Sikkim and Bhutan.

In the inner Himalayan river valleys there was not enough level land where agriculture could be profitable. There were also disputes about the sharing of waters from the tributaries and water-channels. This necessitated interference from persons in authority. The village council, therefore, became a well-established institution and a chief or raja came to coordinate and control the village councils. The gorges of the rivers are deep and wherever the valleys widen up a principality arose to guide and control the smaller valleys in the neighbourhood. The inhabitants are well built and are forced to work hard on their fields to earn their sustenance. They keep oxen to plough the fields; cows for manure and ponies for carrying men and loads. In the valleys they grow rice and higher up in the terraced fields millets, pulses and wheat.

In ancient times, we hear of few rulers in these principalities. It seems the people were governed by their own local councils. Enterprising people from these areas often went to India and sometimes to Tibet and brought back with them ideas they had learnt about Hinduism or Buddhism in their sojourns. They and their opinions were given due respect by the village elders and their councils.

South of these inner Himalayan principalities were the Tarai lands extending from one end of the country to the other. In ancient times the Tarai was not unhealthy. No doubt, there were malarious swamps and marshy forests but there were extensive areas with stately 'sal' forests and deep green paddy fields. These were the granaries both for the hilly tracts in Nepal and the plains of India. Two areas in the Tarai could bc named here: one around Butwal and connected with Palpa in the interior and with Kapilvastu in the plains; the other around Raxaul which was connected with the valley of Kathmandu in the hills and Mithila in the plains. These Tarai areas were the homes of the Lichhavis and the Vrijjis at the time of Gautam Buddha.

In the easternmost Tarai we find the Kirati people who were more given to hunting wild animals in the forests than to clearing the forests and cultivating grain therein. The oldest Sanskrit classics mention the Kiratis in the eastern Himalayas, the foothills and the eastern Tarai. The Kiratis seem to be of Kolarian origin mixed with Tibeto-Burman people coming from Kham or eastern Tibet through the Lohit, the Tawang gap and the Chumbi valley.

The Kiratis were sturdy people depending on hunting and shifting cultivation which is prevalent to this day in parts of eastern Nepal, the Assam Hills and Burma. Sometime before Gautam Buddha the Kiratis invaded the Nepal valley and established their rule. The Vansavalis generally put them after the Gupta and Ahir dynasties in Kathmandu valley. The Vansavalis merely say that the Kiratis came from the east. Their first king was Yalamber. The Kirati rulers have peculiarly non-Sanskritic names, like Hriti, Sthunba, Luk, Thor, Thoko and Khimbu. The period of the Kirati rulers is placed from about 700 B.C. to about 100 B.C. The Kiratis in the Kathmandu valley were conquered by the Chandra Vanshi and Surya Vanshi dynasties. The Kiratis, however, continued to have their own independent principalities to the east of the Kathmandu valley and in the low-lying eastern Tarai.

As we have already said above the Lichhavis were republican people living in the areas around Butwal and Palpa. They were one of the Vrijji people who were occupying most of the Tarai between the Rapti and the Baghmati, as also north Uttar Pradesh and Bihar.

The Lichhavis are known to have lived in this area from the earliest historical times. They were governed by their tribal councils, and the rulers were appointed by common consent. The tribes sometimes fought bitterly with one another and are known to have been involved in internecine war at the time of the Buddha. However, the Lichhavis were the most civilised people inhabiting Nepal at the dawn of history. The Buddha was born at Lumbini in the Nepal Tarai and he spent his youth and part of his latter life in this area. The history of the Buddha, however, is part of the well known history of "Buddhism' and need not be elaborated here. The Lichhavis and the other Vrijjis, however, were pre-dominant political entities in central Nepal in the days of the Buddha and thereafter.

The main source of our knowledge of the early history of the Kathmandu valley is the indigenous history of Nepal, which was translated into English by Munshi Shew Shunker Singh and Pandit Shri Gunanand and edited by Daniel Wright, the Residency Surgeon at Kathmandu from 1863 to 1876. This knowledge is supplemented by inscriptions of some of the local kings and by the descriptions of Buddhist Chinese pilgrims who visited the sacred places of their religion in Nepal.

This indigenous history opens with the sentence, "The Valley on the Southern side of the snowy range, which is within Sumeru (The Himalaya), which was created by Ishwar (who emanated from the great Ishwar, the first Buddha-) was formerly known as Nag Hrad *i.e.* the tank of the serpent".[1]

It seems certain that about 2000-1500 B.C. the valley of Nepal was a big lake. It might have been infested with Himalayan water snakes. This lake was visited from time to time by sages from India and Tibet. Just as lake Mansarowar is visited by hundreds of Hindu and Buddhist pilgrims in our own times, similarly Nag Hard in Nepal must have attracted wandering sages from the South and the North. The sheer physical beauty of the lake with a surface area of over 500 square kilometres in such high altitudes must have given a peculiar charm and ennobling atmosphere to its banks. Indian sages must have found its banks and its waters very welcome to their philosophical minds and nomadic habits. The Parbatiya history records that in very early times the sage Bipaswi came to the lake from a city known by the name of Bandhumati and resided for some time on the mountain, which he called Jat Matrochcha (Nagarjun).[2]

Later Sikhi Buddha visited the lake and resided on the mountain which was called Dhyanochcha (Champadevi) because of the meditation practised by the sage there. Still later Biswabhu Buddha came from a country called Anupam and resided on the mountain called Phulchok. It was about this time that the hillock on which Swayambhu Nath temple is built first shown above the surface of the water and the sage Biswabhu pointed out to his disciples the place through which the water of the Nag Hard should be made to run out.

The task of cutting out a channel for the water of the lake was left to another sage, Bodhisatwa Manjusri, who came from Tibet. He examined the terrain and decided to cut a passage through the low hills on the Southern side between Champadevi and Phulchok. He then cut through the mountain called Kotwaldar, the place where the Baghmati to this day passes out of the valley.[3]

The draining out of the lake prominently put out two mounds in the bed of the lake, namely Swayambhu and Guheswari, and the sage Manjusri built a town called Manju Patan from the Swayambhu hill to Guheswari. He also installed a king, by name Dharmakar, in the new town and himself returned to Tibet.[4]

It is not certain as to when this took place. But we might place this event sometime about 1000 B.C., Manju Patan was afterwards visited by Krakuchhand Buddha, Kanak Muni Buddha etc. The valley was gradually reclaimed from marshes and slowly the entire plain was brought under cultivation. In time the entire valley became a prosperous colony of settlers from East, West, North, and South. The orthodox history of Nepal records the coming of Pandit Dharma Sri Mitra from Benares.[5] Raja Gunkamdeva from Gaur[6] the Kirati[7] rajas who came from Eastern Nepal; Raja Dharma Datt[8] from Kanchi (who is said to have built the temple of Pashupati and presented much wealth and many valuable articles to the shrine as also to have built a chaitya to the North-west corner of Pashupati); and Rani Pingala from Marwar.[9]

It was some time during these early years of cultivation in the valley that the great sage Ne came to Nepal. It is from him that Nepal derives its name. He is said to have lived at the junction of the Baghmati and the Keshwati (for Vishnumati) and to have instructed the people living in the vicinity in the true path of religion. He also ruled over the country.[10] Afterwards, he installed as King the son of a cowherd named Bhuktamana. Eight kings of this dynasty are said to have reigned in Nepal.[11] The last of them, Yaksha Gupta by name, had no issue and an Ahir, Bara Sinha by name, who came from the plains of Hindustan ruled over the country.[12] The Kiratis from the eastern Tarai over-ran the valley about 700 B.C.

The orthodox history of Nepal records that it was during the reigns of these Kirati kings that both Gautam Buddha and Ashoka visited Nepal. Confirmation of these facts is obtained from the stupas and pillars of Ashoka and the records of the journeys made by Fa-hien and I-Tsing to these places. The Lumbini forest, which was marked by a stone pillar by Asoka as the place where the great Sakya-Muni Gautam Siddharth, the Buddha was born, is situated amidst the thick forests of the Tarai of Nepal. Again tradition has it that Kapilvastu, the capital city of the Sakyas, was situated in the Tarai and that the Buddha visited the valley of Nepal and lived there for some time. He is said to have established a great 'Vihar' and to have made Saliputra, Maudgalyayana and Ananda his disciples in this valley. He is said also to have accepted here the offerings of Chuda, a nun.[13] This is not confirmed from Buddhist sources. We only know that in an internecine war the Lichhavis had over-run Kapilvastu and the majority of the inhabitants of the town had migrated to the Kathmandu valley. On their pressing requests Ananda once came to the valley to give solace to the Sakyas. It was after the return of Ananda from the valley that the disciples were allowed to wear shoes in cold climates by the Buddha.

Ashoka is said to have come to Nepal and built five stupas in Deo Patan presumably to commemorate the abode of the Buddha when he was in this valley. All the five stupas are in existence to this day. He is also said to have married his daughter Charumati to Devapala, a Kshatriya by descent. It was Charumati and Devapala who founded and peopled the town of Deo Patan round the five stupas erected by Ashoka.[14] This is again not confirmed from Buddhist texts, and the visit may have been by a high dignitary sent by Asoka. However, this event fixes the time of Sthunko between 245 and 220 B.C., the second definite date in Nepalese chronology.

There were in all twenty-nine Kirati Kings, the last of whom, Gasti by name, being hard-pressed by the Lunar or Chandra Vanshi raja Nimikha, fled from his capital. After five long reigns, the Chandra Vanshi rajas, gave way to the solar or Surya Vanshi dynasty founded by Bhumi Varma. According to the orthodox history, Nepal had become predominantly Buddhist during these long centuries, and the valley was dotted with 'Vihars' for Buddhist monks and nuns. A special sanctity attached to Deo Patan and its Ashokan stupas and the 'Vihar'established there by Charumati, his daughter. Learned and pious men came to

Charumati's vihar from distant places and held discourses on the paths of virtue taught by the great Buddha.

Tradition says that Sankaracharya, the prophet of Hindu renaisance, came to Nepal during the reign of Brikhadeva Verma, the eighteenth king of the Solar dynasty.[15] On his arrival in the valley, he found that there were no learned Buddhists in Nepal. The four Hindu castes had all become Buddhists. Of these some lived in 'vihars' as Bhikshus; some were Shravaks, also living in 'vihars', some were Tantriks, and called themselves Acharyas; and some were Grihastas, following the Buddhist religion. The first two categories had no learned men to argue with him; and the Grihastha Acharyas, who were prepared to argue with him, were soon outmatched. These he ordered to do 'hinsa' (*i.e.* to sacrifice animals) which is in direct opposition to the tenets of the Buddhist religion. He likewise compelled the Bhikshunis or nuns, to marry, and forced the Grihasthas to shave the knot of hair on the crown of their heads, when performing the 'churakarma' or first shaving of the head. Thus he placed the Vanaprasthas (ascetics) and Grihasthas on the same footing. He also put a stop to many of their religious ceremonies. There were at that time some 84,000 monks of the Buddhist religion, whom he searched out and majority of these Buddhists, he converted to Hinduism. In place of the Buddhist religion he propagated the Shaiva Hindu religion in Nepal. There were, however, a few Buddhists still left in the country who were respected by the people for their piety and learning. Even Sankaracharya was obliged to leave Buddhists in some places as priests of temples, because he could not find other persons worthy enough to carry on the religious services in these ancient and highly consecrated temples.[16]

In the reign of Vishwadev Varma, the 31st king of the Surya Vanshi dynasty, the Vikram era was introduced in Nepal. The throne now passed on to Ansu Varma, a Thakuri Rajput, who had married the daughter of Vishwadeva Varma. This raja founded the Thakuri dynasty which gave 18 rajas to Nepal.

The names of some of the Surya Vanshi rajas are also known from inscriptions of early Nepal. Most of these inscriptions are dated. There are, however, great differences of opinion regarding the eras used in the different inscriptions. The later inscriptions of Ansu Varma and Jayadeva II refer to one era and the earlier inscriptions to another era. It is, however, generally agreed that Ansu Varma ruled in the Valley of Kathmandu, a few years before the visit of Hiuen Tsang to the neighbourhood in 646 A.D. Dr. R.C. Majumdar has examined the various theories about the eras used namely those of Pandit Bhagwan Lal Indraji, Dr. Flect, S. Levi and

Dr. R.G. Basak and offers a tentative chronology of the Suryavanshi or Licchavi Kings of the Kathmandu Valley as follows:-

1.	Jayadeva		(2nd century A.D.)
2.	to 12		(3rd and 4th century A.D.)
13.	Vrsadeva	:	
14.	Shankardeva	:	C. 400-460 A.D.
15.	Dharmadeva	:	
16.	Mandeva		C. 460-495 A.D.
17.	Mahideva		C. 495-510 A.D.
18.	Vasantdeva		C. 510-520 A.D.
19.	Udayadeva	:	
20.	Mandeva II	:	C. 520-610 A.D.
21.	Guna Kamadeva	:	
22.	Sivadeva(?)	:	
23.	Narendradeva(?)	:	529-610 A.D.
24.	Bhimdeva(?)	:	
25.	Sivadeva II	:	

I

daughter = Ansu Varma.

The social history of the different principalities of Nepal, as of her southern neighbour India, is principally the history of social and religious reformers. In the earliest days we find learned sages coming from distant parts of India, Tibet and Mongolia with retinues of their disciples, some of whom remained as permanent settlers in the valley. The next great epoch in the history of the Nepal valley was the coming of Gautam Buddha or Ananda to the banks of the Baghmati and the acceptance of the teachings of the Buddha by the inquisitive and the prosperous people living in the valley. The whole valley gradually became Buddhist in culture, architecture and social life, and the coming of the Emperor Ashoka or his emissary put a seal on the Buddhist way of life in the valley. Deo Patan was endowed with five stupas and a number of 'vihars' sprung up from the donations of the pious and the prosperous. The ascendancy of Buddhism was proclaimed by building the Swayambhu Chaitya on top of the highest ridge in the valley. But throughout this period of religious and cultural predominance of Buddhism, Hinduism remained subservient but still alive. The temples of Pashupati Nath and Guhyeshwari, which perhaps the Hindus themselves had inherited from the earlier people in the valley, were always respected by the rulers as well as the ruled throughout this period. Hinduism again became dominant in a new form, partly influenced by the Mahayana form of Buddhism and partly by the Vedantic philosophy of Sankaracharya in the 9th and 10th centuries A.D. Another influence was afterwards added to the religious complexities of Nepal when Gorakhnath brought Tantrik practices and Matsyendranath to Nepal. It is said that Gorakhnath came to Nepal in the reign of the 8th Thakuri Raja, Bardeva by name.[17]

It is said that on account of the Nag-Sadhana or worship of the snakes by Gorakhnath, the valley was visited by a terrible famine which came in the wake of a drought which lasted for nearly twelve years. The people were in great distress and Raja Bardeva, much troubled in his mind, saw no means of relieving the sufferings of his subjects. One night the young Raja overheard the conversation between Bandhudatta Acharya of Triratna Vihar and his wife. The wife asked the Acharya the cause of the drought and its remedy. The Acharya replied, "the only one who is able to put a stop to this is Aryavalokiteshwara, who resides in Kapotal mountain; and he cannot be brought except by the prayers of the ruler of the country. Now the Raja is young and foolish, and the old man his father, Narendradeva, is living in a lonely 'vihar' because he and his son do not agree.

Having overheard this, the raja returned to his palace, and next morning he went to his father and fell at his feet. He brought the old raja home with him, and sending for the aged Acharya, asked the lafter to do something to relieve the distress of the people. The Acharya and Raja Narendradeva, then, performed elaborate religious ceremonies and propitiated Machchindranath or Matsyendranath by consecrating him the ruler and protector of the valley of Nepal. The deity was then brought to the banks of the Baghmati and a great jatra or moving fair was held in his honour. The valley, then, had a plentiful rainfall and everyone rejoiced and accepted Machchindranath as the protector of the valley.[18]

The deity is placed in a temple at Patan and to this day, once every year Machchindranath is taken out in a jatra procession from his temple to the banks of the Baghmati and back again. The Machchindra Jatra is the greatest festival-of the valley and Hindus-from the Maharaja downwards and Buddhists, all take part in it. The jatra is held after the warmest days of summer and is supposed to bring the much needed rain.

The Thakuris were followed in the valley by a collateral line of Vaisya-Thakuris who had been previously ruling in Nayakot. The 5th Raja of this line was expelled by Bamadeva who founded a new Rajput dynasty. These rajas were great builders and delighted in founding new towns. The 3rd Raja founded Kirtipur and the 12th, Bhatgaon or

Bhaktapur. The 10th King of this line, Abhaya Malla was the first raja to hold the surname Malla, because his father, when he heard the news of the birth of his son, was engaged in wrestling and gave the child the name Malla.[19] The name Malla, however, has long historical associations. The Buddha who died at Kusinagar called the Mallas to his death bed, family by family. The Mallas had also shared the republican sovereignty of these areas with their neighbouring clan of Licchavis. The name Malla also occurs in the Institutes of Manu and on the pillar set up by Mana Deva and his mother, Rajyavati, at Changu Narayan in 496 A.D.

The 12th Raja of this Rajput dynasty was ruling in Bhatgaon with his father still ruling in Kathmandu and Patan, when Raja Nanya Deva, who came from the South Karnatak country, entered Nepal and brought the entire valley under his own control. He is also said to have brought the Newars with him. These Newars are said to be the descendents of inter-marriage between Brahmins and Kshatriyas and to have come originally from a country called Nayars.[20] It is difficult for a historian to accept this as a fact. The Newars seem to have lived in the valley from great antiquity. Perhaps a few matriarchal Nayars came with Raja Nanya Deva from South Karnatak and were gradually absorbed by the Newars, who had already settled in overwhelming numbers in the Nepal valley.

The Karnataki dynasty ruled the valley of Nepal for just over a hundred years. Towards its declining days, the valley was invaded by Mukund Sen from the west, namely the country of Palpa and Butwal. It was during this invasion that some Khas and Magar tribes came into the valley and settled there permanently. But a pestilence overtook the invading armies of Mukund Sen and the raja himself escaped from the country in the garb of sanyasi.[21] Great confusion reigned in the three cities and at length the Vaisya Thakuris of Nayakot again seized the throne and ruled the country for the next about 225 years.

About 1320 A.D., the Raja of Ajodhya, Hari Sinha Deva by name fled to Simraungarh when his country was over-run by the Tughlaks. Raja Hari Sinha Deva, with the idol of his family goddess, Turja Bhawani, entered the valley of Nepal in 1324 A.D. He built a temple for Turja Devi at Bhatgaon and, through her influence over the minds of the Thakuris and the people of Bhatgaon, came to be respected as the Maharaja with a nominal superiority over the other Rajas in the valley. His descendents ruled till about 1415 A.D. when the last raja of this line gave his only daughter in marriage to a Malla raja, one of the descendents of the Malla rajas, who had fled to Tirhut on the invasion of the valley by Nanya Deva.

It was during the reigns of the last three rajas of the dynasty of Hari Sinha Deva (about A.D. 1380 to 1415) that friendly envoys were sent to and received from the Chinese Emperor. The orthodox history of Nepal records that Raja Sakti Sinha Deva sent presents to China, which so pleased the Emperor, that he sent in return a seal, with the name Sakti Sinha engraved on it, and in addition the title of Rama, with a royal despatch in the Chinese year 535.[22]

The most important raja of the new dynasty of Malla Rajas was Jayasthiti Malla who reigned about 1425 A.D. He had married the daughter of Raja Shyam Sinha Deva, the last of the line of Hari Sinha Deva. This marriage had greatly added to his prestige.

Jayasthiti Malla was a great law-giver to the valley of Nepal. Firstly, he codified the laws regarding the rights of property in houses, lands and religious endowments. These rights were made transferable and saleable. Secondly, he reformed and reorganised the criminal law. Formerly criminals were awarded corporeal punishments and reprimands only, but Jayasthiti Malla prescribed a scale of fines varying with the criminality of the offences.[23]

Thirdly, this raja reorganised the entire social structure of his people. People were divided into definite castes with fixed places in the social hierarchy. The low caste people were obliged to show proper respect to the people of castes higher than their own. Regulations regarding dwelling, dress and ornaments were made to control the lives of the people. The Bandyas-or Buddhists converted to Hinduism-were classed as Brahmins or Kshatriyas. The Brahmins were graded into numerous sub-divisions. Newars were also divided into Acharyas, Vaidyas, Sresthas and Daivagyas and each group was again sub-divided. The Shudras were divided into 32 groups and the outcastes into 64, depending upon the occupations followed.

Fourthly, he classified houses and lands in different categories varying with their price. Lastly, he standardised the measures for land and commodities. These improvements contributed a great deal to the prosperity of the valley in later years, but with wealth and riches came also laxity in morals, jealousies and mutual heart burnings. Unfortunately in 1472 A.D. the Malla raja divided his kingdom into four parts. Bhatgaon was given to the eldest son, Banepa to the second son, Kathmandu to the third son and Patan to a daughter. Later Banepa was absorbed by Bhatgaon. But still three different lines of Malla princes ruled in the valley from 1472 to the time of their final overthrow by the Gorkhas. To their west was the small principality of Nayakot, which was under the suzerainty of the Malla Raja of Kathmandu. In the 16th century, Patan had again been absorbed in Kathmandu on the extinction of the ruling line, but about 1600 A.D. the line of Mallas of Kathmandu was sub-divided into two, and two independent princes held their courts at Kathmandu and Patan respectively. This line of the Malla Rajas occupied the Western half of the valley, while the line of Bhatgaon Mallas occupied the eastern half. There is not much to be recorded about these different Malla princes. They seem to have had their authority curtailed to a considerable extent by the 'pradhans' or representatives of the different localities in their areas. Surrounded by barren hills, and occupying the most productive parts of the region, these Malla princes never had the necessity of carrying war to their neighbours' domains. They were peaceful and preferred to remain on the defensive. The authority of the raja was, therefore, not supreme; primarily because he was not, and did not try to become, a war-lord with a large disciplined army under his personal command. The authority and dignity of the raja were greatly undermined and there are not a few examples in the history of the Malla princes when the "bharadars" or feudal chiefs and the "pradhans" or representatives of the people turned out their inefficient or licentious rajas without even rising in arms.[24]

In the 18th century, we find that the valley of Nepal was divided into the three principalities of Bhatgaon, Kathmandu and Patan. Different branches of the same family were ruling over these three principalities but there was no confederacy or union of any kind amongst them. There was on the other hand jealousy and ill-will amongst the members of the Malla family, and their mutual quarrels had proceeded to such extremes that not even the greatest danger to their power and existence could forge them into a federal unit capable of resisting any aggressor with a united army. In 1736, Nar Bhupal Shah, the Gorkha ruler, crossed the river Trisuli and attacked the raja of Nayakot. The Gorkhas were defeated and thrown back. Nar Bhupal Shah, however, sent his son Prithvi Narayan Shah to Bhatgaon to learn the practices of the civilised Malla Durbar, and Ranjit Malla readily accepted him as a welcome guest. It was this experience of the Mallas that helped Prithvi Narayan Shah greatly in his conquest of the Nepal valley; and all this he owed to the hospitality of a Malla prince. In 1769, Prithvi Narayan Shah again came as a guest to Ranjit Malla's court after his conquest of Kathmandu and Patan and the old prince, realising that the country did not need his peaceful rule any more, abdicated in favour of the Gorkha raja and retired from statecraft to lead a hermit's life at Benares.

The last Malla king of Kathmandu was Jai Prakash Malla. He ascended the throne against the wishes of a number of important and powerful castes. To secure his own position, he had to ask his younger brother Rajya Prakash Malla to leave his domains and the latter's supporters-the "Thoris"-to absent themselves from his durbar. Rajya Prakash quietly accepted his brother's orders and lived peacefully at the court of Vishnu Malla at Patan. The "Thoris" did not accept their loss of power meekly. They tried to set up one of Jai Prakash's other brothers, Narendra Prakash, as the chief at Deo Patan. This attempt was suppressed with great cruelty, but the "Thoris" persisted in their opposition to Jai Prakash. They succeeded, however, in putting Jyoti Prakash Malla, the 18-month old son of Jai Prakash, on the 'gaddi' with the Rani as one of their supporters. Jai Prakash Malla had to leave his kingdom for some time and his enemies persisted in turning him out successively from Mata Thirtha, Godavari and Gokarna. At length he settled at Guhyeshwari, from where he managed to collect a small army and re-establish himself at Kathmandu. He had then to turn out his old 'bharadars' and to administer the country with the help of entirely new men. Such was the political condition in the principality of Kathmandu when the Gorkhas planned their attacks on it. For some years victory lay with Jai Prakash Malla, and the Gorkhas were turned out from Nayakot which they had occupied in 1736 and again in 1748. In 1768, however, Prithvi Narayan Shah attacked Kathmandu at the head of a large army from Gorkha. He was helped by numerous disaffected chiefs from Kathmandu and Patan. He also timed his attack when Raja Jai Prakash Malla was residing near the temple of Telaju and preparations were being made for the procession of the Indra Jatra. The city was quite unprepared for a surprise military attack. Jai Prakash Malla fought bravely but his good fortune was gone and the valley of the Baghmati passed from the hands of the Mallas to those of the Gorkhas.

In the third principality of Patan, petty squabbles were going on as to who should be the chief while the Gorkhas were threatening their neighbouring kingdoms. About 1750, Vishnu Malla died childless and Rajya Prakash Malla, the exiled brother of Jai Prakash Malla, was placed on the throne by the powerful group of the six 'pradhans'. These 'pradhans' found that Rajya Prakash did not see eye to eye with them in many matters of administration and they caused the unfortunate man's death by blinding him. Then for some time the 'pradhans' called Ranjit Malla from Bhatgaon to rule over the principality, but Ranjit Malla, not liking to work under their instructions, returned to Bhatgaon leaving the 'pradhans' to administer the country as best as they could. It was at this juncture that Jai Prakash Malla established himself for two years at Patan, but again the 'pradhans' were successful in ousting him by placing the maternal grandson of Vishnu Malla on the throne of Patan. This young prince was also killed in turn by them and they invited Dalmardan Shah, the brother of Prithvi Narayan Shah to rule over them. He in his turn, retired to his native place after his experience with the ways of the 'pradhans'. For the last three years of their hegemony the 'pradhans' put a nominee of theirs-Tej Narsingh-a scion of the line of Vishnu Malla on the throne. In 1768, Patan was conquered by Prithvi Narayan Shah. The ruthless Gorkha prince put all the six 'pradhans' to death for their murderous intrigues, and maladministration.

It was in these circumstances that the Gorkhas stepped in from the Western mountains into the fertile valley of Kathmandu and established their sway over the indigenous people. The old story was repeated again namely that the hardy mountaineers came in to establish their rude justice in green valleys where the people at the top had fallen a prey to interminable intrigues amongst themselves and languid enervation and decrepitude by a life of luxuries and debilitating pleasures of the flesh.

Notes

1 Wright's History of Nepal, p.77.
2 Ibid.
3 Wright's History of Nepal, p. 78.
4 Ibid., p. 79.
5 Ibid., p. 84.
6 Ibid., pp. 85-86.
7 Ibid., pp. 89-90.
8 Ibid., pp. 92-93.
9 Ibid., pp. 104-105.
10 Wright's History, p. 89.
11 Ibid., p. 108.
12 Ibid., pp. 108-109.
13 Ibid., p. 110. The Buddha came to Nepal in the reign of Jitedasti, the 7th Kirati King.
14 Ibid., pp. 110-111. "In the reign of Sthunko (the 14th Kirati Raja), Asoka, the Raja of Pataliputra having heard of the fame of Nepal as a sacred place, and having obtained the permission of his spiritual guide, Upagupta Bhikshu, came on a pilgrimage to Nepal, accompanied by his family and followed by a large number of his subjects".
15 Wright's History of Nepal, p. 118.
16 Wright's History of Nepal, pp. 119-120.

17 Wright's History of Nepal, p. 140.

18 The Gorkhas consider Gorakhnath as the special protector and ruler of their race. The Nepalese coins are issued iin the name of Gorakhnath and the ruling prince. The above story to some extent testifies to the conflict between Gorakhnath and Machinadranath and the races respectively protected by them.

19 Wright's History of Nepal, p. 162.

20 Ibid., p. 167.

21 Ibid., p. 171, et, seq.

22 Wright's History of Nepal, p.180;. Also Perceival Landon, Nepal, Vol. I, p. 37.

23 Wright's History of Nepal, p. 182.

24 For example, see Wright's History of Nepal, pp. 208-209, wherein the Vamsavali says: "His subjects seeing his (Sadashiva Malla's) wickedness, determined to take vengeance. So one day, as he went towards the Manohara, they assaulted him with sticks and clubs and he was compelled to take refuge at Bhatgoan (where he was kept in confinement).

"The people, after having expelled Sadashiva Malla, made his brother Siva Singh Malla King."

See also wWright's History of Nepal, p. 222, where the Ranis and Maijus *i.e.* mother and step mother of Bhaskara Mall nominated a distant relative as the next heir.

Also in the same book, p; 223, where some durbar officials made the son of Jai Prakash Malla king over five villages; p. 225 where Jai Prakash Mall is reported to have said that Thapas, Budhathokis, Bistas, Baghis and Basnyats were his enemies because they had said to his father that they would not take him as king; pp. 250-252 where an account is given of the king-making practices of the sixi Pradhans of Lalit Patan.

Fourteen

The Expansion and the Containment of the Gorkhas

Gorkha was one of the twenty four principalities between the Gandak and the Kosi rivers. Drabya Shah the youngest son of the Raja of Lamjung, was called by the Brahmins and the Rajput emigrants of Gorkha to rule over the principality in 1559 A.D. The family of Drabya Shah had migrated to the Nepal Himalayas after the sack of Chittor by Allaudin Khilji and one of the scions of this family, Bhupal Rana by name, carved out a principality for himself around Ridi on one of the tributaries of the Gandak in 1495 A.D. Bhupal Rana assimilated the family with the new people under him. Two of his sons are known to history as Kancha Khan and Micha Khan. It appears that the eldest son predeceased his father and the youngest and the middle one were called by their Gorkhali names. After the death of Bhupal Rana, the principality was divided between the two surviving sons; Kancha Khan getting the western portion and Micha Khan the eastern portion. Later Micha Khan had to move north into the Magar country, and the family ultimately established itself as the rulers of Lamjung. The elder branch of the family ruled at Lamjung and it was the youngest son of the Raja of Lamjung who came to occupy the principality of Gorkha. The elder branch tried to incorporate Gorkha into its domains, but Drabya Shah, the then ruler of Gorkha, managed to keep the identity of his domains separate from Lamjung and as an important rival to it. This was achieved by Drabya Shah by bringing the Magar and Gurung localities to the north and the east of Gorkha under his control.

Drabya Shah's grandson Rama Shah became the raja of Gorkha in 1605 A.D. He was a good administrator and an able military commander. At one time he occupied the Kerong fort and adjoining areas in the north but later he had to yield the fort to Tibetan authorities and to be satisfied with the possession of the pass over Rassnagarhi. To the south, Rama Shah's dominions almost touched the Tarai lands. The Gorkha Raja thus came in touch with the Tibetans in the north and the Mughal Subedars and Fauzdars in the south.

Rama Shah gave the first rudiments of organised administration to his kingdom. The principal minister of the king was the Chautaria, who was a near relation and a confidant of the king. He looked after the affairs of the State when the ruler was away from his capital or was a minor. The administrative offices were manned by Kazis who carried out the raja's orders and maintained the records. The kingdom was divided into 7 thums or districts by Rama Shah and each was entrusted to an umra or high official. Usually the umra was also a sardar or army officer. He collected the rent dues from the tenants and the octroi or trade dues from merchants and craftsmen, kept a small armed force ready for law and order duties and supervised the judicial tribunals of his thum, which consisted of a ditha or magistrate who was assisted in civil cases by a Bichari. The administration was simple and owed complete loyalty to the person of the ruler. Even then, it was superior to what obtained in other principalities in the neighbourhood.

From the time of Rama Shah to the conquest of the Kathmandu valley by Prithvi Narayan Shah the history of Gorkha is a story of local wars with the neighbours and the elder branch of Micha Khan's family ruling at Lamjung. Gorkha managed to keep its separate identity throughout this period, and established contacts with Tibet, the Malla principalities of the Kathmandu valley and the Indian rajas of North Bihar.

Prithvi Narayan Shah was born in 1723 A.D. His mother was a daughter of the Raja of Palpa, but his early education was looked after by his stepmother the senior Rani Prabhawati. She even sent him in 1736 to Bhatgaon where the ruler had invited the heir apparent of the Gorkha raj to live with the Bhatgaon princes and later be a counterpoise to the opponents of Bhatgaon in Kathmandu and Patan. This gave an opportunity to the young Gorkha prince to know the local feuds of the Malla princes at first hand. In 1737, his father attacked Nayakot and Tanhou but was defeated in both adventures. Young Prithvi Narayan was recalled from Bhatgaon and in 1739, he was proclaimed co-regent with Rani Prabhawati due to the illness of his father. In 1742, he ascended the throne on the death of his father.

Prithvi Narayan Shah had set his heart on the conquest of the Kathmandu valley. The gateway to the valley was the fortress town of

Nayakot which the Gorkha forces were unable to take in 1737. On ascending the throne, Prithvi Narayan Shah collected his army and made another bid to take Nayakot. He, too, was defeated by the forces of Jai Prakash Malla of Kathmandu. Prithvi Narayan Shah was greatly distressed and retired to Benares for some time. He brought back with him a few Hindustani soldiers who were later to train the Gorkha soldiers in the use of guns. Prithvi Narayan Shah also introduced the practice of enrolling men from all castes into his army. Hitherto only the Thakurs or Khas Kshatriyas took part in battles which decided the fates of rulers and local chieftains. But Prithvi Narayan Shah's army included men from all the castes in his principality namely the Rajput settlers, the Khas descendents of earlier chieftains, the Magars, the Gurungs and even the Bhotia highlanders. This ensured that after every battle it would be much easier for the Gorkha army to replenish its ranks and face the enemy again with larger forces. The new castes that were enrolled also fought with great zest to deserve their enrollment.

Prithvi Narayan Shah also tried to get the cooperation and good will of the other hill rajas in his crusade against the Malla princes of the Nepal valley. He sent his emissaries to the chaubisi rajas in his immediate neighbourhood. He was not successful in securing armed help from other rajas but he secured his rear by his diplomacy. Most important of all, the raja of Lamjung became a friendly sympathiser, which greatly helped Prithvi Narayan Shah's thrusts to the east.

In 1745, Prithvi Narayan Shah collected a large army and again attacked Nayakot. The Gorkha army captured the fortress after heavy fighting. Jai Prakash Malla could not send a large army to take the field as the noblemen of Kathmandu were against him for the harsh treatment he had meted out to his brother. The small Newar force sent by Kathmandu was easily defeated by the Gorkhas and Nayakot finally passed to their control. In 1746, Prithvi Narayan Shah took possession of some villages to the east of Nayakot and had them fortified. In 1751, he had to relinquish these villages after a minor setback. But the Gorkhas continued their presence in Nayakot. His strategy was to capture the fortresses on all the important routes into the Nepal valley and then take over the valley itself.

As these plans became known to the neighbouring chaubisi rajas, they were alarmed and Lamjung and Parbat attacked the Gorkhas in 1755. Prithvi Narayan Shah's army defeated the allied forces but peace was concluded on terms very favourable to the invaders. Prithvi Narayan Shah resumed his encirclement of the Nepal valley and captured most of the hill-tops to the northwest and north-east of the valley. In 1757, the Gorkhas attacked Kirtipur, the strong fortress between Kathmandu and Thankot. Kirtipur was defended by a combined force of all the three rulers of the valley. The Gorkha army was defeated and Prithvi Narayan Shah himself narrowly escaped with his life to Nayakot.

This was a great victory for the Newar rajas but this was not followed by an attack on Nayakot and the other hill fortresses surrouding the Kathmandu valley which were still in the occupation of the Gorkhas. For this Jai Prakash Malla and the Pradhans or the elder men of the valley were to blame. Jai Prakash Malla had forfeited the confidence and respect of his native soldiers, local men of influence and the brother chiefs of Patan and Bhatgaon. He now recruited a force of mendicants from the Tarai and some Hindustanis. This further strained the loyalty of the Newar army. At the same time Prithvi Narayan Shah pressed with his policy of encirclement of the valley and its blockade. Gorkha success in the blockade led to loss of prestige of the Newar rajas and even the native population looked forward to relief from scarcity of salt and yarn in the victory of the Gorkhas.

In 1762, Prithvi Narayan Shah attacked Makwanpur-the principality to the south of the Nepal valley which was ruled by his father-in-law. The Gorkhas easily conquered the place, gained a good treasury and completed the blockade of the Nepal valley from the south. The raja of Makwanpur sought help from Mir Kasim, the Nawab of Bengal. Mir Kasim was at that time keen to test his own army in battle as his ultimate aim was to throw off his subservience to the East India Company. Mir Kasim precipitately sent his army under Gurgin Khan to restore the raja of Makwanpur to his throne. This army was defeated by the Gorkhas near Hariharpur in January 1763, and the Makwanpur raj finally became a part of the dominions of the Gorkhas. During the next few years the Gorkhas pressed their blockade of the Nepal valley and fought occasional battles with the chaubisi rajas in the west and petty chieftains to the east of the Nepal valley. Jai Prakash Malla, as the last resort, appealed to the East India Company for help. In 1767, the Governor of Bengal authorised Thomas Rumbold, their chief agent at Patna, to open negotiations with Prithvi Narayan Shah offering mediation between him and the rajas of the Nepal valley. As there was little response from Prithvi Narayan Shah an army was sent under Captain Kinloch to raise the blockade and join the forces of the Malla rajas in the Nepal valley. This force of about 2520 men reached Hariharpur but was decisively defeated by the Gorkhas (October 1767) in an engagement near the fortress of Sindhuli. Captain Kinloch retreated to the Tarai areas after losing more than two-thirds of his men. The East India Company, however, stopped further interference in the affairs of the hill areas because of other pressing engagements elsewhere. The complete failure of the Kinloch expedition gave enormous prestige to the Gorkha army and its opponents gave up all hopes of success against them.

Immediately after their victory over the British, Prithvi Narayan Shah again turned his attention to Kirtipur. This was his third attack on this fortress and this time he won (December 1767). The fall of this redoubtable fortress heralded the conquest of the valley by the Gorkhas. In September 1768, Prithvi Narayan Shah's army captured Kathmandu while Jai Prakash Malla and the population were taking part in a local celebration. Two days later Patan also surrendered to the Gorkhas and about a year later Bhatgaon was also conquered where Jai Prakash Malla received a mortal wound and died a few days later. Now the entire Nepal valley was under the Gorkhas and Prithvi Narayan Shah permanently shifted his capital to Kathmandu.

The conquest of the Nepal valley freed the Gorkha forces from the blockade of the valley; and they turned westwards and eastwards seeking new adventures and conquests. The Gorkhas, however, had to fight several engagements in the west with the chaubisi rajas but after their defeat at Satahun in 1770, they retreated east of the river Marsyangdhi which remained the boundary of the Gorkha raj in the west for many years.

To the east of the Nepal valley the Gorkha armies swept everything, before them. They reached the banks of the Arun in 1772 and captured most of the Limbu country. In 1773, they conquered the Morang country which was under Kirati rulers. A few years earlier the raja of Sikkim had taken the district of Ilam from the Kirati rulers. Prithvi Narayan Shah re-captured Ilam but stopped his armies at the traditional boundaries of the Kiratis in the east so as not to offend Lhasa which was the protector of Sikkim at that time.

In January 1775 Prithvi Narayan Shah died. The whole of eastern Nepal from the Gandak to its present boundaries in the east had been incorporated in the Gorkha raj by Prithvi Narayan Shah. He had fought the hill rajas, Mir Kasim, the British and the Newar Chiefs and by his tactics had outmanoeuvred them all. He had introduced muskets and guns in his army but had not brought in European or foreign officers. He expelled the Roman Catholic missionaries and the Kashmiri and Tibetan traders domiciled in the Nepal valley as the did not trust them and did not want possible centres of subversion inside his own dominions.

After Prithvi Narayan Shah's death his son Pratap Singh ascended the throne. He died in 1777 when his son Ran Bahadur was only three and half years old. The queen mother Rajendra Lakshmi became the regent, but the entire period of her regency was a period of political instability and turmoil. She died in 1786 and Bahadur Shah, brother of Prithvi Narayan Shah, took over as the regent. The Gorkha army, however, had not been affected by the ups and downs of the court officials at Kathmandu and had continued its pressure on the neighbours of the kingdom in the west. Several indecisive battles were fought with Lamjung in 1777, 1780 and 1782. At last in 1784 Lamjung was captured almost without firing a shot. Palpa, Keski, Rising, and Tanhau were taken over easily by the Gorkha armies. So also most of the other chaubisi principalities. In 1787, Parbat and Piuthan were captured. Jajarkot and Salliana obtained peace by agreeing to the suzerainty of the Gorkhas. In 1790, the Gorkha army under Amar Singh Thapa reached Dailekh. In the same year other units of the Gorkha army captured Jumla and Amar Singh's forces arrived on the banks of the Kali after conquering Doti and Achhan. By this year the Gorkhas had conquered the entire country of Nepal as we know it today *i.e*: from the river Kali in the west to the borders of the district of Ilam and the Singh Leela ridges of Kanchan Jungha in the east and from the Tarai lands to the snowy ridges of the Himalayas which have been the traditional boundary between the Himalayan principalities and the dominions of the Dalai Lama in Tibet. About this period Kumaon was rife with intrigues in the ruling family and the administration was fast becoming chaotic. The Gorkhas crossed the river Kali early in 1790. One army occupied the northern areas of Dharchula and Pithoragarh and the second army under chautariya Bam Shah, Jagjit Pande and Amar Singh Thapa taking a southerly route occupied Almora meeting little resistance from the defenders (1791). The army continued its march towards Garhwal and occupied Srinagar. The Gorkhas had now reached the banks of the Jamuna and were planning further advances to the west when news reached them of the invasion of their country by the Chinese. The army was directed to hand over the Garhwal territories to the raja of Garhwal and the Kumaon territories to Harakdev Joshi, and return to fight the Chinese. But the end of the war with China sent the Gorkhas westwards again. Kazi Amar Singh Thapa imprisoned Harakdev Joshi and the Gorkhas took over the administration of Almora directly. The Raja of Garhwal was also pushed out from Srinagar and both he and Harakdev Joshi, who had managed to escape from prison, sought refuge in the dominions of the East India Company.

Amar Singh Thapa now led the Gorkha armies across the Jamuna and by 1809 he had conquered most of the hill states between the Jamuna and the Sutlej including Sirmur or Nahan, Dharmapur, Hinaur and the twelve Thakurai States in the interior Himalayas. By this time, the British had entered into a treaty with the Sikhs under Ranjit Singh, restricting the Sikhs to the west of the Sutlej and taking the Sikh principalities of Patiala, Kapurthala and Malerkotla on the left bank of the Sutlej under their protection. The British through their local commander at Ludhiana intimated to Amar Singh Thapa that the Gorkhas should confine their operations to the hills in order to avoid interference with the possessions under the protection of the British Government. They also informed the Sikh chiefs under their protection that they were not to take sides in any conflict between the Gorkhas on the one side and the hill rajas or Ranjit Singh on the other. The British, however, took Pinjor below the main Himalayan ranges, and although the Gorkhas were in possession of the valley of Dehradun to the east of the Jamuna. Amar Singh Thapa accepted this arrangement and evacuated the Pinjor valley although it had earlier belonged to Sirmur and Hinaur.

Amar Singh Thapa was keen to take the fort of Kangra. The raja, however, sought the help of Ranjit Singh and the end of hostilities saw the Sikhs in virtual possession of the fort. The confrontation with the Sikhs thus brought the Gorkha expansion on the west to a halt at the banks of the Sutlej. In the east also the British had taken the Dev Raja of Bhutan and the raja of Cooch-Behar under their protection, which barred further expansion by the Gorkhas in that direction. Sikkim was the only principality left which was not definitely under British protection and the Gorkhas took possession of slices of territory from Sikkim upto the river Teesta from time to time.

In the later part of the eighteenth century Tibet had come under the protection of the Chinese. The Dalai Lama was accepted as the head of State but he also entertained a Chinese representative or Amban who sometimes interfered in the exercise of political power by the Dalai Lama. Both Tibet and Nepal had been using Malla coins for purposes of trade. These were silver coins, and were called the Mahendra Malli. In the time of Jai Prakash Malla these coins were greatly debased. When the Gorkhas came to power in the Nepal Valley, they replaced the old coins in the valley and issued fresh coins with standard silver content. The Gorkhas wanted the Tibetans to do the same and accept proportionate number of new coins in exchange for the old debased coins. The Tibetans would not agree to this. They insisted that the Gorkhas, as successors of the Mallas, were responsible for debasing the currency and they must agree to replace the old coins at par with the new Gorkha coinage.

About this very time a bitter feud took place between the sixth Panchen Lama and his brother the Samarpa Lama for political ascendency at Lhasa. The Samarpa Lama had to leave Tibet and he sought asylum at Kathmandu. The Tibetans wanted the Gorkhas to surrender him but the request was refused. This further stained the relations between the two countries. Finally, in the summer of 1788, the Gorkhas invaded Tibet in force. One body of troops marched up the Trisuli river and captured Kerong. The other army marched up the Bhotia Kosi and captured Kuti. Both these units were to converge on Shigatse from where the expedition to Lhasa was to be under the command of Damodar Pande. But before the Gorkhas reached Shigatse, peace was concluded and the Tibetans agreed to the terms of the Gorkhas, namely, restoration of Gorkha coinage which had been stopped, acceptance of a Gorkha representative at Lhasa and of Nepalese courts in Tibet to try cases involving Nepalese subjects. The Tibetans also agreed to pay Rs. 3 lakhs per year to the Gorkhas. At the same time the Nepalese accepted the Chinese Emperor as the overlord of Tibet and to send a goodwill mission every five years to the Chinese Imperial Court at Peking. This arrangement had been arrived at with the active participation of the Chinese Amban at Lhasa. The Tibetans, however, felt aggrieved and refused to carry out the stipulations of the treaty. Hostilities broke out again in the summer of 1709 and continued for the next two years much to the disadvantage of the Tibetans.

The Chinese Emperor had been told that the Nepalese had submitted to him and an amicable arrangement had been arrived at between the two vassal states of Nepal and Tibet. When the details of the hostilities of 1789-91 and the treaty were known in Peking, the emperor was angry and sent a large army under Fu-Kang-an or Ru Thwang with instructions to destroy the Gorkhas. The Gorkhas had to retreat before superior forces and Shigatse, Kerong and Kuti, which had been occupied by the Gorkhas since 1789, were evacuated after sharp encounters. As the Chinese army approached the Nepalese boundaries, they prepared for a determined war and at the same time approached the British Indian government also for military help. The Chinese Commander also wrote to the British asking them to help him to destroy the Gorkha armies or at least not to help the Gorkhas in their war against the Chinese. The British merely offered the good offices of a British mediator to negotiate peace terms between the Chinese and the Gorkhas. The Gorkhas were disappointed at this and decided to obtain peace on their own initiative. By this time the Chinese had reached the banks of the Betravati, where the crossing of the river was stubbornly opposed by the Gorkhas.. The Chinese suffered heavy losses and as winter was approaching which would have made the recrossing of the snowy ranges hazardous, they agreed to negotiate for peace. The Gorkhas agreed to surrender the remains of the Samarpa Lama, who had died in the meanwhile and all the treasures he and the Gorkhas had brought from Tibet. The Nepalese accepted the Chinese Emperor as arbitrator between them and Tibet and agreed to send a mission to Peking every five years with gifts. The Gorkhas also agreed to the traditional boundary between Tibet and their country and surrendered the privileges accorded to them by the earlier treaty. In return the Chinese agreed to withdraw from all the Nepalese territories occupied by them, and to award a Manchu royal warrant for the Gorkha king. The Chinese army then returned to Peking. Thus ended the war between the Gorkhas and the Chinese. The result was that the ambitions of the Gorkhas for expansion in the north at the expense of the Tibetans were finally abandoned.

Fifteen

Nepal and East India Company

By 1767, Prithvi Narayan Shah had conquered Bhatgaon and Patan and was threatening to occupy Kathmandu. Jai Prakash Malla, the ruler of Kathmandu, as a last resort, sought the help of the East India Company through its Agent for trade at Bettiah. The Capuchin missionaries also sent information about the plight of the Malla rulers to the officers of the Company. Verelst, who was the Governor at Calcutta, directed Rumbold, the Company's Chief officer at Patna, to inform Prithvi Narayan Shah about the Company's displeasure for attacking Kathmandu and to ask him to withdraw to his own territories failing which the Company would expel him by force of arms from the Kathmandu valley. At the same time an expeditionary force was organised under Captain Kinloch at Patna, and Rumbold was told to despatch it to Kathmandu only if he considered that the success of the venture was beyond doubt. The troops under Kinloch proceeded in great haste to the Kathmandu valley via Janakpur and Sindhuli. They had been informed that if the company's troops did not reach the valley in time, the Gorkhas would have captured Kathmandu and it would be extremely difficult to dislodge them from the valley thereafter. At Sindhuli, the Gorkhas inflicted severe losses on the Company's troops and Kinloch decided to retreat to the Company's territories. Of the 2520 sepoys who went with the expeditionary force, hardly 800 returned. Captain Kinloch, for a few months, occupied portions of the Tarai lands in Bara, Routhehat and Persa belonging to the hill rajas but these were relinquished by the Company after the bloodless entry of Prithvi Narayan Shah into Kathmandu in the middle of 1768.

The East India Company, however, wanted to buy fir trees from Nepal and open trading routes to China through Nepal and Tibet. The Company wanted fir trees for its ships to be made or repaired at Calcutta docks, and at that time it was thought that the hinterland of China was more easily accessible through Nepal than by the long circuitous sea route through the South China Sea. It was also generally held that there were several gold mines in Nepal and that the Company would collect handsome profits by buying cheap gold in Nepal. In 1770, therefore, the company sent a special representative to Kathmandu to the court of the Gorkha Raja. James Logan, an adventurer who had travelled widely in the hills, was selected for this assignment because of his contacts with Jai Prakash Malla of Kathmandu and Raja Karan Singh of Morung. Prithvi Narayan Shah, however, was convinced of the hostility of the British. Logan was stopped at the borders and on Prithvi Narayan Shah's orders was asked to return to the plains. This was in keeping with the policy of Prithvi Narayan Shah of expelling all foreigners from his dominions such as Capuchin missionaries, Kashmiris, Yarkandis and other Muslim traders, and Gosain merchants from India.

The expansion of Gorkha authority in the hills brought in its trail border disputes with the East India Company. Under the Mughal emperors parts of the Tarai lands were settled with the hill rajas and the arrangements continued from generation to generation provided the hill rajas, who were in occupation, paid the dues of the empire. In 1771, the Chief of Darbhanga informed the Company's government that the Tauter parganas on the Gandak had been occupied by the raja of Nepal although they belonged to the Sarkar of Tirhut in the Suba of Bihar. He said that the raja paid only Rs. 12,000/- per year for the parganas which could be auctioned for a much larger sum. He suggested that the raja of Nepal be expelled and the entire Suba of Bihar brought under the direct control of the Company. Meanwhile Prithvi Narayan Shah sent his agent Dinanath Upadhyaya to Darbhanga to represent to the Company's officers that these parganas had been settled with Makwanpur and as Makwanpur had been conquered by the Gorkhas, the parganas should be confirmed with the raja of Nepal on payment of the customary dues. The Company decided to accept the request of the Nepal raja as the alternative was an expedition to subdue the raja, the success of which could not be guaranteed, and the result of prolonged hostilities would be frequent inroads by the Gorkhas into the Suba of Bihar which would materially prejudice the collections of the Company.

As Prithvi Narayan Shah had forbidden the entry of foreigners into his dominions, the British sought the friendship of other hill rajas who would allow fir trees and tar to be exported to the Company's dominions. British traders were welcome in Morung in the east and Kumaon in the west. The raja of Morung wanted to send his troops to help the Malla princes of Kathmandu valley through Darbhanga but the local agent of the Company had refused to allow the troops to operate through the company's dominions. The raja then approached the Governor for military help and a joint attack on the Gorkhas on behalf of Adbhut Singh son of Ranjit Malla of Bhatgaon who was living in exile at Benares. On the other hand, Prithvi Narayan Shah, also wrote to the Company that Buddh Karan, the minister of the raja of Morung who had usurped authority by getting the lawful ruler assassinated should not be helped by the British.

The Company had its own internal problems and Warren Hastings did not want to interfere in the affairs of the hill rajas unless he was compelled to do so. Warren Hastings asked the Nepalese to send an accredited representative to settle problems of mutual concern. Dinanath Upadhyaya was then sent by Prithvi Narayan Shah to Calcutta. Warren Hastings wanted the Nepalese agent to follow him to Patna. Leaving his camp at Patna, Warren Hastings had to proceed in a hurry to Benares. When Raja Chet Singh defied Warren Hastings, Mrs Hastings asked the agent if the Gorkhas would send a contingent of hill troops to help her husband. Dinanath Upadhyaya readily agreed to the proposal and on his request the Gorkhas sent an army through Makwanpur. When Mrs. Hastings learnt that the insurrection of Raja Chet Singh had been suppressed, she asked the Nepalese agent that the Gorkha troops should return to their country. This was done, and Warren Hastings greatly appreciated the friendship shown by the Gorkha raja. He also confirmed that Routehat was part of Makwanpur and the Company had no claims on it. He also affirmed the earlier decisions of the Company to confine its interests to the plains below the hills in the Gangetic Valley and not to interfere in the affairs of the hill rajas. This allowed the Gorkhas to extend their conquests in the Himalayas.

Warren Hastings was keen to open trade routes with China through the Himalayas and had sent several officers to investigate and report on the trade prospects through Tibet and on the best routes to be followed for such trade. In 1784, he decided to send Foxcroft to Nepal, to open Nepal to the Company's trade. It is not known whether Foxcroft was received by the Gorkha raja, but British traders were not allowed into Nepal.

When Lord Cornwallis came to India, the hill rajas who had been expelled by the Gorkhas approached the Company for military help to regain their lost principalities. Lord Cornwallis refused to get involved and the policy of non-interference of Warren Hastings was continued. The Company, however, in 1788 refused to allow a consignment of 500 muskets to be taken to Nepal from Calcutta port. The Gorkha raja had to swallow this sour pill as best as he could.

The Gorkhas' war with China offered a great opportunity to the Company to press for the opening of Nepal to their trade. When the Chinese army defeated the Gorkha garrison at Shigatse, the Gorkhas ordered Amar Singh Thapa to return to the capital from Kumaon and Garhwal with his armies. They also asked for help from the Rohilla Chief, Faizullah Khan, who informed them that he could not send his troops into the hills without the consent of the Nawab Wazir of Lucknow and the East India Company. The Gorkha raja then pressed the Governor General for military help. He had earlier asked for ten pieces of canon and ten European sergeants to train his troops. He now requested for two battalions of Europeans and one of sepoys with military stores and a suitable number of guns to be sent for his help. In order to prepare favourable grounds for military help, the Gorkhas concluded a commercial treaty with the Company on March 1, 1792 through the good offices of Gajraj Misra, the Rajguru at Benares and Qadir Khan, the Company's munsif of Benares . The treaty stipulated that 2-1/2 % duty would be levied on imports by either country at their market prices. Further the merchants of either country were to be indeminified of the loss due to robberies etc. by the Zamindar of the area within which the incidents took place.

But Lord Cornwallis was not prepared to send military help to the Gorkhas.1 He merely offered to help the Gorkhas to negotiate peace terms with the Chinese. For this purpose he decided to send Captain Kirkpatrick with a contingent of the Company's troops to Kathmandu. The Gorkhas realised that the Company did not want to help them and only wanted to get benefits for itself by offering mediation. The Gorkhas then came to terms with the Chinese on their own and decided to revert to their policy of excluding all Europeans from Nepal.

The Gorkhas informed the Company about the end of the war with the Chinese and asked Kirkpatrick not to proceed to Nepal. Kirkpatrick asked the Gorkha raja to allow him to meet the raja in the interests of the friendship between the two States. After much persuasion the raja agreed to receive Kirkpatrick. The raja, however, objected to the military surveyor accompanying Kirkpatrick. The visit by the surveyor was, accordingly, dropped by the Company. Captain Kirkpatrick was then asked by the Company to get as much information about Nepal as possible and the only result of his mission was a first-hand report about the Nepalese and their country by one of the Company's European officers.

Inspite of the coldness of the Nepalese the Company was keen to explore the possibilities of expansion of trade with Nepal and the Chinese and Tibetan territories. In 1795, the Company sent Abdul Qadir to Kathmandu with merchandise valued at nearly Rs. 15,000/-. Abdul Qadir also carried the request of the Governor General that freebooters in the trade routes and areas be punished severely by the two Governments. The Nepalese Government agreed whole heartedly to this request. At the same time, the disputes regarding the border between Morung and Purnea were also discussed by the Nepalese with the Company's agent. The Nepalese also pressed that the parganas of Kashipur and Rudrapur then under the Nawab Wazir should be handed over to the Gorkhas as they had previously been held by the Chand rajas of Kumaon and in recognition of the helpful attitude of the Gorkhas to the Company during the Rohilla War. As usual Guru Gajraj Misser persuaded an unwilling Nepalese government to accept the mission of Abdul Qadir so that the relations between the two countries were not strained further. As a result of the mission, the two governments amicably settled the boundary dispute in Morung but the Company conveyed to the Nepalese that it would not press its ally- the Nawab Wazir-to accommodate the Gorkhas' claims to Rudrapur and Kashipur which were entirely within the exclusive jurisdiction of the Nawab Wazir. Trade prospects with Nepal were rated low by Abdul Qadir and he suggested that it would be better for the Company to open trading depots for China and Tibet trade within its own territories.

In 1799, Wazir Ali claiming to be the rightful heir of Nawab Wazir Asaf-ud-daulah, who had died in 1797, killed Cherry, the Company's Resident at Benares and escaped to the Tarai of Butwal. There he was received by Raja Prithvipal Singh of Palpa who held the Butwal parganas from the Nawab Wazir. The Governor-General asked the Gorkha Raja to apprehend Wazir Ali if he entered Nepal and to hand him over to the troops of the Company and Nawab Saadat Ali, who had been put on the gaddi at Lucknow by the Company. This occasion was fully utilised by the Gorkhas for their own purposes. They deputed their own army on the border to apprehend Wazir Ali and knowing that the raja of Palpa-Butwal had incurred the displeasure of the Company decided to annex Palpa to their own dominions. Raja Prithvipal Singh of Palpa was called to Kathmandu to attend the coronation of the infant prince Girvan Yuddha Bikram Shah in March 1799 and detained there on one pretext or the other. He was allowed to return to Palpa only after Ran Bahadur Shah was forced to retire to Benares. When Ran Bahadur returned to Kathmandu, he again persuaded Prithvipal Singh to visit Kathmandu. Prithvipal Singh was then kept in virtual confinement and was killed in 1804 on charges of complicity in the murder of Ran Bahadur Shah. After that Palpa was formally and finally annexed by the Gorkhas.

Ran Bahadur Shah had left Kathmandu on 27 May 1800 for Benares. When Lord Wellesley learnt of these developments, he immediately appointed Captain Knox to attend on Ran Bahadur. The Governor-General wanted to get detailed and accurate information about the happenings in Nepal. As the ex-ruler had sought asylum in their territories, the Company was determined to extract the maximum concessions from the new government in Kathmandu as a quid pro quo for not allowing Ran Bahadur to return to Nepal. In the alternative, the Company was prepared to help Ran Bahadur Shah to re-establish his authority in Nepal provided he was prepared to offer concessions to the Company for profitable trade between the two countries.

Gajraj Misser was asked by the Company to help them in their negotiations with the Nepal durbar and also Ran Bahadur Shah. The latter wanted military assistance from the Company for which he would pay on his return to Nepal but he was not prepared to offer other concessions. As the Company did not agree to his proposal, he became disillusioned with the Company and decided to return to Nepal on his own. This was stoutly rejected and Ran Bahadur Shah was told that he could not leave Benares without the express permission of the Company. At the same time a treaty with the Nepal durbar was proposed in 1801 which stipulated that a resident would be appointed by the Company at Kathmandu and a Vakil by the Nepalese at Calcutta and that Vijaypur parganas would be settled in favour of Ran Bahadur Shah who would either live in his jagir or stay in Benares and get the income of his jagir in instalments from the Nepal government. This treaty was agreed to by the Nepalese deputies but it had to be ratified by the Nepal durbar. Under this treaty Captain Knox was appointed Resident at Kathmandu. Captain Knox arrived in Kathmandu with the draft treaty but found the durbar still in two minds about the British connection. Emissaries on behalf of the raja of Butwal wanted Captain Knox to arrange the Company's protection to the raja. Captain Knox was sold to the proposition but the Governor-General did not want to get involved in the intrigues between the Gorkha raja and his feudatories. Similarly, the suggestion of Captain Knox that Damodar Pande and Bum Shah should be offered pensions by the Company's Government was also turned down. Ran Bahadur Shah was also not idle. He sent a message to the government of Nepal that the Company was in no position to send an army to Nepal and there was no justification for a treaty. He added, "Do not by any means give credit to Gajraj Misser. If you do your lives will be a sufferance of hardships; by giving a daughter in marriage a son-in-law is obtained but no son-in-law is obtained by giving up a wife."

While Captain Knox was in Kathmandu a big change occurred in the administration there. The senior Rani of Ran Bahadur Shah, Tripur Sundari Devi, came to Kathmandu and was received by the populace and the troops as the lawful guardian of the infant raja. She appointed Damodar Pande as her Prime-Minister. She was also opposed to the stipulations in the treaty regarding her husband Ran Bahadur Shah. She thought that as a Hindu wife, it was her duty to see that her husband was well looked after and she wanted the matter to be left entirely to her. The treaty had been ratified by the Nepal durbar on 28th October 1802 but no action was taken to implement the terms. At long last in March 1803 Captain Knox left Kathmandu without any definite arrangements for the jagir of Ran Bahadur Shah. Captain Knox suggested that Ran Bahadur Shah should be allowed to regain power in Nepal on condition that the principality of Kumaon was handed over to the Company. The Governor-General, however, did not want to enter into any engagements with Ran Bahadur Shah as that would lead to the employment of the Company's troops in the hills. The Governor-General also abrogated the treaty of 1801 and removed the restrictions on Ran Bahadur Shah's movements so that he was free to go to Kathmandu, if he so desired. The allowances to Ran Bahadur Shah were also stopped after giving him one month's notice. Ran Bahadur Shah returned to Nepal early in 1804. There was no opposition from Rani Tripur Sundari Devi and the erstwhile Prime Minister Damodar Pande and his son were imprisoned. Bhim Sen Thapa was now made Prime Minister and Amar Singh Thapa, the army general, was sent to the west to conquer new territories in the hills. Ran Bahadur Shah also ordered one of his uncles Sher Bahadur, to accompany Amar Singh Thapa. On Sher Bahadur's refusal, he was insulted in open durbar and sought to be imprisoned. In a rage Sher Bahadur wounded Ran Bahadur Shah fatally with his sword. Sher Bahadur himself was killed by Bal Nar Singh. These events in April 1805 left Bhim Sen Thapa in virtual control of the administration. He persuaded Rani Tripur Sundari not to immolate herself on the funeral pyre of her husband Ran Bahadur Shah. At the same time, the raja of Palpa, Damodar Pande and several others were charged with conspiracy to murder Ran Bahadur Shah and were put to death.

The Gorkhas and the East India Company faced each other in the Tarai in the low lands below the hills from the Sutlej in the west to the

Teesta in the last. Both these powers had displaced earlier rulers in the Tarai and in those turbulent years the exact limits of the dominions that had been conquered had not been defined. It was after the Gorkhas had consolidated their positions in the hills and the Company had organised its conquests in the plains that the officials of the two governments, on their respective frontiers, began to examine old records and revised or contested claims forgotten in the hurry and carelessness of easy triumph. For the Gorkhas, the Tarai was their main source for the supply of food-grains to the army and every acre of it was precious to them.

Disputes now arose about Tarai lands in several districts. When Palpa was absorbed in Nepal, the Gorkhas proceeded to occupy the paraganas of Butwal and Sheoraj which the Raja held from the Nawab Wazir of Oudh. The Raja of Palpa had been in communication with the Company's authorities and one of his officers had persuaded the Company to agree to his holding Butwal as on a sub-lease from the Company. The Gorkhas occupied Sheoraj and a large part of Butwal. On remonstrance from the Company, the Gorkhas offered to hold Butwal on payment of the usual rent from the company. Sir George Barlow, who was then the Governor-General, agreed to relinquish the Company's rights on Sheoraj which had been occupied by the Gorkhas before 1801, when Gorakhpur was ceded to the Company by the Nawab Wazir, but he desired them to vacate Butwal. The dispute, however, dragged on till the outbreak of hostilities between Nepal and the East India Company in 1814.

In 1811, another serious dispute arose in district Saran in North Bihar. Bir Kishore Singh, the Zamindar of Bettiah, who was under the Company's protection, forcibly occupied twenty-two villages belonging to the pargana of Routehat which at that time was actually under the control of the Gorkhas. The Gorkha Tehsildar Lachhmen Giri and his escort were killed and the property and cash of the Nepal government were taken away by Bir Kishore Singh. The Gorkhas lodged a strong protest and desired the Company to punish Bir Kishore Singh or allow them to punish him. The Magistrate of Saran, however, sided with Bir Kishore Singh and reported to his superiors that the Gorkhas had been the aggressors. Later the matter was referred to Nepalese and Company's Commissioners, while all the twenty-two villages were evacuated by the Gorkhas and allowed to be under the control of the Company's representative. The officer of the Company was contemptuous of the claims of the Gorkhas and pressed the Governor-General to occupy the villages permanently.

The Gorkhas were greatly agitated. They had either to submit to the behests of the Governor-General or defend their claims by force. The

Prime Minister Bhim Sen Thapa, as also the leaders of the army, held that the rightful claims of the Gorkhas should not be surrendered. They felt confident that the Gorkha army could stand up to the Company's forces in case of war. A minority group, however, headed by the Rajguru pressed that no power in India had been able to wage a successful war against the Company's forces and advised that another effort be made to come to some mutual understanding with the Company's officers even if half of the disputed villages had to be surrendered. The latter view prevailed and an accredited representative was deputed to negotiate a settlement with the Governor-General. The Governor-General had already decided on war and the Nepalese representative was unceremoniously asked to return to Nepal after his camp was ransacked and his papers seized.

The Governor-General had decided on war primarily on three considerations. Firstly, he wanted physically to separate the two warrior races of the subcontinent *i.e.* the Sikhs and the Gorkhas. Secondly, he wanted to annex the territory between the Jamuna and the Kali rivers where the rulers displaced by the Gorkhas had sought help from the East India Company. These territories would provide an alternative route to the Company in the west for trade with Tibet and China apart from the routes in the east through Bhutan and Sikkim. Thirdly, it was decided that the Company should extend its control over the entire low-lands below the hills on its northern boundary with Nepal so that the base of the hills should form the frontier between the two states.

The war started in 1814 and continued for the next two years. Colonel Ochterlony was the Commander and political representative of the Company at Jalandhar. He had watched the activities of Amar Singh Thapa, the Commander-in-Chief and the plenipotentiany for his King in the areas west of the Jamuna. He felt certain that he could defeat the Gorkhas effectively in this area and assured the Governor-General accordingly. The Governor-General decided to attack Nepal at four points. Colonel Ochterlony was to attack Amar Singh Thapa who had his forces between Bilaspur and Nahan. A second division was to attack the Gorkhas in the Doon Valley and expell them from Garhwal and Kumaon. The third division was to enter Nepal through Syuraj and Palpa. The fourth division was to enter the valley of Kathmandu through Makwanpur. On all these fronts efforts were made to subvert the loyalty of the local Gorkha Commanders and to gain the support of the local chiefs. Amar Singh was promised great rewards if he deserted his master's camp. So also the Chautariya Bum Shah, a collateral of the King-who was controlling Doti and Kumaon. The Gorkha army and its commanders, however, did not succumb to the temptations offered by the Company and fought doggedly for their country. The local chiefs whose territories had been annexed by the Gorkhas naturally sided with the Company. After the war, all the chiefs in the area between the Ganga and the Sutlej were restored in their principalities. Only Kumaon and parts of Garhwal which included the routes to Tibet through Niti and Mana passes were annexed by the Company as also the Dehra Dun valley.

In the first battles the Company's troops were defeated in Makwanpur, Dehra Dun and East Almora. But in the Malaon area the Gorkhas were decisively defeated and were allowed safe conduct only when they promised to evacuate all the lands to the west of the Kali. A peace treaty was then negotiated which was notified by the Nepal durbar only when Ochterlony, now a Major General, crossed the Churiaghati pass into the Valley of the Baghmati. The treaty enjoined that the whole of the Tarai lands from the Kali to the Teesta were to be handed over to the Company; Nepal was to renounce all claims to the territory lying west of the river Kali and undertake not to disturb the raja of Sikkim in the peaceful possession of his territories and to abide by the arbitration of the Company in case of any boundary disputes. The Gorkhas were also forbidden to take or retain the services of any Europeans or Americans without the consent of the British Indian Government. Nepal was also to accept an agent of the Company who would reside in Kathmandu. Lastly, the Company wanted to give pensions to certain chiefs of the Nepal Government ostensibly on the ground that their interests had suffered because of the cession of Nepalese conquests. There was great opposition to the grant of pensions to Nepalese Chiefs by the Company in the durbar and the Governor-General agreed to abrogate this provision of the treaty. The Nepalese were wise in insisting on this point and it was only because the British Indian Government did not have paid agents in high places in Nepal that the country could preserve its independence.

The treaty of Segouli, however, marked the end of the epoch of expansion. In the North, the snow-clad Himalayas forbade permanent conquest and the British in 1816 set definitive limits to the Gorkha Kingdom in the East, South and the West. The Gorkhas were now confined to the mountainous country between the Kali in the West and the Teesta water-shed in the East. At the same time most of the land they had occupied below the inmmediate foot-hills of the Himalayas had to be surrenderd by them to the East India Company, which they regained from time to time as quid-pro-quos for services rendered. The East India Company had also succeded in separating the warlike Gorkhas from another militant Indian power namely the Sikhs in the Punjab. This removed the danger of any possible Hindu-Sikh coalition threatening the

Northern and Western frontiers of the Company's territories by a surprise concerted attack.

Note

1 See Minute by Comwallis, dated Oct. 3, 1792 in *Political Proceedings*. Oct. 3, 1792 (Cons. No. 17) which summarises the position:
The Commercial treaty that we have concluded with Nepal, and the friendly advances lately made to us by the Rajah should induce us to endeavour, as far as it can be done by safe and justifiable means to preserve him and his country from destruction, and it is equally incumbent upon us not only to avoid giving offence to the Chinese, but to neglect no opportunity that affords a prospect of opening a communication with an officer of rank in that State. The union of these objects renders it necessary for us to be extremely delicate and circumspect in our correspondence.

Sixteen

Rule by the Queens (1816-45) and the Ranas (1846-1951)

Bhim Sen Thapa, the Prime Minister, with the backing of the Regent Maharani continued to rule his truncated country with a stong hand from 1816 to 1832. He insisted that the Company's Resident in Nepal should have no contacts with any one in the country except the Prime Minister and such intercourse was to be confined to the minimum requirements laid down in the treaty of Segouli. He realised that the Company wanted to include Nepal in its system of subsidiary alliances of protectorates and his efforts were directed to save his country from such a fate. He laid down what later became the traditional policy of Nepal namely to keep the Company totally in the dark as to whatever transpired in the mountains and to keep it apart from internal disputes between the local chiefs and families of Nepal. Bhim Sen also invented the political fiction that Nepal by a treaty was bound to respect the Chinese Emperor to whom gifts were sent every five years since 1792, and that unwelcome diplomatic moves by the Company would jeopardise Nepal's relations with Peking. That was a polite way of refusing to accept such requests from the Company. Bhim Sen had a healthy respect for the Company's military strength and his aim was to avoid any clash of arms but at the same time to preserve the independence and sovereignty of his country *vis-a-vis* the Company's Government in India.

The death of Maharani Tripur Sundari in 1832 made the political life of the country extremely unstable. Bhim Sen had followed Ran Bahadur Shah and the Maharani Tripur Sundari in their exile and had only returned to Kathmandu with them. On the assassination of Ran Bahadur Shah in 1804 he had been appointed Prime Minister by the Regent Maharani, which office he held till 1837. But he derived his authority from the

Regent Maharani and when on her death the young king started to withdraw his support from the Prime Minister, the latter's troubles started. The young king began by encouraging Ranbir Singh, the brother and rival of the Prime Minister, and giving the latter pin-pricks every now and then. At the same time, the two queens of the new king were both ambitious women and they started intrigues with different factions in order to secure the Prime Ministership for their own nominee. The senior queen called back the Pandes to the royal durbar. The Pandes were themselves keen to take revenge on Bhim Sen who had ousted the family from all positions of authority since 1804. Ranjang, the son of Damodar Pande who had been murdered in 1804 now pressed the claims of his family for royal favours. The senior queen kept drumming into the king's ears that he was a tin-god and incapable of standing up to his Prime Minister. She wanted the young king to dismiss Bhim Sen and make Ranjang the Prime Minister. In this she had the tacit blessings of the Company's Resident also, who was apprehensive of the military strength of Nepal and the absolute control that the Prime Minister exercised over the Nepalese army, some 30,000 strong, at that time.

In 1837, the king disregarded Bhim Sen's advice as to who should lead the quinquennial delegation to Peking. He also restored to Ranjang Pande all the lands and offices the family had lost to Bhim Sen. Bhim Sen's nephew Matabar Singh was also removed as Governor of Gorkha and replaced by a Pande.

At this time suddenly the senior queen lost her young son. The Pandes insinuated foul play by the Prime Minister, and persuaded the king to arrest Bhim Sen on the charge and put him in prison. At the baseless and whimsical decision of a weak king, the most powerful administrator in Nepal was dragged from his high office and thrown in chains in a dirty prison cell. Not only Bhim Sen but his nephew Matabar Singh was also imprisoned. That the other chiefs accepted such injustice proved that the king's authority in Nepal knew no limits. The plotters of the Pande family, however, dare not execute their rival because he staunchly refused to admit any guilt and the depravity of the plotters was revealed when they drove the aged Prime Minister in 1839 to commit suicide on hearing the false news that his wife had been compelled to walk the streets of Kathmandu to the magistrate's Court.

The enormity of the crime and the tragic end of a great Prime Minister shocked the Chiefs and the people of Kathmandu. Ranjang Pande, who had obtained the office of Prime Minister through the intrigues of the senior queen, tried to assuage public opinion by instigating war against the

Company. The Pandes sent agents to Maratha, Sikh and Rajput chiefs for a war to throw out the British from India. Lord Auckland, the Governor-General in India had entertained plans for a second Nepal war in 1840 when his difficulties in Afghanistan forced him to abandon direct intervention in Nepal. He then authorised the Resident at Kathmandu to work for a change in the office of Prime Minister.

Towards the end of 1840 a disorderly military tumult threatened the Residency and on that pretext Hodgson, the Company's Resident, forced the King to throw out the Pandes and entrust the affairs of the Kingdom to the Brahmin Raj Guru and the Chautariyas, collaterals of the royal family. With the appointment of Lord Ellenborough as the new Governor-General, the Company's policy towards Nepal, however, underwent complete change. Ellenborough, following the Company's Afghan policy, directed the Resident to stop forthwith any participation in the intrigues of the Nepal durbar. Hodgson could not go back on what he had solemnly asserted to the King, the ministers and the chiefs without loss of face. He preferred retirement and Ellenborough sent Major Lawrence in his place assuring the durbar at the same time that the Company's relations with Nepal were to be restored to their former basis of strict neutrality.

In 1841, the senior Maharani died. Even during her lifetime her son and heir apparent had started on his career of irresponsible oppression of the common people as also of the chiefs. After her death the junior Maharani seemed to most of the chiefs the only person who could place some restraints on the young prince. At length, the chiefs led by the chautariya Fateh Jung who was a collateral of the royal family and the Prime Minister, called upon the king and persuaded him to sign a proclamation resting full powers of State on the junior Maharani. This is an example of the ancient Hindu tradition of responsible public opinion asserting itself even before an absolute Hindu monarch.

The junior Maharani placed effective curbs on the whimsical actions of the heir apparent Surendra Vikram and thereby endeared herself to the people and the noblemen at Kathmandu. With supreme powers vested in her, the junior Maharani decided to debar Surendra Vikram from the throne and clear the way for her own son to become the heir apparent. She kept her own counsel and started careful preparations to achieve her aims. She decided to bring back the Thapas to power, planning that out of gratefulness to her, they would get rid of Surendra Vikram. She sent for General Matabar Singh, a nephew of Bhim Sen Thapa, who was then residing in Simla and made him Prime Minister. He was Prime Minister from December 1843 to May 1845, when he was mysteriously shot dead. The junior Maharani turned then to Gagan Singh, a favourite of hers, and made him Prime Minister. At the same time, Kazi Jung Bahadur was raised to the rank of a General and three regiments at Kathmandu were placed under the latter's command. On the 14th September 1846, General Gagan Singh was also shot dead in his own house. The perpetrators and instigators of this crime could not be caught or traced. The junior Maharani was wild with rage and sending for all the prominent people in Kathmandu to assemble in the palace grounds, called upon them to name and surrender the culprits. At the same time Jung Bahadur with the three regiments under his command was called to standby. When some of the prominent people protested against the charges levelled at them by the Maharani, who was the lawful regent, the Maharani characterised the protests as treason. At this turn of events, Jung Bahadur brought his soldiers to the assembly place in the palace and ordered ruthless shooting of all the protesters. In the melee that followed most of the prominent persons amongst the Pandes and the chautariyas were killed. Appalled at the enormity of her outrageous actions, the junior Maharani prevailed upon the weak king to appoint Jung Bahadur as the Prime Minister and the Commander-in-Chief. This was the only step that would have saved the royal family from the anger of the families of the prominent chiefs and noblemen in Kathmandu. The gamble worked. Jung Bahadur ordered all the regiments at the capital to assemble at the parade ground. The palace was surrounded by the infantry-men of his three regiments and their muskets were got ready with lighted front fires. Jung Bahadur harangued the troops in a long speech and promised that, although they had lost their commanders whose dead bodies were placed before them, but that they would be sincerely and steadfastly looked after by him in future. He told them that the regent Maharani, after quelling the treason of their erstwhile commanders, had appointed him their Commander-in-Chief; and therefore, he exhorted them to obey him in future. The soldiers agreed to follow him and their junior commanders swore loyalty to him as Jung Bahadur had already announced numerous promotions. The different regiments retired to their quarters alongwith their new commanders. The day's massacre, however, left the populace stunned and leaderless and Jung Bahadur emerged as the new arbiter of the country.

The junior Maharani, however, continued to press Jung Bahadur to get rid of the heir apparent. The new Prime Minister refused to oblige, but showed utmost courtesy to the Maharani. The Maharani then inspired a plot to get rid of Jung Bahadur. The latter, in mortal danger of his life, laid bare to the Raja the conspiracies ordered by the Maharani to get rid of the heir apparent and obtained his approval for the deportation of the Maharani to Benares. But when the time came for the departure of the Maharani, the Raja accompanied her to Benares inspite of the pressing requests of the Prime Minister. This happened on 23rd November, 1846. When the Raja did not return early to Kathmandu, his son Surendra Vikram was formally installed as the Raja. On learning of this development, the Raja returned to Nepal and sent his emissaries to the capital with orders under his own hand and addressed to the general public, and in particular the soldiers to kill Jung Bahadur. The royal letter fell into the hands of Jung Bahadur who read it to the soldiers assembled by him at the Kathmandu parade ground. At the end of his harangue, he asked the soldiers if any of them would like to carry out the Raja's order thinking it to be according to "dharma" and if so, he welcomed such a soldier to shoot at the speaker. The soldiers were taken up by the charisma of their commander and acclaiming him confirmed their total alienation from the Raja. The Raja was then intercepted in his way to the capital by Jung Bahadur and kept under strict surveillance at Bhatgaon.[1]

Jung Bahadur had seven brothers and he built his career on their unquestioned loyalty to him. He had put his brothers to command his regiments and one of them to control his personal office as Prime Minister. It was not only that Jung Bahadur was the Prime Minister and Commander-in-Chief of Nepal but also that each one of his brothers, his sons and his nephews was holding an important office of State. The government of Nepal thus became a family concern of the family of Jung Bahadur. The family's hold on the affairs of State was strengthened by Jung Bahadur obtaining from the Raja of Nepal, who was locally called the Maharajadhiraj, the title of Maharaja to be bestowed on the head of the Rana family who occupied the office of Prime-Minister. This was further fortified by Jung Bahadur by arranging the marriage of his daughter with the heir apparent. This ensured that the future Maharajadhiraj of Nepal was a close relation of the Ranas. Jung Bahadur could establish this type of family supremacy in Nepal only with the active support of the British in India. Jung Bahadur had a clear appreciation of British power in the geo-political conditions of the Indian subcontinent. He gave unstinted support to the British and in return obtained for himself and his family the support of the paramount power in South-Asia. Jung Bahadur offered the services of the Nepalese Army to the British during the Sikh wars and again in 1857. On the latter occasion, an army group of about 12,000 infantry men and 5000 gunners accompanied by an even larger number of supporting personnel helped quell the '57' rising in Oudh. In return the British returned a number of taluqas or groups of villages in the Uttar Pradesh and Bihar Tarai which had been taken over by the East India Company in the Nepal War of 1814-16.[2]

Jung Bahadur was one of the most astute and consummate administrators of his time in South Asia. In 1850, he visited England. Since the 12th century A.D. Hindu princes from South Asia had not undertaken sea voyages. Jung Bahadur and two of his brothers braved the religious objections of the Brahmins in undertaking the visit. He visited the naval dockyard at Southampton, the arsenal at Woolwich and the manufacturing cities in Lancashire. He was now convinced, more than ever, that no combination of Indian princes could match the East India Company's troops and artillery and that the soundest policy for Nepal was to be loyal ally of the British Power in India. However, he was equally sure that the British, should not be allowed to mix with the Nepalese themselves or through their agents. The Resident at Kathmandu could not move out of the Residency without the knowledge and the permission of the Prime Minister and he was expected not to talk or meet any of the Chiefs, nobles or publicmen of Nepal. The arrangement was that the Prime Minister of Nepal would do nothing to harm the interests of the British and the British would take no steps against the interests of the Prime Minister and his family-who, by 1847, had become the hereditary arbiters of Nepal. After the Second Sikh War, the junior Sikh Maharani had taken refuge at Kathmandu. Jung Bahadur allowed her to stay in Nepal but strictly forbade any political activity by her against the East India Company. So also in 1859, Nana Sahab, Azimullah Khan, some descendants of the last Mughal emperor Bahadur Shah and of the last Nawab of Oudh Wajid Ali Shah sought refuge in Nepal and obtained asylum on condition that they would engage in no political activities against the British in India. This was a step also to emphasize the fact that Nepal was an ally of the British Government in India but was not a vassal or subsidiary state.

Jung Bahadur was convinced that no Indian armies could fight the British forces successfully. This was why he offered help to the British during the Sikh Wars and the 1857 uprising in Oudh. But for his armed intervention, the general uprising in Oudh would have taken considerably more time to be controlled by British arms alone. As a reward for this, Jung Bahadur secured the return to Nepal of all the disputed territories in the Tarai which had led to the war of 1814-16 and which had been ceded to the East India Company at the end of that war. The Nepalese had ancient claims to these lands, whereas Kumaon and the hill states to the left had been conquered by the Nepalese only in the years between 1790 and 1804, and their acquisition by the East India Company had been accepted as final by all parties at the Nepal Durbar.

There was, however, the defeat of the Nepalese at the hands of the Chinese and the Tibetans in 1792 to be avenged. At that time, the Nepalese had lost some of the districts on the Kuti and the Kerong passes to the Tibetans. In 1854, the quinquennial mission to China had returned to Kathmandu with the news that the Chinese Emperor had to face the Taiping rebellion and was in no position to come to the help of the Tibetans in case of war with Nepal. The conditions in Lhasa were also favourable for a Nepalese victory as the Regent Lama Yeshi Gyatso Rating and the Chief administrative officers were working at cross-purposes. Jung Bahadur decided to take advantage of these conditions, and a short war was fought in the summer months of 1855 and all the districts ceded in 1792 were recovered. This was confirmed by the treaty of 1856 under which the Tibetans, in addition, agreed to make an annual payment of Rs. 10,000 to Nepal; to accept a Nepalese Agent at Lhasa; to exempt Nepalese traders from import duties and to accord to them the most favoured terms. This was acclaimed as the recognition by Tibet of the superior strength of the Nepalese army and its vindication by the recapture of all the districts ceded in 1792. Jung Bahadur now became the national hero of all Nepal.

It was at this time that Jung Bahadur played the trump card of his career. He had always displayed enigmatic and charismatic traits of his personality at opportune moments. In July 1856, he ostensibly retired from the office of Prime Minister and entrusted its responsibilities to his next younger brother Ban Bahadur. There was great consternation amongst the leading men at Kathmandu as no one could assess the motives of Jung Bahadur or predict the course of events. Many thought that Jung Bahadur wanted to become the Maharajadhiraj of Nepal. The Raj Guru led a deputation to Jung Bahadur to assure him that the crown of Nepal could be offered to him peacefully if that was what he wanted. The reply of the ex-Prime Minister was characteristic of the man. He told the deputation that he would not be party to dethrone the Maharajadhiraj whom he had himself put on the throne of Nepal. But he added that he would be available in case the country needed him at the helm of affairs. This was both an assertion of loyalty to the Shah ruler and a warning. The upshot was that the Maharajadhiraj, as the scion of the family of Prithvi Narayan Shah, conferred the principalities of Kaski and Lamjung, which had no rulers at that time, on Jung Bahadur with the title of Maharaja. This honour was to be associated with the office of the Prime Minister of Nepal who was now to enjoy all sovereign powers in Nepal. After this signal honour, it was incumbent on Jung Bahadur to assert publicly his loyalty to the Shah Maharajadhiraj and his family and to resume the office of Prime Minister.

Nepal was administered with a strong hand by Jung Bahadur from 1846, when he first assumed power till his death in 1877. He is remembered best as the ruler of a Hindu Kingdom who abolished the practice of sati or burning of widows, and consolidated the administrative system that continued in its essentials till 1951.

Jung Bahadur's elder surviving brother Ranudip Singh became the Prime Minister after his death, and Dhir Shamsher, the last surviving brother, the Commander-in-Chief. In 1881, Surendra Vikram Shah, the Maharajadhiraj died and was succeeded by his grandson Prithvi Bir Bikram Shah then in his sixth year. In January 1882, a conspiracy was detected against the Prime Minister and the Commander-in-Chief in which the eldest son of Jung Bahadur, Jagat Jung, was suspected to have been involved. Jagat Jung was exiled to India and twenty-one persons found guilty of conspiracy to murder the Prime Minister and the Commander-in-Chief were sentenced to death. Dhir Shamsher who was the dominant Rana personality after Jung Bahadur died in 1884. Ranudip Singh, who was mild by nature, allowed Jagat Jung to return to Kathmandu in 1885. This led to a bitter power struggle between the sons of Jung Bahadur and Dhir Shamsher. After the death of Ranudip Singh, Jagat Jung would have become the Prime Minister according to the order of succession envisaged by Jung Bahadur. This was not acceptable to the sons of Dhir Shamsher. In November 1885, fearing that Jagat Jung might be restored to office as Commander-in-Chief, they conspired to kill the Prime Minister Ranudip Singh, Jagat Jung, and Juddha Pratap Jung, Jagat Jung's eldest son. Bir Shamsher, the eldest son of Dhir Shamsher, now assumed office of Prime Minister.[3] In 1887, Khadga Shamsher the Commander-in-Chief was removed from office and sent as a state prisoner to Palpa when his conspiracy to kill the Prime Minister misfired. In 1888, Ranbir Jung, one of the sons of Jung Bahadur, who had escaped to India tried to organise an armed revolt in Palpa, the Baghmati Tarai and Kathmandu but without success. Thereafter there was comparative quiet in the family of the Ranas and when Bir died in 1901, Deva Shamsher, the Commander-in-Chief, succeeded as the Prime Minister. Deva Shamsher was cast in a different mould from the rest of the Ranas. He had given the fullest support to Bir in all his efforts to improve the collection of state dues from land, enhancement of the state's share of local taxes, reform of the criminal law, abolition of taxes on pilgrims etc. He now expressed himself openly in favour of greater consultation between the Maharajadhiraj and the Maharaja Prime Minister in affairs of state and in the abolition of the Nepalese custom of bonded labour who or whose ancestors had voluntarily sold themselves into such bondage. He ordered the abolition of the custom in his principalities of Lamjung and Kaski as also in Kathmandu. He had, however, to annul the decree on the vehement protests of the other Ranas and the upper classes who all benefited from the custom. On 26th June 1901, Chandra Shamsher, the Commander-in-Chief, forced Deva to sign his retirement in favour of his brother. Deva was then asked to leave the valley of Kathmandu and was practically interned at Dhankuta from where Deva conveniently exiled himself to British India. Deva tried to organise a plot against the life of his brother in 1903 when the latter was on a visit to India. The British-Indian Government was, however, wholly in favour of Chandra Shamsher and saw to it that Deva was first safely moved to Benares and later to Mussoorie. His pension of Rs. 4000 per month was continued by the Nepal durbar.

Chandra Shamsher ruled Nepal as Prime Minister from 1901 till his death in 1929. He was the most astute of the Ranas of his time. He had been involved in the conspiracy organised by Khadga Shamsher against Bir Shamsher in 1887, but had been pardoned by his uncle. He had also agreed to Bir's inclusion of several of his sons from other than high caste wives in the succession list. He was the senior commanding general in Bir's time and had devoted himself to improving the efficiency and discipline of the Nepalese army. In 1891, Chandra had agreed to the proposal of increasing the recruitment of the Nepalese in the British Indian Gorkha battalions from nine to fifteen and to allow the reruitment without 'let or hinderance'. In 1892, Lord Roberts came to Kathmandu to review the Nepalese army. Chandra availed of this opportunity to come nearer to the highest officers of British India. He had further occasions to improve his personal standing with the British officers in India while he held charge of the foreign affairs desk at Kathmandu. Like Jung Bahadur, Chandra Shamsher was an admirer of the British and a great advocate for Nepal's reliance on the British connection.

When the First World War seemed imminent and in fact a day before war was actually declared, Chandra had informed the Resident at Kathmandu: "I request you to inform his Excellency the Viceroy, and through him the King Emperor, that the whole military resources of Nepal are at His Majesty's disposal... Though far from the scene of actual conflict we yield to none in our devotion and friendship to His Majesty's Person and Empire... May I say I am speaking to you in double capacity: firstly, as Marshal of the Gorkhas and secondly, as Major-General in His Majesty's Army." It appears the message was drafted by the Resident after a talk with Chandra who had come to the Residency on learning that hostilities might commence any time in Europe between Great Britain and Germany.[4]

In the First World War, the Gorkha regiments under the British fought gallantly in several war theatres including France, Gallipoli, Suez, Palestine, Iraq and Persia. Since 1908, the strength of the Gorkhas had been fixed at twenty battalions forming ten rifle regiments. In addition Chandra sent another ten regiments of the Nepalese army to assist the British Indian garrisons in the North West Frontier and the United Provinces of India, relieving to that extent European regiments in India assigned to internal security duties. The British acknowledged this help rendered in time of need and concluded a new treaty with Nepal in 1923 which confirmed all the previous agreements and treaties between the two parties but changed the modes of address of certain personages. The Maharajadhiraj of Nepal was to be addressed as His Majesty instead of as His Royal Highness, the Maharaja Prime Minister as His Highness instead of as His Excellency. Similarly, the resident was now called an Envoy and not a Resident. In effect, however, foreign relations of Nepal continued to be controlled by New Delhi. No Europeans could be employed in Nepal without the sanction of the Government of India and the right to import arms and ammunitions freely into Nepal was limited by the clause that this concession would be applicable only so long as "the intentions of the Nepal Government are friendly and that there is no immediate danger to India from such importation.[5]

Chandra was a cautious ruler, careful about security, and orderliness of administration but mild and skilful in execution of State policies. His elder brother Khadga Shamsher, who was Governor of Palpa, tried on Chandra's assumption of office to rouse the local garrison against a younger brother occupying the office of Prime Minister when an elder brother was available. Chandra called Khadga's battalion to Kathmandu and persuaded Khadga to leave Nepal and reside permanently in Saugar in Central India with a handsome pension from the Nepal government.[6] We have already noticed his handling of Deva, the deposed elder brother. Within two years of Chandra's assumption of office, Gehendra Shamsher son of Bir Shamsher and Fateh Shamsher son of Dhir Shamsher and brother of Gehendra, who had actively helped Chandra in deposing Deva, committed suicide. Gehendra had developed new models of rifles and guns to be manufactured in Nepal itself and was popular with the army. Fateh was one of the Secretary Generals. After the death of Fateh, Chandra appointed his own son Mohan as the sole Secretary General, although he was only 16 years of age.[7] These carefully thoughtout arrangements ensured that in future there was to be no internal conspiracy against Chandra's life as had been the case with all the previous Prime Ministers.

Chandra is credited with several administrative reforms by British historians, but most of them were undertaken only to project a favourable image of Chandra before the British public and to enhance the state revenues which to all intents and purposes became the perquisites of the Maharaja Prime Minister. When Chandra died in 1929 he left a fortune of 40 million pounds sterling to his sons in addition to several palaces, shares in British and Indian joint-stock companies and costly jewellery.[8]

Chandra abolished the practice of sati or the self-immolation of a widow on the funeral pyre of her dead husband. Chandra was keen to be known as the Lord William Bentinck of Nepal. As a matter of fact, however, Jung Bahadur had decreed that no widow, who had duties towards her children or her husband's family or the state was to be allowed to burn herself with her husband's dead body and Bir Shamsher had ordered that no rite of sati was to be allowed except under his personal orders. The rite of Sati, occasionally indulged in by high-caste widows had practically disappeared from Nepal, but Chandra must get credit for his unequivocal and unconditional abolition of the rite.

Chandra also abolished the custom of bonded household servants; mistakenly alluded to as slavery by British officials and historians. In times of acute scarcity people who could not buy food bonded themselves and their children to others who undertook to feed them and thus save their lives. The plight of a woman in such circumstances was harsher still. If she bore children, they were at the mercy of the master and could be sold to others. It was this custom which Deva in his short rule of a few months had promised to abolish. Chandra, in 1924, abolished the right of the master to sell the offspring of a bonded woman, or the services of a bonded person without his or her consent. Such masters numbered about 15,000 and the bonded persons were between 50 and 60 thousand. These persons still remained as personal servants with their masters but the rights about sale of their services and their offspring were bought over by the government at a cost of 37 lakhs of rupees, which came from the treasury attached to the Pashupati Nath temple. In other words, these rights were now purchased by Pashupati Nath and no Nepalese dared interfere with the rights now vested in the protector deity of the kingdom. This was a great achievement for Chandra. He managed to abolish bondages derogatory to human dignity which were, in some aspects, indistinguishable from certain characteristics of slavery in a singularly Nepalese way; displeasing neither the masters nor the bonded persons. Jung Bahadur had forbidden men and women of higher castes, forty castes and subcastes were enumerated by him, to sell themselves or their children into bondage. Deva had freed all bonded women in Kathmandu and his own principalities of Lamjung and Kaski. But the customs lingered on as no complaints came to higher officers that the orders were not being implemented. Chandra now consummated the progress by vesting the rights of sale in Pashupati Nath by buying the same from the masters. This ensured that such rights would not be exercised in future in Nepal as no one dared to interfere with the rights of Pashupati Nath. So there was now the biggest moral pressure against the old customs, and they were finally abandoned.

Chandra also abolished the inter-district octrois and duties in Nepal. He also built a light railway in the Tarai to prove to the world that Nepal was not without a railway line. However, he refused to build a motor road to Kathmandu. He was still unsure of the British connection. A good motor road to Kathmandu would have facilitated the conquest of the valley by British arms, whenever Britain wanted to annex the Kingdom. This rule was followed by his successors till the nineteen-fifty's and one could see till then thirty or forty porters carrying on their shoulders and bamboo-poles a limousine on the rough track from the Tarai to the Kathmandu valley for the use of the Ranas.

Chandra did not believe in educating the masses. He was only interested in educating his officials at the lower and intermediate ranges of the administration. For them he opened the Tribhuwan Chandra College at Kathmandu in 1918. He also built the light ropeway from the railway terminus at Bhimphedi to Kathmandu. This he had purchased from the British Indian government who had used it in the third Afghan War, Kathmandu, itself, had electricity, a number of motorable roads for the city and the entire valley, piped water supply and an allopathic military hospital.

He also reorganised to some extent the Nepalese battalions on the lines of the Gorkha battalions in British India. The field service manuals of the British were translated into Khas-Kura or Gorkhali and promotion examinations were started. He also started the practice of payment of all officers and men in the army in cash from the government treasury, so that they would not be attached to the officers who raised them but to the state. But the men were now enlisted for short periods and there was great paucity of barracks even in Kathmandu. And the worst feature was that commanding Lieutenant Colonels and above were Ranas born in the family of the Prime Minister and most of them lacked military training and experience. Inspite of these drawbacks, however, the Nepalese army brought credit to itself wherever it went inside or outside the country. For the Nepalese, army life has always been attractive. The men from the mountains are hardy and live in conditions of acute scarcity and discomfort. The one sure way to make good in life is to join one of the Gorkha battalions. There are hardly any other worthwhile occupations for the healthy mountaineers. If Britain is a nation of shop-keepers, Nepal is a nation of soldiers.

Chandra was succeeded by his brother Bhim Shamsher in 1929. Bhim died in 1931 and was succeeded by the last of the brothers Juddha Shamsher. In Nepal, the sons of the ruling family of Ranas were classified as A, B and C class Ranas, depending upon the standing in the caste hierarchy of their mothers and their family background. Bir Shamsher had elevated his son Rudra, a C class Rana, to the status of A class Rana. Rudra thus came to occupy senior positions and was the senior General now next in succession to Juddha. Bhim Shamsher had also elevated his sons who had class C status and posted them to Palpa, Birganj and Eastern Nepal as commanding Generals. Yuddha and the sons of Chandra Shamsher did not like these actions of the former Prime Ministers. Chandra was cautious in this matter also. He did not disturb Rudra's elevation to A class status and was content by having his own sons and younger brothers in the most important offices in the State. Rudra was not aggressive or ambitious. He became the Commander-in-Chief when Yuddha became the Maharaja. He is reported to have gone shortly afterwards to Yuddha to know his views on the succession list. Yuddha is reported to have assured him that he had no intention to change the order of succession. However, three years latter, in 1934, Yuddha called all the C class Ranas to his palace and peremptorily asked them to resign all claims in the succession list. When Rudra agreed to do so, the rest followed suit. Rudra was then sent as the district officer to Palpa but most of the others were deprived of their offices and Commands and exiled to India.

In the same year *i.e.* 1934, by a new agreement the Envoy at Kathmandu became British Minister Plenipotentiary and the Nepalese were allowed to open a Legation in London. However, the British Indian

Foreign Department continued to handle Nepal desk of the British Government as also the relations with the Arab principalities in the Persian Gulf.

Yuddha, like all his predecessor Ranas was totally wedded to the British connection. At the time of the Munich crisis he offered eight Nepalese battalions for garrison duties in India. He was thanked but the offer was declined. The offer was renewed on the outbreak of war in 1939. This time the offer was accepted and Yuddha sent the promised eight battalions with his eldest son General Bahadur in overall Command.

After Dunkirk, some of the councillors including General Padma Shamsher, the Commander-in-Chief and next in line of succession to Yuddha, thought that the German army would be victorious in the war in Europe and that Nepal should be prepared for such an eventuality. Yuddha Shamsher, however, remained unconvinced. He also felt honour bound to help Britain in her time of dire distress. Yuddha allowed the British to increase the number of Gorkha battalions in the British army and at the end of the war there were forty Gorkha battalions in all with the British with ten more battalions under training in the Regimental centres.

Yuddha remained unaffected during the Cripps Mission, the Quit India Movement of Gandhi and the Japanese conquests of Malaya and Burma. In 1942, when rail transport was disrupted in U.P. and Bihar, the Maharaja allowed British war planes to fly over Nepal. An airfield was also laid near Birganj, opposite to Raxaul in British India, to facilitate communications between Delhi and Kathmandu.

After the war, Yuddha laid down his office as Maharaja in November 1945, and like ancient Hindu Rajas decided to devote the rest of his life to peaceful contemplation and observance of religious behaviour prescribed in the sacred Hindu texts. He was then sixtytwo years of age. His decision was entirely his own, and was a rare event even in Nepal. He left Nepal with his enormous personal wealth and went to Hardwar, where the Ganges emerges from the Himalayas onto the plains of Northern India. He might have retired earlier but he wanted to be at the helm of affairs till final victory had been won in the Second World War and till the question of succession was well settled. The sons of Chandra Shamsher headed by Mohan were for tightly controlled Rana rule whereas Padma Shamsher, the only class 'A' Rana son of Bhim Shamsher, was known for his liberal views and his determination to push through political reforms. Mohan and his brothers wanted to have Padma passed over, but Yuddha gave his verdict in favour of Padma on the ground that he was the rightful heir.[9] Yuddha was not in favour of yielding to Chandra Shamsher's sons mainly because any deviation from the accepted succession list would have, strengthened the hands of Chandra Shamsher's sons and his own sons would, in all likelihood, been deprived of their rightful claims once Mohan, Chandra Shamsher's eldest son got control of the kingdom. This is evident from the fact that Yuddha's eldest son Bahadur continued to hold the very important office of Secretary General under Padma.

Padma Shamsher inaugurated the process of political change in Nepal. From December 1945 till April 1948 when he resigned his office, he had devoted himself to the encouragement of all progressive forces in the country. He wanted to start with democratically elected panchayats in the villages and thus to associate the people in the administration of their own local affairs. This was not acceptable to most of his Rana cousins and in February 1948 he left for India ostensibly to apprise himself about the shape of things to come in that country. Padma stayed in Delhi and in April sent in his formal resignation to Kathmandu. Mohan Shamsher, however, had already shifted to the Singh Durbar, the official residence cum office of the Maharaja Prime Minister. Already in December 1947, the British Residency had been transferred to independent India. At the same time, the rights and privileges obtained by Britain in Nepal had been relinquished. Padma had thought that India had stepped into the place occupied by Great Britain and that Nepal's ties with independent India should be patterned on the model of Nepal's ties with the British authority in India. But most of the Ranas considered Nehru's India as an ally of the dispossessed masses of Nepal and to sageguard their own personal interests they considered themselves in the camp opposed to independent India. This led to the British Minister becoming Ambassador, followed by ambassadors from India and the U.S.A. In 1950, however, during the Hyderabad episode Mohan agreed to send ten battalions of the Nepalese army to help India. Perhaps, he would not have refused the help sought by India as India was then fighting a defiant subsidiary ruler belonging to the Muslim faith.

Mohan was totally opposed to the new constitution inaugurated by Padma. He and his brothers had decided to fight for the rule of the Ranas and the implementation of the new constitution was made impossible by the ordinances promulgated by the new Maharaja under the new constitution.

In November 1950 King Tribhuwan sought refuge in the Indian Ambassy and later went to Delhi in an Indian plane. The King, his three sons and his eldest grandson left the country. Mohan Shamsher, in a hasty decision, announced that the King should be presumed to have abdicated as also his eldest son and eldest grandson in favour of Prince Gyanendra, the elder of the two grandsons of King Tribhuwan still remaining in Nepal. This was not accepted by the people, the army and the noblemen of Nepal. Even Great Britain did not accept the new position. Sensing that he and his brothers were left alone, Mohan decided to capitulate. The end of the rule of Ranas had been ushered in by the peaceful revolt of the King with India's active backing.

King Tribhuwan returned to Nepal in January 1951 amd a series of events took place in quick succession heralding the end of the era of the Ranas. In April 1951, the King proclaimed the termination of the hereditary Prime Ministership in the family of the Ranas, and most of Maharaja Prime Minister's powers were taken over by the King. He also became the Commander-in-Chief of all Nepalese forces. In December, 1957 Mohan Shamsher, now over seventy years of age, left his native country and retired to Bangalore in South India. Three Ranas who had been Maharaja Prime Ministers of Nepal were then in India, Yuddha in Dehra Dun, Padam in Ranchi and Mohan in Bangalore. The Ranas were still very powerful in Nepal but their absolute control of all important offices of State had gone. The change, however, had been generally peaceful and came from the King himself. King Tribhuwan's eldest son, Mahendra was married to Maharaja Yuddha's granddaughter and a second son Prince Himalaya was married to a great-granddaughter of Yuddha. The sisters of King Tribhuwan were married to Chandra Shamsher's son, the eldest to General Kaiser, the second to General Singha and the third to General Krishna. After the end of the rule of 'A' Class Ranas in 1951, for several years 'C' class Ranas who had been exiled by Yuddha came to hold important offices in Nepal. Even to this day the Ranas hold important appointments in the Nepalese army and the new civil service, but the absolute hold of the Ranas on the administration, the army and all important offices of State came to an end in April 1951.

Notes

1 See Sanwal, B.D.-Nepal and the East India Company, Chapter 20. Jung Bahadur's Early Career.

2 See Sanwal, B.D.- Nepal and the East India Company, Chapter 22, Nepal's War with Tibet and the Sepoy War, pp. 284-297.

3 For details see *Gorkha* by Sir Francis Tuker-Chapter 20. *The House of Shamsher* pp. 162-173 and *A Century of Family Antocracy in Nepal* by D.R. Regmi, pp. 96-121.

4 See *Gorkha* by Sir Francis Tucker, p. 192.
5 *Accounts and Paper*, vol. 14, State Papers. Session Jan 8-October 9, 1924, vol. xxvi (1924) CMD 2112.
6 *Gorkha* by Sir Francis Tuker, page 178.
7 A *Century of Family Aristocracy in Nepal* by D.R. Regmi, p. 119., 122 and 123.
8 *Gorkha* by Sir Francis Tuker, p. 171.
9 D.R. Regmi-Ibid., p. 190.

Seventeen

The Beginnings of Political Awakening

Political activities amongst the people of Nepal started with the First World War and the ferment caused by the mobilisation, experience in fighting and the deaths of thousands of men in the different theatres of war. Previously, it was only the different factions of the ruling class that conspired against each other to get the plums of office, power and privileges. The Thapas, the Chautariyas and the Brahmins connected with the royal household had contested for power from the time of Ran Bahadur Shah to the coming to power of Jung Bahadur. Jung Bahadur, however, had eliminated all other centres of power and concentrated all authority, power and privileges in the Rana family.

Educated Nepalese other than Ranas came in contact with the rising nationalism of the Indian middle classes particularly in Benares, Patna and Calcutta. These were the places where bright Nepalese students went to pursue higher studies and where the discontented and the deprived Nepalese came for succour, consolation and cogitation. Trouble for the Ranas started when these Nepalese elements came in contact with nationalist Indians. During the First World War itself subba Devi Prasad had started, to question the autocratic rule of the Ranas. Devi Prasad had been a senior officer in the Foreign Department of Nepal and had based himself in Benares after his relinquishment of office at Kathmandu. He edited the weekly "Gorkhali" for nearly six years before the paper was finally suppressed by the British Indian authorities in 1922.[1] Another effort was made to start another weekly paper "Gorkha Samachar" from Dehra Dun by Thakur Chandan Singh in 1927-28. But this enterprise had to be closed as the associates of Chandan Singh were bought over by the

Nepal government.[2] It should be appreciated that at that time any writing in praise of democracy in Nepal was construed as treason.

In 1937, Shukra Raj Shastri, a resident of the Kathmandu valley, gathered courage to say that the Newars should be allowed access to higher posts in the administration as had been the case before the conquest of the valley by the Shah rulers and the Thapa and Rana Chief executives. He met Gandhi and told him about the denial of basic human rights to the common people in Nepal. Although Shukra Raj was a man of peace and mild in his use of words, he was sentenced to six months imprisonment.[3]

In 1936, Tanka Prasad Acharya formed a secret organisation-the Praja Parishad or the citizens League-at Kathmandu. The aim of the Parishad was to bring to an end the autocracy of the Ranas by bringing to light the oppression of all other strata of society by the Ranas. At first they worked clandestinely and made propaganda amongst the partly educated masses in the valley. They also published details of the cruelties and oppression by the Ranas in the Hindi weekly "Janata" edited by Ram Vriksha Sharma Benipuri from North Bihar from 20th June 1938 till 1940 when the paper was suppressed by the British Indian authorities. Tanka Prasad had access to the Maharajadhiraj as a Brahmin of high learning. King Tribhuwan lent his willing ears to the Acharya and the aim of the Praja Parishad became the revival of the powers of the King and curbing those of the Ranas. Between July and September 1940 leaflets were distributed all over the country demanding extensive political reforms. The Ranas were warned to mend their evil ways on pain of a call of Satyagraha in Nepal on the lines of Gandhi's movements in India.[4] According to the Ranas, the movement was not as peaceful as it was portrayed. It was alleged that in a secret plot the king was to call all the Ranas and the other members of their families to witness the latest Hindi film from Bombay in his private cinema hall, the cinema hall was to have gunpowder under the floor and at an opportune moment the powder would be lighted and most of the gathering would be annihilated.[5]

The conspiracy was said to have come to the notice of Maharaja Yuddha Shamsher and he lost no time in arresting the suspects-some sixty people in all. Mohan Shamsher was prominent at the trial where even the king was required to own his part. The King, however, kept strictly aloof, assumed a dignified silence and did neither protest nor plead guilty.[6] The others were severely punished. Seven persons were sentenced to death. The Newars, namely Shukra Raj and Dharma Bhatia, were hanged; Ganga Lal and Dasrath Chand were shot dead; two Brahmins, Tanka Prasad and Ram Hari, were not hanged but their sacred Hindu threads were torn off and they were expelled from caste and the seventh Subba Dharm Narain's death sentence was commuted to life imprisonment by the Maharaja. Of the rest six were given life imprisonment; five twenty years imprisonment; another six twelve years and last four six years.

King Tribhuwan was believed to have given his discreet support to the conspiracy against the Ranas and an enquiry was held against the King at the instance of the Maharaja. The King refused to accept the validity of such procedure and refused to admit or deny his guilt. Maharaja Yuddha sounded the heir-apparent Prince Mahendra if he would agree to the deposition of his father and accept the throne himself. On his firm refusal, Yuddha retraced his steps and setting aside the charges, declared the King's innocence. The relations between King Tribhuwan and Yuddha had now become totally estranged and the King decided to visit India for medical treatment. Yuddha delayed his decision but did not allow the King to leave Kathmandu. On being pressed by the King, Colonel Denham White an eminent surgeon and physician from Calcutta was called to examine the King. Colonel White did not think that the thrombosis, from which the King was suffering, was serious; but at the same time advised advanced treatment at his own clinic in Calcutta. Late in 1944, King Tribhuwan went to Calcutta, escorted by Yuddha's eldest son, General Bahadur who was later joined by General Kiran, a step brother of General Bahadur but a 'C' class Rana. The king was allowed to visit Calcutta in his private capacity and 'incognito'. From Calcutta, King Tribhuwan went on pilgrimage to Puri and returned to Kathmandu after visiting Lucknow, Agra and Delhi-all incognito. The King was greatly depressed by the treatment meted out to him and decided to abdicate. This time, however, it was Yuddha's turn to insist that he should wait till Prince Mahendra was a little older.

We had earlier referred to the 'Gorkha Samachar' from Dehra Dun. There was a large population of Gorkhas domiciled in India at Dehra Dun. They were mostly from the families of pensioners from the many Gorkha Regimental centres then stationed at Dehra Dun. The All India Gorkha League was set up at Dehra Dun in 1925 and in 1927 it secured the services of Bahadur Shamsher, son of the deposed Maharaja Deva Shamsher, as President. He was followed by Thakur Chandan Singh who, in collusion with the Ranas of Nepal, brought about the collapse of the Gorkha League. In 1942, a branch of the All India Gorkha League was revived in Darjeeling by Rup Narain Sinha, a barrister. This branch was taken over by Dhambar Singh Gurung, a member of the Legislative Assembly in the province of Bengal, on the ticket of the Indian National Congress. In 1946,

Gurung visited Kathmandu and returned to India as an upholder of the Rana regime. With this development, the Gorkha League at Darjeeling also faded out of Nepalese politics.[7]

After the failure of the conspiracy by Tanka Prasad Acharya in Kathmandu, schemes for political change in Nepal could only be organised in India. The sympathies of King Tribhuwan for a new scheme of things in Nepal curbing the power of the Ranas were well known. In 1946, a Nepalese National Congress (NNC), modelled on the Indian National Congress was established in Calcutta. The object of the NNC was to bring about the end of Rana autocracy and to establish a progressive democratic regime under the aegis of the King. It developed close links with some of the Indian Congress leaders in Patna and Calcutta and was supposed to have leftist leanings. The first President was B.P. Koirala. The NNC concentrated its attention on the jute mills at Biratnagar near the Bihar border. A strike was organised in early 1947 at Biratnagar by Koirala. He was arrested, but was released by Maharaja Padma, when the NNC threatened to organise peaceful satyagraha in all parts of Nepal to secure his release.

With the ushering in of independence in India, Maharaja Padma decided that the time had come for Nepal to effect political changes in its own territories. He announced the creation of municipal and district boards to look after local affairs as the first steps towards a modern democratic constitution. He declared that the judiciary would function as an independent organ of state in future. The surplus from the revenues of Nepal used to become the personal property of the Maharaja and no accounts were ever published. Padma Shamsher announced that he would publish an annual budget and provide for larger sums of money for education for both boys and girls. He also guaranteed freedom of the press, of speech and of association throughout Nepal. To place his earnestness for reforms before the people of Nepal, he called Sri Prakash, a liberal political leader from Benares and R.V. Singh, Professor of Political Science at Lucknow University to advise him on constitutional reforms. On this, two Rana members of his council said the Maharaja was going too far and resigned. Most of the other Ranas were of the same view. However, in spite of vehement opposition from the other Ranas, Maharaja Padma went ahead with his scheme of reforms and his advisers from India, working day and night, gave him the blue print for a new constitution of Nepal. The new constitution was inaugurated by Maharaja Padma Shamsher on 26th January 1948. For the first time, the rulers of Nepal had accepted the necessity of a written constitution which introduced the ideas of civil liberty, independent courts, elected representatives at the village panchayat level and of a popular ministry at the headquarters of the government. The new Reforms Act, however, laid down in the preamble that the order of succession to the high office of the Maharaja Prime Minister as also of the King would be governed as heretofore by traditions, customs, and usages then prevailing and the then existing rule of succession would for ever remain immutable. The control of the civil and military administration was to be absolutely in the hands of the Maharaja Prime Minister; who would, however, have on his council two popular ministers besides others nominated by the Maharaja. The Reforms provided for an upper house of thirty members who would be entirely nominated and a lower house of between 60 and 70 members, of every five of whom two would be nominated. Further, the Speaker and the Deputy Speaker would be nominated by the Maharaja. In the case of the upper house, the Commander-in-Chief *i.e.* the Rana, next in order of succession to the Maharaja's office would be the Chairman and a Vice Chairman was to be nominated by the Maharaja. The elected members were to have the same restrictions on speeches in the lower house as the ordinary citizens of Nepal and they were forbidden to debate any matter which would affect the privileges and the dignity of the King or the Ranas. The lower house and the ministry were to have no control over finances and the budget was to be proposed and presented at the discretion of the Maharaja.

However, it was laid down that the administration of villages and towns would be carried out by panchayats elected on adult franchise. Their powers, however, were strictly limited to social and civil services and for finances they depended totally on what the Maharaja Prime Minister would allot to them.

Such was the broad outline of Padma's scheme of reforms. It was a great step forward from the unlimited and irresponsible autocracy of the Rana family and the Indian advisors thought that it was a beginning towards responsible government. But just as the reforms by the liberal Governor-General Ripon were left unimplemented in practice by the bureaucracy and the conservative rulers of India, so also Mohan and the other Ranas never implemented the provisions of the Reforms Act. If Padma, with his liberal views, had been allowed by his cousins to bring in peaceful changes as in his Reforms Act, the history of Nepal might have been different. But the Reforms Act remains the key to the understanding of political developments in Nepal in the last fifty years. If one takes out the reference to the Rana family, the Act is very much the model for the government of Nepal from 1960 to 1990.

After the Second World War, the political balance of power in south and south-east Asia had been totally upset. India and Pakistan which till August 1947 formed the British Empire in India, had millions of native soldiers who had shared defeat and then victory with the British soldiers and there were the Indian industrialists producing war goods, the local traders and contractors arranging for war time necessities and the hangers-on who benefited by their easy access to the British. There was a lot of money in the country and there were lots of people who had held responsible assignments in war time. At the same time the U.S. and the U.K. soldiers were anxious to return home and had little sympathy for their compatriots who wanted to stick to the countries then ruled by Britain. Wavell in India, General Marshall in China and Padma Shamsher in Nepal were convinced that the times had changed and autocratic rule could not be continued any longer for the benefit of an alien ruling class or irresponsible and inefficient native family groups. But in Nepal, there were Ranas like Mohan and others who were not prepared to preside over any diminution in the powers of the Rana family. They failed to appreciate that they had no powerful supporters in high quarters in India once the British left; and the monopoly of power exercised by them had alienated the King, the Brahmins, the Newars, the Rais and the Kiratis and even the 'C' class Ranas. Even the Nepalese army, most of whose regiments had seen service in India, and the Nepalese soldiers demobilised by the British, had no heart when the final crisis came, to fight for the personal privileges of the Commander-in Chief Kaiser or of the then Maharaja Prime Minister Mohan.

Padma, inspite of his clearer understanding of the forces released by the war, was not a determined administrator who could carry his own family and the country with him. He pushed through his reforms with great perseverence, the epitome of which was the inauguration of a written constitution in January 1948. His meeting with the Indian leaders bore little fruit. The leaders of the National Congress were too busy with their own day-to-day developments and Padma found them unwilling to back his progressive policies. Padma decided to abdicate and allow Mohan and his brothers to run Nepal according to their perception and policies. Nepal which was ripe for constitutional reforms was thus denied the benefit of having them from the Rana family. The other centre of authority, by moral right and by constitutional fiction, was the Maharajadhiraj. When Jawahar Lal Nehru decided to back the King, it became clear that the reforms had to come from that quarter.

Mohan stalled the implementation of the reforms and decided to face the rising tide of expectations from Nepalese citizens other than the

Ranas. His first steps were to find friends outside Nepal. He had set himself against Nehru and the Indian National Congress. The British Legation at Kathmandu reporting to the Foreign Secretary at New Delh now became the British Embassy working directly under London. The Nepalese Legation at London also became an embassy. The United States and Chiang-Kai-Shek's China were contacted. In May 1948, Mohan started negotiations with the governments of the United States, China, Tibet, France, and the Netherlands, for opening formal links and assistance in developing bilateral trade. In February 1949, Nepal applied to the United Nations for admission. At that time, Russia vetoed the request as it was not satisfied with Nepal's claim to sovereign status.

In his domestic policies Mohan was against any dialogue with political parties. We have already mentioned the Biratnagar jute mills strike in 1947 and the arrest of the NNC leader B.P. Koirala and his subsequent release by Padma. In January 1949, B.P. Koirala was rearrested in Kathmandu along with twenty other members of the NNC. They were convicted on the charge of inciting violence and working against the constitutional position of the Ranas. B.P. Koirala went on hunger-strike in jail and he was only released for medical treatment and exiled to India. In his place the NNC elected his half-brother M.P. Koirala as President of the NNC in late 1949. The two brothers, however, did not share each other's views and, true to their middle class origin and outlook, their petty personal ambitions and political manoeurvings clashed much to the detriment of political development in Nepal. But more of this later.

In 1948, the Nepal Democratic Congress was founded in Calcutta with Mahindra Bikram Shah as President and S.P. Upadhaya as General Secretary. It had the support of most of the 'C' class Ranas and other exiles from Nepal. One of the main objects of the organisation was to take revenge on the 'A' and 'B' class Ranas and to curtail their prerogatives. In March 1950, the Nepal Democratic Congress and NNC merged to form the Nepal Congress or NC. The exiled Ranas thus came to form an important faction in the N.C. Subarna Shamsher became the Treasurer of the party and Mahabir Shamsher, who was a wealthy house-owner in Calcutta, gave generous donations for the propaganda efforts of the NC. The NC had already forged links with the King. These links were strengthened when the 'C' class Ranas, as an elite group which nursed grievances against the Ranas, gave their backing to the NC.

A one-time splinter group of the NNC led by D.R. Regmi organised the Praja Panchayat at this juncture. The NNC had rejected the new constitution as a specimen of sham reforms but Regmi's views were that the common people should not fail to take advantage of the provisions regarding civil liberties as conceded, to whatever limited extent, in the constitution. Regmi thought that by publicly declaring their readiness to work out the constitution, his associates shall force the hands of the Ranas to implement the same and in the event of evasion, they will be able to expose the negative aspects of the Ranas' actions.[8]

The Praja Panchayat was formally established at Kathmandu on Dashera Day 1948. It was to work for the success of the new Constitution and it dissociated itself from the activities of the NNC whose objective was the immediate establishment of a responsible government. For a week or so the Panchayat was allowed to organise meetings and enrol members, but immediately thereafter public meetings and processions were banned by a notification of the Police Superintendent at Kathmandu.[9] The only course open to the sponsors was to go underground or to remain dormant. The effort of Regmi to win Mohan Shamsher's sympathies thus came to naught. Mohan was determined to have no truck with political parties and on assumption of office as Prime Minister one of his first action's was to ban all activities by the NNC.

The Communist Party of Nepal was also founded about this time by Man Mohan Adhikari and his friends. Adhikari was then a member of the Politbureau of the Communist Party of India. Later the party was headed by Pushpa Lal and others. The Communist Party of Nepal, the CPN was the prime mover in the strikes in the jute mills of Biratnager in 1947. Tanka Prasad Acharya, who helped organise the 1940 plot against the Ranas, professed himself to be a Marxist but he never joined the CPN. He was, however, a prominent worker in forging leftist unity amongst the political parties in Kathmandu. Dr. K.I. Singh also was considered to be a Marxist but he had generally kept himself within the Nepal Congress.

It needs emphasis, however, that all political parties in Nepal insisted upon their separate identity from similar organisations in India. This was necessary because Dr. Ram Manohar Lohia, of the Socialist Party of India, and Jai Prakash Narain of the Indian National Congress had escaped to Nepal in the 1942 Quit India movement, had been arrested there but with the help of Nepalese sympathizers had managed to escape from Nepalese jails to the Tarai forests of Nepal. With these contacts, the Indian leaders often attended meetings of parallel Nepalese parties. Nepalese political leaders had, therefore, to assert again and again that Nepal's independent status would be preserved and that any political activity in Nepal would be conducted only by Nepalese citizens.[10]

A sullen confrontation now existed in Nepal with political parties on one side and Mohan and his family on the other. The political parties wanted responsible parliamentary rule under the King whereas the Ranas refused to make any concessions. Inspite of the new constitution, civil liberties were curtailed drastically by official ukases. For example according to the rules made under the provisions of the constitution guaranteeing rights of assembly, organisation and free speech there was little chance of even minimal exercise of these rights; meetings could only be held at a place fixed for the purpose by the police authorities, with their express permission, and after a written application had been presented to the policc 48 hours earlier with details of the topics to be discussed and the names and addresses of the convenors and participant speakers. Under these rules the organisers and speakers were answerable for any untoward disturbances or loss of life or property during the meetings. At the same time, the police were empowered to send an observer with powers to interrupt the speakers and stop speeches altogether at his discretion.[11]

No organisation, educational institution, hospital, library, club etc. could be started without police permission, applied for two months before the same was to be started. The aims and objects and the names and addresses of the sponsors had to be supplied to the police and the police had powers to check the accounts and the proceedings book and close the organisation if they found its functioning unsatisfactory.[12]

Further a Censor Board was established which scrutinised the manuscripts for all publications as also any proofs at the printing stage.[13]

The promises of Maharaja Padma were ignored and political dissent was curbed with a heavy hand. Political activists were detained without trial and only those detenues were released who promised loyalty to the Ranas in future. The confrontation was complete but the very air of Kathmandu was full of a revolutionary fervour. A great change in the political set-up was imminent, and this was brought about by a royal coup. The Ranas under Mohan held absolute power in Nepal and the only other source of legal and moral authority and power was the monarchy. The intelligentsia of Nepal had greatly contributed to this end. Jung Bahadur and Chandra had catered to their backing and had inspired books in English about themselves.[14] . But eminent Nepalese writers like Surya Bikram Jnawali and Chitta Ranjan Nepali had written in Nepali and made national heroes of Prithvi Narayan Shah, Amar Singh Thapa and Prime Minister Bhim Sen Thapa. The people in Nepal had come to admire and adore these historical personages and in contrast to be disenchanted with the Ranas.

Secondly, King Tribhuwan who was no supporter of the Ranas, inspite of marriage alliances, had come in contact with the new Indian rulers and had secured their full backing in case he asserted his legal and moral authority. An indication of the way the wind was blowing was evident when the Indian ambassador to Nepal, C.P.N. Singh presented his credentials to the King without going through the Rana Prime Minister. Mohan did not give due weight to what this signified namely that the balance of political forces in Indo-Nepal relations had been tilted by India in favour of the King. Yuddha had retreated in the Ranas confrontation with the King when he publicly submitted that the King had no charges to face for the 1940 plot against the Ranas. With India now acknowledging the King as the supreme political authority in Nepal, the position of the King vis-a-vis the Rana Prime Minister was greatly strengthened.

Notes

1 D.R. Regmi,-*A Century of Family Antocracy in Nepal*, p. 165.
2 Ibid p., 166.
3 S.V. Francis Tucker,-Gorkha, p. 251. D.R. Regmi,-*A Century of Family Antocracy in Nepal*, p. 172.
4 D.R. Regmi,-*A Century of Family Autocracy in Nepal*, p. 176, et seq.
5 Sir Francis Tucker,-*Gorkha*, p. 208 et seq.
6 D.R. Regmi,-Ibid., p. 181.
7 Sir Francis Tuker,-*Gorkha*, pp. 223-4.
8 D.R. Regmi, *A Century of Family Autocracy in Nepal*, p. 21.
9 D.R. Regmi, -*A Century of Family Autocracy in Nepal*, p. 223.
10. D.R. Regmi, -Ibid., p. 228.
11 D.R. Regmi, -Ibid., p. 228.
12 Ibid., p. 228.
13 Ibid., p. 229.
14 Cavenagh Captain O. -*Rough Notes on the State of Nepal* (Calcutta, 1851); Reminiscenses of an Indian Official, London 1884; Landon, P-Nepal (2 vol.) London 1928.

Eighteen

King Tribhuwan's Revolution and the Quest for Parliamentary Democracy

On 6th November 1950, King Tribhuwan left his palace at 9.45 am. for a family outing. He was accompanied by his two queens, by the heir apparent Prince Mahendra, and the latter's two brothers and eldest son. The party was escorted by the royal guard stationed at the palace. As the cavalcade passed the gate of the Indian embassy, the King and all his party entered the embassy, met the ambassador and sought asylum. The guard provided by the Rana Prime Minister was taken aback and did not prevent the king from entering the embassy. When the matter was brought to the notice of the Maharaja Prime Minister, the Ranas were totally confounded. Indian Prime Minister Nehru sent a special plane to Nepal the very next day and King Tribhuwan and his family came to Delhi. Things had moved swiftly and peacefully. Mohan Shamsher held counsel with his family. It was announced that the King was dethroned and Gyanendra, a four year old son of Prince Mahendra, who was not the eldest, was crowned King by the Ranas. Mohan had made a mistake. He took the stand against the monarchy without the backing of India. Yuddha Shamsher was faced with the same choice when he finally withdrew the charges against the King that the latter had taken part in the conspiracy organised by T.P. Acharya in 1940. The British Government in India had also then advised that no action be taken against the King and that it stood neutral between the Prime Minister and the King. On that occasion also Prince Mahendra had refused to be a party to the deposition of the King. The solidarity of the Shahi family had saved it then and now again in 1950. India refused to accept the claims of the infant King and treated Tribhuwan as the dejure King of Nepal and Mahendra as the heir apparent. Great Britain followed India's lead.

1950 was a year that saw great changes in Nepal and Tibet. On 7th October the Chinese had invaded Tibet in strength and as India was unable to send any help, the Dalai Lama was forced to submit. Nepal was also invaded by units of the Mukti Sena or liberation army organised by the Nepali Congress. It was commanded by General Subarna Shamsher and financed by Mahabir Shamsher. Both these Ranas had been exiled from Nepal in 1934-35 by Yuddha. They had, therefore, scores to settle with the ruling circle of Ranas in Nepal. In eastern Nepal Tarai, Biratnagar was taken by the Mukti Sena after the Bada Hakim or district officer surrendered to G.B. Yakhtumba, formerly of the Burma Rifles, who was accompanied by the NNC leader B.P. Koirala. In the west, General Rudra, a 'C' class Rana was commanding the Nepalese forces. He was arrested by Mohan on suspicions of having sympathies with the NC. But his soldiers revolted and General Rudra and his forces joined the N.C. The Mukti Sena in the west *i.e.* Gorakhpur region was commanded by Dr. K.I. Singh and the revolt by General Rudra greatly helped its success in the western Tarai. In the Central Sector, Birganj was taken by the Mukti Sena under Mahendra Bikram Shah. This was an important post on the way to the Kathmandu valley and Mohan sent a strong force to Birganj, which was retaken after about five weeks.

In these circumstances both the Rana ruling classes and the Indian Government were not averse to a compromise settlement. Almost throughout the year 1950 talks had been going on between Nepal and India about the constitutional reforms inaugurated by Padma. Nehru advised that Nepal should be a strong independent and progressive country. He did not want any major upheaval in Nepal in view of the developments in China and Tibet. He pressed the emissaries of the Rana regime who had come to Delhi to find a middle way which would ensure the progress of Nepal and the introduction of some steps towards democracy.[1] The King had assured Nehru that he was working for and he wanted to establish a democratic system of government.[2]

The King and the Rana government in Nepal, with the good offices of the Indian government, agreed on further steps towards constitutional reforms. The Ranas agreed to have popular majority in the council of ministers and to universal manhood suffrage as early as possible. The assembly was to frame the new constitution under which Nepal would be governed. The King was to return to Kathmandu, and the crowning of the young Gyanendra was to be forgotten. Mohan had now yielded much more than what Padma had done earlier. Mohan knew that the era of Rana rule was coming to a close in the aftermath of World War II and he now submitted gracefully.

Even before the return of the King, Mohan Shamsher announced several reforms. On 8th January 1951, political parties were legalised and all political prisoners, not guilty of violence, were released. Tanka Prasad Acharya of the Praja Parishad was also released. He now formed the United Front Party with Gauri Bhatt Pradhan, a Newar communist, as the General Secretary. D.R. Regmi, the Brahmin leader of the splinter Nepali National Congress returned from Benares and started political work from a peaceful and responsive standpoint. The Brahmins and the Newars were now being fostered not only by the NC and the King but also by the ruling Ranas. Mohan Shamsher also promised to form immediately a new government with seven Ranas and seven outsiders. He also promised an independent judiciary and an annual publication of the public budget.[3]

King Tribhuwan returned to Nepal in February 1951. On 18th February a new cabinet, responsible to the King, was appointed with Mohan Shamsher as the Prime Minister and having five persons from the Rana group and five leaders of the Nepal Congress chosen by the King.[4] The new Cabinet was not welcome to M.P. Koirala and Dr. K.I. Singh whose claims to office had been disregarded. Dr. K.I. Singh led his forces against Bhairawa where he had a good following. He was arrested by the Indian armed police, which had been called in. He was later released but rearrested and sent a prisoner to Kathmandu, when he started robbing the rich to distribute their wealth to the poor in the name of fighting Rana autocracy (February and April to July 1951). In April, the Gorkha Dal (organised by the Ranas as a counterpoise to the Mukti Sena) broke open the Kathmandu jail to secure the release of their leader Bharat Shamsher. Bharat was the son of Babbar who was the Defence Minister at the time. Bharat had been arrested under the orders of the Home Minister B.P. Koirala. The Gorkha Dal also organised an attack on the official residence of the Home Minister. B.P. Koirala, however, applied the Public Safety Act ruthlessly and within a few hours the leaders of the Gorkha Dal were apprehended and put in jail.

B.P. Koirala, instead of relying on the established organs of law and order, started backing the Raksha Dal which was the new name given to the Mukti Sena. Its members were unpaid and had not been properly encadred. The organisation became uncontrollable and the citizens of Kathmandu greatly resented its over-bearing attitudes and exactions. In

October 1951, a violent clash took place between students and members of the Raksha Dal in Kathmandu in which several students were seriously injured. Maharaja Mohan Shamsher called at the hospital where the students had been admitted. The conflict between the Ranas and the NC had now come to the surface.

On 2nd October 1951, King Tribhuwan appointed a 35-men Advisory Committee. Mohan objected to this step taken by the King without first consulting the cabinet. On the other hand, B.P. Koirala supported the action of the King. For immediate political gain, the NC had worked against the principle of responsible government and provided strength to the authority of the King and independent exercise of authority by him. On 10th November, the NC members of the cabinet resigned. But before quitting office the Home Minister B.P. Koirala declared an amnesty, on his own, and released among others the leaders of the Gorkha Dal. The resignation by the Nepali Congress members led to the ouster of the Prime Minister Mohan Shamsher also.

The NC had been complaining to the King about obstruction by the Ranas in all measures of administrative betterment. The King had already abolished the right of succession to the Prime Minister's and other high offices in the Rana family and had proclaimed himself the Supreme Commander of all Nepalese forces. He now decided to inflict a mortal blow to the rights and privileges of the Rana family. He appointed a new cabinet of twelve members, of whom eight were members of the Nepali Congress. The President of the Nepali Congress M.P. Koirala was appointed as Prime Minister and Foreign Minister. Finance went to Subarn Shamsher and Surya Prasad Upadhya got the important portfolio of Home. Kaiser and Mahavir Shamshers, brother and son of the Maharaja Mohan were inducted as ministers but Mohan Shamsher was dropped. The King had finally ended the monopoly of the Rana family to the topmost position in the governance of the country. At the same time, B.P. Koirala, the Home Minister who had fought tooth and nail with the Rana Prime Minister was also dropped. This was the King's compromise formula. Babbar, the Defence Minister and the Rana second in succession to Mohan had already been dropped after the demonstrations by the Gorkha Dal headed by Babbar's son, Bharat Shamsher, Babbar had then been replaced by S.P. Upadhaya.[5] The new ministry was broad-based as it included a Gurung, a Yami,-a Shaha and a Thulung besides the Ranas, Thakurs and Brahmins. And they were all the nominees of the King and not of any party or organisation.

The experiment faced trouble from the very beginning. Maharaja Mohan Shamsher, who was over seventy years old and a sick man, realised that the rule by the Rana family was over and like his predecessor Padma left Nepal to settle down in Bangalore. The Ranas were still the most powerful groups in the government and the army of the country, but a peaceful revolution had taken place and the Ranas had to occupy important offices of State on individual merit and share them with 'C' class Ranas whom they had exiled in 1934. The credit for this should go to the farsighted Padma and the extremely conservative but politically mature Mohan who in the valedictory appraisal by the King had "accommodated himself to the new situation." The Ranas, however, controlled the Gorkha Dal, which represented the interests of the soldiers in Nepalese, Indian and British armies. Soldiering is the primary outlet for most of the people of Nepal and the livelihood of the dominant groups in all of rural Nepal depends on the remittances sent by the soldiers to their homes.

The King had not liked the way B.P. Koirala had handled the Home portfolio, and the encouragement he had given to the Raksha Dal, which had become the unruly oppressor of the valley and the Tarai. The Mukti Sena, turned into the Raksha Dal, had now attracted many anti-social and good-for-nothing elements. There had been no screening and no regular absorption of the screened personnel into State cadres. The blame for this was squarely placed on B.P. Koirala by the people and the King. B.P.Koirala was also unhappy that he was not appointed the Prime Minister and the rivalry of the two half-brothers undermined the reputation of the Nepali Congress.

Kunwar Indrajit Singh, Dr. K.I. Singh of the newspapers, was also on the war-path.[6] In January 1952, Dr. K.I. Singh, then interned in the Baraf Bangla, the coldest house in the Singh Durbar Complex, managed to arouse the Raksha Dal to free him and hold the place against M.P. Koirala government. B.P. Koirala had relied on the Raksha Dal to fight the Gorkha Dal and K.I. Singh, nominally a leader of the Mukti Sena, was not put in jail but was placed under house arrest in the Baraf Bungalow in the custody of the Raksha Dal. K.I. Singh and the Raksha Dal demanded dismissal of the M.P. Koirala government and formation of a new all party government with K.I. Singh as Prime Minister. The Nepalese army was called in and Indrajit Singh with some armed men of the Raksha Dal escaped to Tibet. From Tibet, Indrajit Singh organised despatch of Chinese Communist literature to Nepal. He left the Nepali Congress and became an outstation member of the Left United Front then organised by Tanka Prasad Acharya.

In October 1951, the King had appointed a 35-member Advisory committee. In July 1952, he added another 21 members. This time M.P.

Koirala raised no objections. He had tried to keep the posts of party President and Prime Minister to himself, but in May 1952 at the Janakpur Conference of the party, he was forced to withdraw his candidature in favour of B.P. Koirala. B.P. now started dictating to the cabinet. The party asked M.P. to drop Bhadrakali Mishra who had contested against B.P. at the annual conference of the party for the president's post, and reduce the strength of the cabinet to seven members. M.P. refused to oblige and B.P. Koirala retaliated by asking the other party members to resign from the cabinet. Only three NC members namely Subarna Shamsher, Ganeshman Singh and S.P. Upadhaya submitted their resignations. On this, B.P. suspended M.P., Mahabir Shamsher and Bhadra Kali Mishra from the Nepali Congress. There were now charges and counter charges between the brothers. Ultimately M.P. Koirala put in his resignation on 6th August which was accepted by the King on 14th. On the same day the King, ignoring the NC completely, appointed an Advisory Council of five to run the government. Kaiser Shamsher became the Chief Advisor. The other advisors were Mahabir Shamsher, Khadgman Singh, Lt. General Surendra Bahadur Basnyet and Bhagwati Prasad Singh. Except General Basnyet, the others had been in the previous cabinet.

The Nepal Congress was now divided into four groups. The largest group was led by B.P.. M.P. had formed his own group which he named as the Rashtriya Praja Party in 1953. B.P. Mishra turned his group into the Jan Congress and Balchandra Sharma and Kedarman" Byathit" formed a socialist congress group. The King could now safely ignore the NC with whose help he had curbed the powers of the Rana family. The army and the newly appointed civil servants were loyal to him. The King now added to his power through a special Emergency Powers Act, enacted by the advisory council. The Interim Government Act of 1951, pending a new constitution to be framed by a Constituent Assembly, had bound the King to consult his ministry on all his actions. The special Emergency Powers Act now empowered him to act on his own in enforcing laws and issuing ordinances, and all provisions of the previous Act not compatible with these powers of the Crown were to be set aside. Only the NC under B.P. and the banned Community Party of Nepal opposed the new Act. The political climate had undergone a seachange in Kathmandu. Ministers were now to be appointed not as representatives of political parties but as individuals acceptable to the King. A member of a small party could now aspire to be the Prime Minister. Mass contact or backing by a great political party was at a discount. The Nepalese called it "chakari" or "service" of the King.

On 15th June, the King appointed M.P. Koirala again as Prime Minister. He was then the president of the Rashtriya Praja Party. He took office along with Mahavir Shamsher, Naradmuni Thulung and two other ministers. The Nepalese Congress under B.P. the Gorkha Parishad under Mrigendra Shamsher and D.R. Regmi's Rashtriya Congress did not cooperate with M.P. each party leader expecting to be called by the King to become Prime Minister as soon as M.P. was forced to resign.

The King was ill and had to go to Europe for medical treatment. Before leaving the Capital, he delegated his powers to a "Rajkiya Parishad" or Privy Council. The result was that, in his absence, the council of ministers and the Privy Council worked at cross purposes. There were differences about most matters of State and in the absence of the King these could not be resolved.

In September elections were held for the city board at Kathmandu. M.P.'s party failed miserably at the elections and all the other political parties pressed that there should be a national government composed of the different political parties that had won in the city polls. B.P. was arrested but at the same time M.P. started negotiations with the Nepali Congress whose President was B.P.; the Praja Parishad whose President was Tanka Prasad Acharya and the Rashtriya Congress of D.R. Regmi. The NC proposed the names of B.P. Koirala, Subarna Shamsher, S.P. Upadhaya and Rameshwar Singh for ministers posts. M.P. would have none of these persons in his Cabinet and the talks with the NC were broken off.

In November 1953, the Supreme Court allowed the appeal of B.P. Koirala against his internment. M.P. was so upset with the judgement that he changed the Interim Government Act in early 1954. The directive principles were made unjusticiable and the executive powers of the State were emphatically vested in the King including the power to grant clemency, appoint the Prime Minister and the power to finally pass any law or ordinance. A proclamation on these lines was announced on 13th February 1954.

Armed with these powers, the King on 18th February reconstituted the council of ministers. It was now called a national cabinet and included political leaders of different parties who were prepared to serve the King in their individual capacities. At the same time he undertook to have fair and independent elections held early for a Constituent Assembly. The Advisory Assembly was also reconstituted. Its membership was increased to 106, which included M.P. Koirala's Praja Party with forty-five members as against the Nepali Congress's five.

In the national cabinet M.P. Koirala was named as Prime Minister. There were two more persons from the Rashtriya Praja Party namely Mahabir Shamsher and Naradmuni Thulung. Tanka Prasad Acharya represented the Praja Parishad, Kaiser Shamsher was an independent, D.R. Regmi and B.K. Misra represented the Rashtriya Congress. Both the Nepali Congress and the banned Communist Party criticised the national cabinet. In October 1954, King Tribhuwan left for Europe for medical treatment. Crown Prince Mahendra was appointed Chairman of the Privy Council which was to exercise royal powers during the King's absence.

The Advisory Council in its very first session in July 1954 had defeated two official bills. In its second session in November, the council, going beyond its powers, pressed the cabinet to agree that no bill be sent for approval to the King without the approval of the majority in the Advisory Council.

On 10th January 1955, the NC sent a call for a civil disobedience movement to press for early general elections and restoration of civil liberties. The Crown Prince promised to take suitable action and the movement was not pressed. On 30th January, the Advisory Council rejected one of the budget demands, and on 31st January, M.P. Koirala submitted his resignation. In February, Prince Mahendra went to Nice to meet his dying father and returned with full royal powers to deal with any contingency in Nepal. In March, Tribhuwan died and Prrince Mahendra became the King of Nepal on 13th March 1955.

The new King was in no hurry to form a new government from representatives of the people. Tanka Prasad Acharya had been appointed in January as the acting Prime Minister after M.P.'s resignation. He continued on this post till 13th July 1957. Later on 26th July, King Mahendra asked Dr. K.I. Singh to form the government. He was, however, dismissed on 14th November, 1957.

On 1 February 1958, Mahendra appointed a Commission to draft a Constitution for the country with Sir Ivor Jennings, a British academic, as the Chief Advisor. In May 1958, a caretaker Ministry was appointed headed by Subarna Shamsher, a Nepali Congress leader. It included Ramadhir Subba of the Gorkha Parishad, D.R. Regmi of the Rashtriya Congress, Chandra Bhushan Pande of the Praja Parishad and two nominees of the King, Purendra Bikram Shah and Bhupal Man Singh Karki.

Elections to the Pratinidhi Sabha (house of representatives) were held early in 1959 and out of 109 elected seats, 74 were captured by the Nepali Congress, 19 by the Gorkha Parishad, 5 by the United Democratic Party, 4 by the Communist Party,2 by the Acharya group of Parishad and 1 by the Mishra group of Praja Parishad. On May 4, the caretaker government submitted its resignation and Mahendra asked B.P. Koirala leader of the Nepali Congress to form the Government.

The B.P. Koirala government took office on May 27, 1959 and was dismissed on December 15, 1960. It had to tackle intricate domestic and foreign issues and to safeguard vital national interests of the country. It was settling down to business when suddenly it was dismissed by the King on December 15, 1960. With its dismissal parliamentary government came to an end in Nepal.

Notes

1 India's Foreign Policy 1946-61. "Steps towards Democracy", (pp. 435-7) Nehru's speech on 6th December '50.

2 Ibid., Nehru's speech in the Rajya Sabha, 20th December 1960.

3 Sir Francis Tucker,-*Gorkha*, pp. 261-2.

4 The cabinet of 18th Feb, 1951 consisted of Maharaja Mohan Shamsher P.M.; Gen. Babbar Shamsher (Defence); B.P. Koirals (Home); Gen. Subarn Shamsher (Finance); Chudraj Shamsher (Forest); Ganeshman Singh (Industry and Commerce); Nripjang Rana (Education); Bhadrakali Misra (Transport), Yagya Bahadur Basnat (Education) Bharat Mani Sharma (Agriculture & Food).

5 The new ministry consisted of: M.P. Koirala, P.M.; S.P. Upadhaya; Kaiser Shamsher (Ind.); Subarna Shamsher; Naradmuni Thulung; Mahendra Bikram Shaha; Sharda Shamsher (Ind.); Bharakali Misra; Mahabir Shamsher; Ganeshman Singh; Khadgman Singh (Ind.); Bhagwati Prasad Singh (Ind.); and as deputy ministers: Nar Bahadur Gurung (Ind.) and Dharma Ram Yemi (Ind.).

6 He claimed to be a distant relation of the royal family. He had been in Burma before 1942, when he settled at Nautanwa in India near the Gorakhpur border with Nepal, as a homeopathic practitioner. He joined the Nepali Congress, led the Mukti Sena on the Gorakhpur Sector but later split from the Koirala brothers.

Nineteen

King Mahendra Opts for King's Rule

Crown Prince Mahendra had become King of Nepal on 13th March 1955, on the death of his father King Tribhuwan. He was born in 1920 and was married to Yuddha Shamsher's granddaughter. He was educated in British-Indian Schools and in the U.S.A. He was ambitious and was keen to rule his Kingdom as a Hindu King *i.e.* an absolute sovereign dedicated to the betterment of his country and his subjects.

He was sagacious and from the day of his accession he decided to work for King's rule in Nepal. He knew that Nehru and the Indian people were backing parliamentary democracy in Nepal modelled on the Indian experiment. Mahendra, therefore, had to seek support from his country's other great neighbour, China. China had asked for diplomatic relations through its ambassador in Delhi in late 1954 about the time of Nehru's state visit to China. On return from China Nehru had said that diplomatic relations between China and Nepal were matters to be decided by the Nepalese themselves.[1] King Mahendra invited the Chinese Ambassador in India to Kathmandu, and held long and secret negotiations with General Yuan-Chung-hsien for several days in late July. The Chinese ambassador in India was also accredited to Nepal although no resident embassy had been established at that time. King Mahendra had, thus, taken his first steps to notify to New Delhi that he was plumping for a new direction in governing Nepal. In July 1955, there was no popular ministry in Nepal and the decision to have direct contact with the Chinese was the personal decision of King Mahendra. This was followed by King Mahendra issuing state pardon to Dr. K.I. Singh who was in China and who returned to Nepal shortly afterwards. King Mahendra gave active encouragement to the pro-China enthusiasts in Kathmandu. These were left-wing politicians and intellectuals who considered India to be tied to the imperialist camp and who also wanted their country to have a political profile of her own and distinctly different from India's. In January 56, the King asked Tanka Prasad Acharya to form the government with instructions that he was to take steps to finish the "special relations" with India and seek changes in the 1950 Indo-Nepali trade treaty and establish direct trade with third countries. Within a month of the Acharya ministry's inauguration General Yuan arrived from New Delhi for a four day visit and with promises of aid and political support. Vice Premier Ulan-fu from China came to a Hindu King's coronation in May 1956 and was warmly welcomed inspite of the fact that communist China was a sworn enemy of all absolute monarchs and feudal societies. King Mahendra, however, was not only keen on befriending China but also to make concessions urgently desired by the Chinese. On September 20, 1956 Nepal agreed to withdraw its military escorts at Nepal government offices in Tibet within six months and surrendered all the extra-territorial rights and special privileges secured to Nepalese citizens under the 1856 treaty with Tibet made by Rana Jung Bahadur. In addition all previous agreements between Nepal and Tibet were abrogated.[2]

This was followed by Premier Chou-En-Lai's visit to Kathmandu from February 25 to 28, 1957, who during his visit spoke of "the blood ties between Nepal and China". Later the Chinese started their propaganda for "Bhotia raj" and a federation of autonomous states in the Himalayas.

New Delhi was taken by surprise but the mild-natured Nehru preferred to play down the obvious change in Nepal. In October 1956, President Rajendra Prasad of India, paid a state visit to Kathmandu to renew friendly ties but his remarks that "any threat to the peace and security of Nepal is as much a threat to the peace and security of India", was greatly resented and his remarks that "your friends are our friends and our friends yours," was countered with officially inspired propaganda that India wanted to foist her own enemies on Nepal. In plain words King Mahendra had given notice to India that Nepal's special relations with India were over as far as he was concerned and that he had opted for Chinese friendship equal in all respects with Nepal's friendship with India.

Dr. K.I. Singh, however, was against opening Nepal to the Chinese and was for further strengthening of the bonds with India. He had paid a visit to India in October 1956 and had been received by Nehru and other Indian leaders. In December, Acharya, the King's new Prime Minister, also visited India but he had a cool reception.

Chou-En-Lai's visit to Kathmandu had provoked alarm in Nepal, and even the King realised that he had gone too far. On July, 14, King Mahendra dismissed the Acharya ministry and appointed a new government headed by Dr. K.I. Singh.

Dr. K.I. Singh's ministry reverted to the traditional foreign policy of Nepal of close friendly ties with India. Dr. Singh announced that China and the Soviet Union need not have resident embassies at Kathmandu and that Nepal would also not extend its diplomatic relations beyond the then existing level. He refused to formalise relations with Pakistan and also supported India's stand on Kashmir explicitly and unreservedly. On November 19, 1957 the Singh ministry was dismissed as the King feared that continuation of the ministry may curtail his own powers considerably. Immediately thereafter, the King pursued his policy of direct linkage with China by calling it "diversification" of diplomatic relations. Nepal had diplomatic relations with only five countries when Dr. Singh's ministry was dismissed but by mid 1960 Nepal had established, at considerable cost, diplomatic relations with twentyfour. The King also went on a state visit to Moscow in June 1958 to strengthen his personal position.

The 1950-51 revolution in Nepal had promised elections and an elected government in two years. This promise could not be disregarded and the elections were ultimately held in 1959. The Nepali Congress gained over two-third seats in the lower house and its leader B.P. Koirala was called upon to become first elected Prime Minister on May 27, 1959, after King Mahendra had met Nehru in late May. Nehru visited Kathmandu in early June and a joint communique was issued by the two Prime Ministers on June 14, that "there was an identity of views, as the policies of the two countries, both in the international and domestic spheres, were animated by similar ideals and objectives."[3]

King Mahendra kept aloof from these public statements and was known to have inspired public criticism of the Nepalese Prime Minister's common stand on the Tibet question with Prime Minister Nehru and it was put out that Nepal should be neutral as between India and China on the Tibetan issue. This was the King's policy and it was noticed that the Chinese ambassador to India and Nepal, Pan Tsu-Li, had visited Kathmandu in May and again in October 1959 and had established contacts with the King. Anti-Indian propaganda was started in Kathmandu about the proposed Gandak barrage and about Nehru's statement in Parliament on November 27, 1959 that "any aggression against Bhutan and Nepal would be regarded as aggression against India".[4]

Because of the King's backing to the pro-China lobby, B.P. Koirala had to soft-peddle his foreign policy. He sent one of his then close associates Dr. Tulsi Giri to the anniversary celebrations in Beijing in October 1959, followed by his own visit there in March 1960. He rejected joint defence agreement between Nepal and India and also emphasized Nepal's friendship with both India and China. It will be seen that the King had influenced his country's foreign policy decisively and had persuaded the elected head of government to veer round to his views.

King Mahendra was facing a threat to his powers when B.P. Koirala was asked to form the government, following the conventions of Indian democracy. B.P. Koirala stressed that he was the Prime Minister because of the trust the Nepalese people had placed in him, and that he was not a mere instrument to carry out the King's directions. King Mahendra openly canvassed, his theory of the hereditary ruler's rights in a Hindu State. He asserted that he would not allow the fair name of democracy to be exploited to do evil rather than good to the people. He emphasized the Hindu ruler's duties by the country which were: to maintain sovereignty of the county; to maintain national integrity; to improve relations with other countries; and to initiate action oriented to public good. He also expressed his determination not to allow any real hindrance along his path.[5]

In September 1960, King Mahendra went to London accompanied by Subarna Shamsher of the Nepali Congress and Deputy Prime Minister. In Paris, Rishikesh Shaha was called from U.N. headquarters for consultations by the King. After his return to Nepal, Yogi Narhari Nath, who claimed to have received support and a donation of Rs. 500 from the King, started his agitation against the land reforms in lands held by Brahmins and others as "birta" lands in Gorkha. The demonstration led by the Yogi was quelled by police firing, in which about half a dozen people suffered casualties. The B.P. Koirala government now had a difficult time. It would not go back on its land reforms and at the same time it would not ignore the agitations inspired and led by Royalists in Gorkha the home of the ruling dynasty. It appointed a judicial Commission under a Supreme Court Judge to enquire into the incidents and to report if the police firing was justified.

Late in October 1960, Dr. Tulsi Giri resigned from the ministry. On 15th December 1960, King Mahendra in a sudden and successful move dismissed the ministry and arrested the Nepali Congress leaders. The Royal Proclamation announced that anti-national elements had received encouragement from the Koirala government and that as it was the King's ultimate responsibility to safeguard nationalism and sovereignty, he had decided to dissolve the cabinet as well as both houses of Parliament.[6]

In 1950-51, King Tribhuwan had led a bloodless revolution against the monopoly of all powers and privileges vested in the Rana family and with promises for the establishment of parliamentary democracy in Nepal. In 1960, King Mahendra successfully enacted another bloodless revolution abolishing parliamentary government, arresting the members of his government who had been responsible to the parliament and assuming to himself all the powers that the King and the Maharaja Prime Minister exercised during the Rana regime. On 26th December, King Mahendra nominated a five-member council of ministers and as Maha Rashtra Nepal-supreme national leader started presiding over the deliberations of his council of ministers.[7]

On 5th January 1961, King Mahendra banned the functioning of all political parties and promised to give his subjects "a partyless panchayat system of government."

Jawaharlal Nehru regretted the setback to democracy in Nepal in a speech in the Indian Parliament. There was no other reaction except a cooling off of relations. The leaders of the Nepali Congress who had escaped to India were completely outmanoeuvred. B.P. Koirala had taken no steps to weaken the King's hold over the army, the secretariate or the numerous political aspirants to office who could hold political power only if patronised by the King. The raids organised by the exiles from India came to nothing as the Indian government did not offer any help or encouragement.

The eclipse of parliamentary democracy was welcomed by China and Queen Elizabeth's proposed visit to Nepal was also not cancelled. The U.S.A. and the U.S.S.R. reserved their comments. B.P. Koirala had lost because he had no military or para-military force with him. The King had won the day. For political support he went on a state visit to China in October 1961. Before that on March 21, 1961, Nepal signed its boundary agreement with China. Nepal had to make several concessions in return for Chinese acceptance that Gauri Shankar or Mount Everest stood at the boundary line, with its south face belonging to Nepal and north face to China. The Chinese maps had been claiming the mountain to be entirely in Tibetan territory. The areas on the Kerong and Kuti passes that Jung Bahadur had taken from the Tibetans in 1856 were returned and the new boundary was fixed according to Tibetan claims. On the whole, however, it was a settlement of Tibet-Nepal boundary which had led to several wars in the past. The boundary was now accepted by China also, the power holding suzerain rights over Tibet. For this reason the boundary treaty was welcome to all sections of Nepalese people.

The Sino-Indian War of 1962 came as a god-send to King Mahendra. The war showed India's lack of military preparedness on the Himalayan borders. Indian democracy had failed to face reality. There were no Indian mountain divisions to face China's divisions on the Himalayan border. India had to suffer defeat and had to make great efforts spreading over several years to build its defence potential in the Himalayas. Till this was done Nepal had little to fear in ignoring India's national interests and its susceptibilities. King Mahendra turned completely neutral.[8] Earlier, on october 5, 1962 the Chinese foreign minister Ch'en Yi had thundered at the banquet given in Beijing to celebrate the first anniversary of the China-Nepal border treaty: "in case any foreign army makes a fool-hardy attempt to attack Nepal... China will side with the Nepalese people, and for every bullet coming from that side, we shall send two...[9] King Mahendra somewhat to his surprise, noticed the reference to the Nepalese people and not to him personally.

The Sino-Indian War cooled down the activities of the Nepali Congress and Nehru, inspite of Nepali aloofness sent Lal Bahadur Shastri to Kathmandu as a gesture of good will. India had accepted that it had no special rights in Nepal. King Mahendra, the ruler of the Hindu Kingdom of Nepal, also hosted in May 1963 a state visit to Kathmandu by President Ayub Khan of Pakistan. Even in the South Asian subcontinent King Mahendra was courting the friendship of those who were to go to war with India shortly afterwards.

King Mahendra had established direct personal rule and a new constitution was given to the Kingdom late in 1962-replacing the 1959 constitution. The new constitution curtailed the right of political association and established a partyless system of panchayati government. The King was himself to preside over a committee of his nominees who were to run the government. The King was given the right to issue ordinances, declare emergency and to suspend any or all the provisions of the constitution. He could also amend the constitution on the advice of a special committee of the National Panchayat. Money-bills could be tabled by any member of the national panchayat but after being passed in the panchayat every money bill as any other resolution required royal approval. The actions of the royal couple and the successor to the throne could not be debated in the national panchayat.

The new constitution provided for elections to the village panchayats on adult franchise. These representatives then elected the members of the district panchayat, who in turn elected the members for the zonal panchayat. The rashtriya panchayat was elected by the zonal panchayats.

It was to consist of 109 elected members and 16 nominated by the King. Of the elected members 4 seats were directly elected by the graduates constituency and twelve were reserved for representatives of class organisations, namely: women, youth, peasants, labour and ex-servicemen.

There was also a Raj Sabha which was modelled on the Privy Council in the United Kingdom. Both houses were to hold their sessions in camera and the public including the journalists could neither watch nor report the proceedings. All knowledge about these came from the official handouts. This provision was removed only in June 1982 when the sessions of the national panchayat were thrown open to the public and the press.

The 1962 constitution was similar in content to the 1948 constitution of Padma Shamsher. The 1948 constitution had discouraged elections on party tickets but the '62 constitution totally banned political parties and the representatives in the different panchayat bodies represented themselves alone.

The King changed his council of ministers from time to time. His success had come from his foreign policy. The Nepalese were happy to see that their King could stand up with dignity against their big neighbour to the south which no Rana Prime Minister had done before. For this success, the King had made friends with China and had agreed to the construction of the heavy vehicle road joining Kathmandu to Lhasa. Kathmandu was also on friendly terms with Pakistan and had opened trade links with East Pakistan. At home, however, there was little success to report. Only the U.S.A. had come to back the King on his experiments with panchayats and the U.S. ambassador in 1963 offered his country's guidance to panchayat development officers.

It was only after a serious heart attack in March 1968 that the King relented and on October 30 of that year B.P. Koirala and Ganeshman Singh were released from prison after having been in jail for nearly eight years. On October 31, the King granted pardon to Subarna Shamsher and twenty-two other Nepali leaders then residing in India. In January 1969, the King pardoned 179 Nepali Congress workers sentenced by different special tribunals in absentia. The King expected the Nepali Congress to work within his partyless panchayati system but B.P. Koirala had different views on the subject. He was working within the Constitution given by King Mahendra in 1960 also when he was detained. He held his own detention morally wrong but he was willing to talk to the authorities. He was for a party system of government under a constitutional monarch. The King turned down the Koirala approach. In his democracy day message on 18, February 1968, the King said: "political party is neither desirable nor can flourish in the present economic, social and political situation of the country". He pointed out that in a country lacking in the means of education, "political parties only confuse the common people, create internal competition and conflict by dividing the national strength and are nothing more than old, rotten means of progress."[10]

The Nepali Congress was not prepared to toe the royalist line but its influence on the polls to the primary panchayats in January 1969 was ominous. Recourse was again had to foreign policy activities. The Prime Minister, Kirti Nidhi Bista, took exception to the speech by Dinesh Singh, India's Foreign Minister on a visit to Kathmandu referring to "special relations" between the two countries. The Nepal government pressed for the withdrawal of the Indian Military Liaison Group and of Indian technicians from Nepalese check-posts. He also announced the unilateral termination of the arms supply agreement with India. At the same time the Dalai Lama's representative for refugee relief operations was also asked to leave Nepal. India yielded to the pressure from Nepal and the King gained open applause from the intellectuals and the officer class. But the relations with the Nepali Congress had deteriorated. B.P. Koirala had retired to India where he had described Nepal's panchayat democracy as a "modernised dictatorship" headed by the King. He alleged that it had been "so constituted as to play an auxiliary role to the monopolist powers of the King."[11]

Nepal's relations with India were also not happy on the trade front. The Indian rupee was devalued in June 1966 but the King refused to allow the Nepalese rupee to slide down with the Indian rupee. The balance of payment's gap with India grew to alarming proportions. For some time the King wanted to bridge the gap with the monetary aid Nepal had been receiving from China and the U.S. But this could not last long and the realities of Indo-Nepalese trade forced the hands of the Nepalese government to restore the value of the Indian currency in term of the Nepalese rupee. From 8 December 1967, however, Nepal linked its currency to the U.S. dollar.[12]

Nepal now took up the question of transit trade rights through India. Under the 1923 treaty between Nepal and the British, the former was allowed to import any trade goods through Indian ports. At that time these were mostly goods produced in Great Britain and imported by the Rana gentry. The goods paid custom duties at Calcutta but on production of a certificate from the Nepalese customs that the goods had been received in Nepal "with customs seals unbroken and otherwise untampered with", the Indian Customs refunded the customs duties paid at Calcutta. Under the 1950 Nepal and India Trade and Commerce treaty, free and unrestricted trade was allowed between the two countries. In other words, Nepal formed a common market with India. Indian manufactures imported into Nepal were to pay the Indian excise which was reimbursed by India to Nepal. In order to prevent smuggling Nepal agreed to impose on its overseas import and export goods customs duties at par with those imposed by India. The Reserve Bank of India also acted as the foreign exchange clearing authority for Nepal. In 1960, a new Nepal and India trade and transit treaty was signed. The treaty allowed freedom of transit, free from customs to goods of either country to and from third countries. This was sbject to avoidance to the maximum extent practicable of diversion of commercial traffic or deflection of trade. The treaty also provided for goods imported at Calcutta to be kept in a bonded warehouse. This was necessary to prevent the flooding of the Indian market by goods imported into Nepal from third countries. The treaty allowed refund of Indian excise duty on manufactures from Indian goods imported into Nepal. However, at the same time Nepal was allowed to impose customs surcharge on imports from India.

King Mahendra's foreign policy of friendship with China and Pakistan was not compatible with a common market with India. Irritants started comming up with Sino-Indian disputes. India objected to sale of heavy-duty truck tyres, petroleum products, construction material ect. to the Chinese in Tibet. King Mahendra had already concluded a trade and transit arrangement with Pakistan. It wanted to have transit trade depots at Wagah for trade with West Pakistan and at Radhikapur for trade with East Pakistan (now Bangladesh). Late in 1964, the Indian government agreed to afford transit facilities at Radhikapur to Nepalese goods exported to East Pakistan. The treaty of 1960 due for renewal for a period of another five years was, however, not renewed in time.

At the same time, Royal Nepal Airlines and Pakistan Airlines, joined by other international Airlines, had started connecting Dacca (and thus Hong Kong) with Kathmandu. Electronic and photographic goods were coming to Kathmandu in bulk and were finding their way into India. Apart from this, the Nepalese rupee was being propped up against market conditions. Nepalese goods mainly rice, jute and sugar were priced out of the Indian Market. This trade deficit was sought to be made good by high import duties levied on Indian goods, coming to Nepal. In short, Nepal started a trade confrontation with India.

In November 1968 a protocol to the 1960 treaty was signed by the two governments. As regards stainless steel utensils and synthetic textiles, it was agreed that Nepal would regulate import of third country raw materials to correspond to the level of export figures of 1967-68. As regards small bulk luxury goods like tape-recorders, watches etc. Nepal was to restrict its imports to its own domestic requirements. Both Nepal and India agreed to rectify trade discrimination against goods from either country. India, however, insisted that import and export trade of Nepal through Calcutta port would be controlled by prescribed documentation in order to prevent unfair trade practices.

Inspite of the agreement, the trade war continued. Small-bulk luxury goods were being sent to Kathmandu as gift parcels to be sold in the lucrative black market in India. Quotas were issued for stainless steel utensils and synthetic textiles exceeding the prescribed 67-68 year levels.

But India had changed in the meanwhile. Raj Bahadur, the Indian ambassador at Kathmandu and senior ministers, like Dinesh Singh and Lalit Narayan Mishra were well aware of the developing situation and were unwilling to overlook their country's economic interests. On 21 May 1969, New Delhi, unilaterally banned the entry of Nepalese manufactures to India. This single step brought the entire export-oriented industrial units in Nepal, which were based on third country raw materials, to the brink of bankruptcy.

When protests were of little avail, King Mahendra decided to bring international pressure on India. Having given up special relations with India, Nepal wanted that trade facilities be granted to her by India in accordance with the Geneva Convention on the transit trade of landlocked countries. Nepalese delegates at ECAFE and other international forums were asked to voice Nepal's protests against India. Abdul Rauf Khan, Pakistani envoy at Kathmandu also joined in the protest.

King Mahendra in his address at the non-aligned summit conference in Lusaka in 1968 demanded "full and unrestricted transit rights", through India. The transit treaty was to expire on 31 December 1970, but no agreement could be reached for a new treaty before its termination. King Mahendra was deeply concerned that India which had been very conciliatory in the past was now reluctant to yield to his demands of unrestricted import and export facilities through Indian territory. His visit to Moscow in June 1970 was intended to obtain Moscow's assistance in getting Nepal's demands accepted by India, but Moscow was not happy with Nepal seeking closer relations with China and Pakistan. The visit yielded little benefits to Nepal.

Nepal's case was that there should be two treaties with India: one for transit facilities in accordance with international practice and the other a trade treaty under which India should be given the same considerations as any other friendly country. Nepal felt that India was not providing unrestricted transit facilities which were essential for expansion of Nepal's foreign trade. It was said that the facilities offered by India compared unfavourably with those offered by Thailand to Laos and Pakistan to Afghanistan. Nepal insisted that she had a right to transit facilities from India in accordance with the most liberal international conventions.[13]

The Indian stand was that there was a deep inter-connection between the existence of a free and open border between India and Nepal and the provision of transit facilities through Indian territory for the exports from Nepal to third countries and imports from third countries into Nepal.[14] Nepal's trade with third countries had expanded from two million dollars in 62-63 to twenty million dollars in 68-69 under the 1960 trade and transit treaty between India and Nepal and, therefore, the contention of Nepal that transit facilities provided by India were hampering expansion of Nepal's foreign trade were not countenanced by India. India was disturbed by the deflection of trade by unscrupulous elements.[15]

Nepal was adamant in her demands and insisted on unrestricted transit facilities for Nepali foreign trade. Indian attitude also hardened and there was a void in the trade and transit arrangements from 31 December 1970. There were anti-India demonstrations in Nepal alleging that New Delhi was starting "economic blockade" of Nepal. But India permitted export to Nepal of all essential consumer articles inspite of the expiry of the treaty. The result was that non-essential goods would have to be smuggled to Nepal and facilities for export of Nepalese goods and "the rent-free" bonded warehouses at Calcutta docks for Nepal were not availabe. Nepal declared that she would become self-sufficient by embarking on a crash industrialisation programme. Subsidies up to eighty per cent were announced to industrial entrepreneurs. A Nepalese Petroleum Corporation was also established to import petroleum products from overseas to replace corresponding Indian supplies. China was also expected to send essential consumer articles and replace Indian imports.

King Mahendra passed away in the midst of acrimonious trade confrontation with India, in which neither side would yield what it considered its vital national interests.

Notes

1 The "Hindu" English daily from Madras. Nov. 15, 1954. 8:4 quoted in "Nepal Strategy for Survival" by Leo E. Rose, p. 207.

2 Nepal-Strategy for Survival by Leo E. Rome, pp. 219-20.
3 Ibid., page 221.
4 Nepal-Strategy for Survival, Leo E. Rose p. 23.
5 *The Nepalese Dilemma* by Tribhuwan Nath, pp. 199-200. Speech by King Mahendra in Western Nepal Tarai on 30th January 1960 when Dr. Tulsi Giri was the Minister in attendance.
6 *Nepal-Strategy for Survival.*, Leo. E. Rose, p.231.
7 The nominees of the King were Dr. Tulsi Giri, Vishwabandhu Thapa, Rishikesh Shaha, Surya Bahadur Thapa and Aniruddha Prasad Singh. The Commander-in-Chief Neer Shamsher was also replaced by a Shaha.
8 He said: "Nepal of today is not that of the year preceding 1951, nor is she in such a condition as she was in till the year 1960 (obvious reference to pro-India stance of the Koirala government). This being a dispute between India and China, Nepal deems it most appropriate that they should resolve it through mutual understanding.... Nepal sees no reason why she should become a victim of the struggle between her two big neighbours, nor in fact, does she want to be in that position".
9 *Nepal-Strategy for Survival* by Leo E. Rose, p. 248, and *The Nepalese Dilemma* by Tribhuwan Nath, p. 375.
10 *The Nepalese Dilemma*-Tribhuwan Nath, page 266.
11 Ibid., page 274.
12 Until 1957 the Nepalese rupee remained linked to the Indian rupee and its conversion rate varied from time to time e.g. between 97 and 205 to the Indian rupee during the fifties. In April 1960 the Nepali Congress government fixed the conversion rate under statute of Nepali 160 rupees to 100 Indian rupees. Since then, there have been great variations between the statutory and the market value of Nepali rupee.
13 Statement by Industry and Commerce Minister Navraj Subedi in national panchayat on 5 August 1970.
14 Statement of Laliti Narayan Misra, India's Foreign Trade Minister in the Indian Parliament, 9th August 1970.
15 Ibid. In the same statement the minister added: "In the result the transit facility is known to have been abused by unscrupulous elements for the deflection of Indian export products and for deflecting via the transit route import from third countries of items which were either prohibited by India or are subject to very heavy duties.... Nepal has conveyed to us that she had no desire to damage or circumvent Indian rules or regulations; and, therefore, procedures for consultation and cooperation to achieve the common ends of India and Nepal, without deflecting Indian trade, remained to be worked out.

Twenty

King Birendra's Legacy of the Partyless Panchayats

King Mahendra had died before government by partyless panchayats had taken roots in the political system of Nepal. The panchayats had been worked by the King's men and there was little contribution from the people, the officers of the government or the ministers appointed by the King towards its development into nationally accepted system of government. The system required sovereign powers in the hands of the king and suppression of all dissent. This had been a new experiment to bridge the gulf between the hardy, poor and illiterate people of the mountains and the comforts, prosperity and knowledge of the twentieth century. A monarchical society of pre-capitalist days was sought to be changed into a developing modern society with electric energy, rapid hill transport based on the passenger bus, and larger foreign trade to pay the costs for the transformation. But such transformation requires tremendous efforts, large investments and an elite dedicated to the service and the greatness of their country. Peter's Russia, Frederick's Prussia and Meiji's Japan were examples to be emulated. King Mahendra had similar plans for his Hindu Kingdom but the men who were selected by him to operate his schemes were mostly men who placed their personal interests above those of the people they had been called upon to serve. Secondly, King Mahendra did not insist on Nepal's own way to modernisation. He had proposed a system of government based on the age-old village panchayats and he himself decided what form the system would have above the village level. In olden times a group of villages had a local chief who had to live with similar petty chiefs all around him. The King had now given the people a district then a regional and at the apex a national panchayat. To begin with the King's officers were guiding and supervising the panchayats at all levels, but the system had no seeds of reforms within itself. No parallel economic and fiscal system was, however, evolved and the educational system was left without a national policy frame. This was to lead to the stagnation of all development efforts and projects in Nepal. Foreigners suggested the projects and offered assistance, which was eagerly lapped. The end reults were not clearly envisaged by Nepalese statesmen and the investments in most cases were counter productive in real terms. The share of agriculture in the gross domestic production increased from 65 to 68 per cent between the second plan (62-65) and the third plan periods (65-70). Agricultural yield also decreased from 1.92 tons per hectare to 1.85 tons per hectare during the same period.[1]

Coming back to the panchayat system, we find that factors had already arisen therein pressing for reforms. Rishikesh Shaha, a directly elected member of the National Panchayat and Krishna Prasad Upadhyaya, Speaker of the National Panchayat, had both been imprisoned by the Prime Minister, Kirti Nidhi Bista. There was thus opposition amongst people of high social status to the King in the National Panchayat itself. In the graduates constituency poll of June 1971, Rishikesh Shaha had united sixteen of the twenty-two candidates to four common demands, namely: (i) the Prime Minister should be elected by a National Panchayat composed of representatives elected by direct vote from the district panchayat level; (ii) the Prime Minister should be responsible to the National Panchayat; (iii) Rule of law must prevail (*i.e.* there should be no arbitrary arrests); and (iv) National Panchayat sessions should be declared open to the public and the press.

A more serious threat to the panchayat system was brewing in the new schools. The Rana regime had deliberately neglected education of the people. For their offices they recruited men with only four qualifications or 'Char Pass' *i.e.* proficiency in the three Rs and acquaintance with the legal codes and procedures. From 1951 onwards, however, education became the nation's first priority. Both the government and the people themselves started opening schools and colleges in every district, town and large village. But the growth was uncoordinated. The result was that about 50 per cent of all candidates for the School Leaving Certificate Examination were from the Kathmandu Valley and about 20 per cent from Kathmandu itself. There were not enough white collar jobs for the large number of young Nepalese who stood qualified. Then most of the jobs available were monopolised by government officials and functionaries for their own wards, particularly in Kathmandu and its neighbourhood. The students were grossly dissatisfied and had already formed the Nepali Vidyarthi Sangathan (Students' Organisation) in 1966. In March 1971, the Students' Organisation decided to hold a demonstration before the Pakistan Embassy to urge the release of Shaikh Mujibur-Rehman. The demonstration was not allowed. The National Panchayat elections had also been a censure for the ministry of Kirti Nidhi Bista. The Foreign Minister Raj Bhandari, the Defence Minister Burhathoki, the Home Minister Upadhyaya and the Education Minister, Pradhan could not be re-elected in the elections held in early 1971. Raj Bhandari was nominated to the National Panchayat by the King and appointed as Foreign Minister. Bista was again appointed as Prime Minister.

B.P. Koirala was in Patna and had been consistently unwilling to support the partyless panchayat system. On 20th April 1971, the Nepali Vidyarthi Sangathan observed 'Students' Day' to mark its fifth anniversary. It was coming up as a new political force in the country. B.P. Koirala on behalf of the people of Nepal, also supported the people of Bangladesh and praised the struggle of an un-armed people against the mighty force of a heartless military dictatorship. This was contrary to the King's policy of friendship with Pakistan dictated by the belief that China and the U.S.A. would not let down Pakistan in any possible confrontations with India. The episode of Ramraja Prasad Singh, a young member of the Supreme Court Bar, was also a challenge to the Panchayat System. Singh's election manifesto declared that the action of the King in 1960 had been unconstitutional and that if elected, he would table a resolution in the National Panchayat seeking its dissolution and a return to the parliamentary system. The police, even under the personal orders of the Prime Minister, was unable to arrest him. He was elected and appeared before the National Panchayat for taking oath on 19th July, some members objected to administration of oath to Singh as he had no faith in the Constitution. The Chairman of the National Panchayat adjourned the House, taking time to give a ruling on the objections. Singh stayed in the House but was arrested at nightfall, was produced before a special tribunal and sentenced to two and a half years imprisonment on 12th August. Shortly afterwards the Chief Election Commissioner resigned. Singh was, however, pardoned by the King and the Chairman of the National Panchayat was directed to administer oath to him. It was said that the King did not like that his action in dissolving parliament, dismissing the cabinet and arresting its members should be brought before the Supreme Court and turned into a matter of public controversy. Later Singh was re-arrested and detained.

There was also great discontent in the press when the government decided to withhold advertisements to journals which did not wholeheartedly support the partyless system of democracy. The majority of newspapers published a common editorial on 9 April, 1971 saying that discontinuance of government advertisements was disigned to hamper development of independent journalism so that the way might be paved for government monopoly in the field. These developments showed that when King Birendra Bir Bikram Shah Deo ascended the throne of his forefathers, he had inherited the legacy of his father of a partyless panchayat system of government which had not taken firm roots and had lukewarm support from the Press and the intellectuals. The students were angry and the pensioners of the British and the Indian armies discontented. B.P. Koirala, the Nepali Congress leader, was in self-imposed exile and had threatened a struggle for parliamentary democracy if the King refused to part with power.[2] He also inherited his father's conviction that as a Hindu Sovereign both the constitution and the government of the country derived their legality from the pleasure and the grace of the monarch personally. The western conception of a social contract between the elected representatives and the sovereign had no place in King Birendra's thinking. Like his father, King Birendra, considered that a political system based on "partylessness" was indispensable for Nepal. King Mahendra in his Constitution Day message of 16 December 1971 had said, "Our system has room for necessary reforms". The same sentiment was echoed by King Birendra in his Democracy Day message of 19 February 1972 that "gradual reforms would be initiated in the system in keeping with the changing needs of the changing times."

After the Bangladesh War of 1971 India had emerged as the most powerful country in South Asia and Nepal took note of the fact that neither China nor the U.S.A. came to the help of Pakistan as the representatives of these two countries had previously assured the Nepalese. The message of the new situation was clear and it was that Nepal had to mend her fences with India on her own.

On 16th April 1972, the selection of ministers was left to Prime Minister Bista when the cabinet was reorganised. This was a departure from earlier cabinets when the ministers were nominated by the King and were personally responsible to him. As King Birendra did not know the different politicians personally, he decided to leave the selection to Bista who enjoyed his confidence.

The political situation in the country was growing more complex. The Nepali Congress under B.P. Koirala was pressing for a government responsible to the elected representatives of the people, drastic reduction in the powers of the King and effective guarantees of personal freedom and freedom of association. Subarna Shamsher along with Surya Prasad Upadhyaya, D.R. Regmi and Keshar Jung Raimajhi were soft-liners who wanted to press for reforms but without recourse to violence. B.P. Koirala while emphasizing the peaceful nature of the struggle for political reforms waged by the Nepali Congress, did not rule out armed struggles for constitutional government. The panchayat system had its stalwarts in Kirti Nidhi Bista and Surya Bahadur Thapa. Bista was for gradual changes in the King's system while S.B. Thapa thought that drastic changes had become eminently necessary in the then existing socio-political conditions in Nepal, though these had to be achieved only through constitutional means which meant by convincing the King through representations, dialogues etc., Tulsi Giri's position was somewhat between the hardline and the reformist approaches of Bista and Thapa.

Indira Gandhi, Prime Minister of India, paid an official visit to Kathmandu between 7 and 11 February 1973. She said that India was a true friend of the people of Nepal in "weal and woe". The emphasis on the people of Nepal indicated that the relations between Nepal and India would now be realistic and mature. Mrs. Gandhi also said that the government of India would not allow insurrectionary activities from India against the government of Nepal and would not want to do so. These clear statements of Indian policy removed the irritants and left little ammunition to the India-baiters in Kathmandu. At the same time, the Indian stand forced the Nepalese government to ponder over its relationship with India and to refrain from an overtly anti-Indian stand. The emergence of Sikkim as a full-fledged state of India in 1975 also pointed to the desirability of better relations between the two countries.[3] India, took little notice of Nepalese objections and China's protests. It was a pointer to the political sagacity of the Chinese with the Russian armies poised on their western and northern frontiers that they would not commit their armies to any action South of the Himalayas. In later years, the efforts of King Birendra to have Nepal declared a zone of peace by China and India were backed by China but ignored both by the Janata and the Congress governments in India. India thinks that the 1950 treaty with Nepal should be the sheet-anchor of Indo-Nepalese relations. The Nepalese government is not prepared to ask for termination of this treaty as such a step will be vehemently opposed by most Nepalese citizens and ex-army personnel. Some people, therefore, interpret King Birendra's proposal of a zone of peace for Nepal as untimely and likely to bring the monarchy itself into the political controversies between the two countries.

Inside Nepal King Birendra's attention was centred round education and economic development. Both were critical for the experiment of partyless panchayats to take root in the public ethos. King Mahendra had set up a committee of intellectuals and educators in 1970 to perpare a new scheme of education which was to be "in consonance with the requirements of the partyless democratic panchayat polity and planned national reconstruction."[4] The National Education System Plan (NESP) or the new education as it was commonly called came into operation in 1971 under King Birendra. The objective of the new education was "to produce citizens who with full faith in the country and the Crown, would conduct themselves in accordance with the panchayat system and meet the manpower requirements of development through the spread of scientific and technical education."[5]

Before 1971, there were few government schools, but individual citizens and communities had started new schools everywhere after the 50-51 revolution. These were run by local committees or individuals. After 1971 the schools were taken over by the government and the local committees were replaced by active workers of the "Back to Village National Campaign" Committee. The campaign was, however, dropped in 1979, and members of the local committees are now nominees of the local, district and national panchayats.

Under the NESP, primary education was limited to 3 years between the 6th and the 8th year âge-limits. The aim was to develop literacy and devotion to the King and the country. The next stage (grade 4 to 7) was intended to build good chäracter amongst the students and to inculcate in them a spirit of loyalty to the King and the country alongwith a sense of discipline and responsibility. The entire education system, at the same time, was given a strong bias towards vocational education.

The results achieved so far under the new education system have evoked little enthusiasm. Those with High School Certificates are little fitted for higher university education or for employment in the private sector. And there are not enough government jobs to go round. The result has evoked great discontent amongst the certificate holders and even university graduates.

The university students have been in the vanguard of opposition to the NESP. In August 1972, the students of Tribhuwan University Kathmandu went on a strike for educational reforms and release of four members of the National Panchayat. Amongst these members was Surya Bahadur Thapa, later a Prime Minister. On 16 August, the students demonstrated against the arrests by a huge march through the streets of Kathmandu. The demonstration was dispersed by batons and canes by the police. Again in April 1974, another student strike led to the closure of the University for nearly five months. The students were dealt with great severity by the government and the university authorities.

On 6th April 1979, a group of Nepali students clashed with the police. The students were marching towards the Pakistan Embassy in Kathmandu to hand in a note protesting against the execution of Zulfikar Ali Bhutto. The clash led to disturbances in most of the eighty odd campuses of the University.

The disturbances spread to schools as well and strikes and violent clashes with the police became the order of the day. Events of great importance now followed in quick succession. On 2 May 1979, King Birendra appointed a royal commission to enquire into the grievances of the students and alleged police excesses. The Royal Commission on 20 May decided that the University and the Ministry of Education should concede all the demands of the striking students. On 23rd May, however, a massive demonstration led by students took place in Kathmandu and two public buildings were set on fire in the heart of the city. The army was called in to restore law and order and on 24 May, King Birendra took the Kingdom by surprise by promising to hold a national referendum to choose the political system the nation wanted. The students had thus forced the government to terminate the NESP and to concede the basic demand of the Nepali Congress that the ultimate arbiters of the national destiny were the people themselves. In other words, the concept of an infallible Hindu Sovereign was modified to some extent and the popular will was recognised as the ultimate guiding principle for the Hindu ruler's actions.

The national referendum was held in May 1980. Fifty-five per-cent of the votes were cast in favour of the panchayat system and forty-five per cent against it. The partyless panchayat system was allowed breathing time by the common people but the extent of discontent was evident by the large minority vote. As regards, the NESP, progressive opinion considered that part of the blame for the collapse of the system should be placed squarely with the elites who were against its bias towards mass-education. Kamal P. Mallu a Professor at the Tribhuwan Univerrsity also thinks that the revolt by students was "the revolt of the masses against the elites who were monopolising power under the partyless panchayat system, of which the NESP was mistakenly considered a sub-system."[6]

The national referendum of May 1980 was a landmark in the recent history of the Hindu Kingdom of Nepal. King Dasrath had asked his ministers to obtain the consent of the people before finalising his decision to handover the kingdom of Ayodhya to Ram.[7] Following the same prcedent King Birendra ordered the national referendum based on adult franchise and secret ballot to obtain the preference of his subjects for partyless panchayat system with timely reforms or the multi-party system. After a judicious and mature consideration of the results of the votings the king announced the third amendment of the constitution embodying some far-reaching reforms in the partyless system. These reforms envisaged direct election to the National Panchayat on the basis of adult franchise and a government answerable to the National Panchayat.

The general elections under the new provisions were held in May 1981 and an elected popular government was installed in power. The Prime Minister, Surya Bahadur Thapa, chose his cabinet colleagues and the principle of the cabinet's responsibility to the National Panchayat through the Prime Minister, was accepted. The elections for the National Panchayat were followed by elections to village and local panchayats and elections of class organisations. The functions and powers of the lower-level panchayats have been enhanced and defined by the Decentralisation Act 1982. With the newly elected pranchayats Nepal tried to reform its political system and gear it up to the requirements of the rapidly changing balance of power in her neighbourhood.

Notes

1 From Nepal government official documents quoted by Devendra Raj Pandey; Economic Reality in Seminar 274, p. 27.

2 Interview with Express News Service of India. *Indian Express*, New Delhi, 20 September 1971.

3 There was standstill agreement between Sikkim and India from 5 December 1950. Political demands were pressed in March-April 1973 and the Indian police had to be called to keep law and order. In 1074 Sikkim became a State associated with the Indian Union. Elections were held in April, 1974 to a popularly elected assembly which on 10 April 1975 abolished the institution of Chogyal, (Cho-religion; gyal-gyalpo or King; hence divinely appointed King) and decided that Sikkim become the twenty-second State of the Indian Union.

4 *National Education System Plan for 1971-76.*, Ministry of Education, Kathmandu, 1971.

5 *National Education System Plan for 1971-76*, Ministry of Education, Kathmandu, 1971.

6 Seminar-274-Nepali Reflection, June 1982, page 45.

7 Tulsidas Ramayan-Ayodhya Kand.

Twenty-One

Nepal in the Nineteen-eighties

King Birendra presides over the destinies of a poor country. The people expected prosperity and a better way of life ever since the revolution of 1950-51. King Mahendra was deeply aware of this but economic growth has eluded both King Birendra and his father. King Mahendra's men had little knowledge of economic principles and little experience of big business. They followed the Indian example of five year plans, but like their neighbours were carried away by the economists from developed countries who only talked and advised about investment rates, inputs and targets, topics relevant to mature economic conditions. Nepal banked heavily on foreign loans and grants and like other developing economies overlooked the basic truth that a nation has to raise productivity and gross domestic product by its own hard labour. The result has been the growth of a near parasitical capitalism that gathers the cream from all economic activities into a second stream of economic storage and consumption commonly called a parallel economy. In these conditions even the shrewd operators fail to realise that they are building their houses on sand and that any strong wind is likely to pull down their houses along with the occupants. They forget the benevolent capitalism of Tatas, Carnegis, Rockefellers, Fords and the builders of Japanese Capitalism. For their personal gains they are prepared to destroy the environment, retard all but their own indigenous manufaturing and harm even the proximate national goals. We shall, however, confine ourselves to some tell-tale figures only. The growth in Gross Domestic Product has hardly kept pace with the growth in population. However, there has been some improvement in the standard of living in the Kathmandu Valley but elsewhere the subjects of the King of Nepal have become poorer. From east Nepal, they flock to Darjeeling and from west Nepal to Kumaon and Garhwal to perform at a pittance the most arduous tasks to keep body and soul together. Their earnings are less than those of indigenous Indians but in adjoining districts of Nepal there is no work and local agriculture cannot provide them with even two poor meals per day.

The share of agriculture in the Gross Domestic Product has fallen from 65 to 60 per cent and tertiary occupations have come up to fill the gap. This is all to the good. But alarm signals have been raised by the planners in that agricultural yield (ton/hectare) has gone down from 1.92 to 1.78 between 1962 and 1980. This is inspite of the fact that the use of chemical fertilisers has more than quadrupled in this period, grant of state loans for agriculture has gone up more than twelve times, more than 1,50,000 hectares of land have been brought under irrigation, use of improved seeds has been pushed more than five times and lakhs of hectares of forest land has been turned into agricultural fields. The positive side, however, is that the growing population is being fed from indigenous agricultural production, part of which is still exported particularly rice to India.

The drawbacks, however, have been forest and mineral developments and manufacturing. The record has been unmistaken failure on all these fronts. The forests of Nepal are being used up so rapidly that total food production will soon come down very considerably because of soil erosion. The statistics give us details of loss of forest or vegetable cover from day to day and this has not abated yet. The income from sale of "sal" wood to India is sizeable but Nepal is trading in the commodity at grave risk to its economy even in the short run. As regards mining, there has been little development to report.

Manufacturing has also been a poor starter in Nepal. There have been small scale mills for husking rice, crushing oil-seeds and sawing timber; mostly for the local or the Indian markets. With the plans came a steel re-rolling mill at Parwanipur; sugar mills in the Tarai, one with Soviet help at Birganj; a cement factory with credits from West Germany; a large tannery and shoe factory with Chinese help; a large saw mill with USAID and modern hotels at Kathmandu and Pokhra. Most of the new units have had to face difficulties because of lack of an industrial climate and manufacturing infrastructure. It will, however, take several years before the existing units make profit and become the centres of manufacturing complexes. The biggest drawback is the growth of highly profitable 'export-import' business encouraged by the government because of the social connections of the promoters. The well-to-do Nepalese are turning to this system of earning an easy bonanza with little investment and very large built-in profits. Manufacturing is more demanding and risky and so far few Nepalese have taken to industry inspite of the incentives provided in the 1974 Industrial Enterprises Act, which reserved all units with fixed capital of over Rs. 2,00,000 for Nepalese nationals or firms in which they had the sole or the major shares. The Nepal Industries Development Corporation, a state undertaking, also gave loans for industrial development at low rates of interest and delayed periods of repayments. But so far there has been little fresh industrial development in Nepal, especially in the seventies amd eighties.

However, great progress has been achieved in Nepal since the 1950-51 revolution. Growth of education has been phenomenal. In the farthest villages children go to school and learn the three Rs. The government is committed to compulsory primary education. Every child in Nepal, if he has merit, can now aspire to higher education and a bright future. This has been the greatest contribution of the monarchy to the country; and has bestowed on every citizen a chance for a better life. Next we must refer to the development of the network of roads in all parts of the country. Complete coverage will take time but in all regions the interior hills will soon be connected to the Tarai and the large towns. Thus the underemployed men of the mountains will have better chance of getting employment nearer to their homes. Thirdly, we should refer to the modernisation process taking place in Nepal. The Tribhuwan University has more than sixty colleges affiliated to it. Some of these are for medical, engineering, geology, agricultural, forestry and animal husbandry disciplines. U.N. and other foreign experts are in great demand and even the training of civil servants is not excluded. The lawyers, the journalists and the retired civil servants are spearheading the formation of a new middle class, and a new dimension is being given to the political life of the country. The partyless panchayat system has trained the people into habits of self government and as the Nepalese middle class is growing, the content of the partyless system is also changing. It has been said that when forty-five per cent of the electorate votes against the partyless system in a closely supervised governmental set-up, it should be interpreted as rejection by the majority. King Birendra has realised the weak support extended to the system and the trend in public opinion for a change in the system. That must be the reason that the King now seemed eager to have the majority of the national panchayat with him and his government. In other words, the Prime Minister had to command the majority in the National Panchayat. At the same time the sittings of the national panchayat were thrown open to journalists and others and the proceedings were covered by the national and the international press. Previously, the government had to issue handnotes giving details of the proceedings; which had to be published without material changes.

Lastly and most important of all, during the last few years, there has been a more realistic and sober appraisal of Nepal's geopolitical position and the compulsion of her history, geography, culture and destiny. The development of responsible and representative government; the establishment of the rule of Law or Dharma with guarantees of fundamental rights and a more realistic and enlightened posture vis-a-vis India and China herald for Nepal an era of cooperative diversification of the economy and national and cultural development undreamt of in any period of her past history. Nepal, the country of the Central Himalayas has to play a distinguished role in South Asia. With its three great rivers namely the Karnali, the Gandak and the Kosi, it has the greatest hydroelectric potential in the region and when Nepal has harnessed this energy, it will have an immense and constantly renewable source for earning foreign exchange. Energy generated from Himalayan rivers is going to be Nepal's primary wealth and her destiny lies in its early accomplishment. Hydroelectric power stations dotted in the different river valleys will not only earn saleable and inexhaustible resources but will also ensure employment, better wages and better life to her citizens living in the inner Himalayan belt. With cheap electricity from its rivers, Nepal can expect rapid exploitation of its mineral wealth. Cement, aluminium and nonferrous metals production could be profitably undertaken once Nepal's giant rivers are harnessed to produce cheap hydro-electric power, more on the lines of the Tenesse Valley in the U.S.A, and the various smaller projects in Japan than as grandiose dams which require enormous capital and latest technology. With cheap electric power Nepal could produce cement, aluminium, and even high quality steel which could compete with similar products in the markets of neighbouring India and Tibet.

It seems certain that the future will see great social and economic progress in Nepal. Economic growth shall enhance Nepal's standing with her neighbours and will give greater confidence to her own citizens in the future well-being of their country. The sooner such a consummation takes place, the better for Nepal, her neighbours and the world. King Birendra has thrown his full weight behind the economic development of Nepal. After his Constitutional Reforms of 1981, he declared on 21 June, 1981, "Since the Nepalese society by now has achieved clear political direction, time has come for implementing economic development programme with dedication and determination". Again in his message to the nation on King Mahendra Memorial and Constitution Day (15 December, 1982) he said that the challenge of the times continued to be one of economic development.

The public sector had taken the major lead in the industrial development of the Kingdom, but most existing industries, including the private ones, operate below capacity and are confronted with the problems of power and raw materials shortage, absence of reliable market and low consumer purchasing power. Poor management has also hampered fuller utilisation of capacity in the public enterprises. The government of Surya Bahadur Thapa came to the conclusion that the process of economic development cannot be effectively advanced unless the country brings about a change in the thinking, outlook and values of society and its individual members towards development.[1]

The government had decided to invite the private sector to play a major role in accelerating the process of industrialisation in the country. According to the new Industrial Enterprises Act, all the sectors, except defence related ones, had been opened to private sector and the public sector was called upon to start a new project only when the private sector did not show any interest. The Foreign Investment and Technology Act had opened the industial sector to foreign capital also. Apart from income-tax, sales-tax and excise reliefs, liberal concessions had been granted to remittances from abroad. Nepal had asked United Nations Industrial Development Organisation (UNIDO) to help mobilise investment, grants, aid, loan etc. from friendly countries. The eighth meeting in this connection was held in late 1982 at Kathmandu where representatives of Algeria, Bangladesh, Chile, China, Egypt, India, Kuwait, Malayasia, Pakistan, the Philippines, Republic of Korea, Romania, Singapur, Sri Lanka, Thailand, Turkey, Venezuela and Yugoslavia participated. Such meetings have been held from time to time in the eighties but foreign investment for new projects in Nepal has been poor, if not disappointing.

However, the death of B.P. Koirala in July 1982 left the democratic forces in Nepal without a popular leader. In the referendum held on 2 May, 1980, Koirala had led the campaign for the restoration of multiparty system of government. He had been charged for treason but had been granted amnesty to enable him to take part in the referendum. His death led to the disarray of democratic forces in the country. His presence in the Kathmandu valley had forced the King to appoint a Commission to check corruption in the administration and to report on the working of the new educational system.

On 11 July 1983, Prime Minister Surya Bahadur Thapa resigned following the passing of a no confidence motion against him in the National Panchayat on charges of corruption. The King then appointed Lokendra Bahadur Chand as Prime Minister. Thapa had visited both

Pakistan and Bangladesh. Following his visit to Pakistan a joint Commission was formed to develop and promote economic cooperation between the two countries. Closer ties with Pakistan were established and the Pakistan International Airlines resumed services to Kathmandu after a lapse of 12 years. Nepal also wanted to be a party to the discussion between India and Bangladesh about use and sharing of river waters. India did not agree. India also protested about increasing discrimination by Nepal on Indian settlers. Nepal, however, achieved higher international status as it persuaded French President, François Mitterrand to pay a visit on 2 May, 1983. He was the first head of a western democracy to visit Nepal. King Birendra was distancing himself from India, and was emphasizing the sovereign and independent position of Nepal in international affairs. He wanted India to agree to his scheme of Nepal being accepted as a zone of peace. India maintained that the 1950 treaty was the sheet-anchor for Indo-Nepalese relations and met all the legitimate security needs of Nepal. Lohendra Bahadur Chand, the Prime Minister, however, imposed restraint on anti-Indian sentiments of the King and avoided open confrontation with India.

In mid-1985, a series of bomb attacks took place in Nepal and eight people were killed. The government arrested more than 1500 persons, and said that the bomb attacks were the handiwork of terrorists opposed to the monarchy, and were operating from Indian territory. This was not so and the Indian police forces mounted an effective search for the terrorists hiding in India. Apart from sporadic terrorist activity, the opposition in the country continued to agitate against the partyless system. Covertly the opposition was against the monarchy. Article 20(2) of the Constitution stated that all powers-executive, legislative and judicial-emanated from the King, and Article 87 placed the King's action outside the purview of the Courts. Similarly, the conduct of the King and members of his family could not be discussed in the National Panchayat. Article 11(2a) banned all political parties and persons detained under the State Offences Act, Public Security Act, Treason Act, Destructive Crimes Act and several other Acts were denied basic human rights for example right to be informed about the grounds for detention, access to lawyers and courts. The real conflict was between a totalitarian monarchy and the rising middle classes' clamour for western type democracy.

The relations with China were actively cultivated. The King profusely thanked China at the inauguration of the $ 20 million water conservation and irrigation project. Chinese help was also sought for the seventh five year plan (1985-90) which was to cost nearly $ 3 billion and was to be financed mainly by foreign loans and grants.

The election to the National Panchayat were duly held in May 1986. Political parties had been banned in Nepal since 1961. The Nepali Congress and the Communists boycotted the polls, but more than 60% of Nepali voters took part in the elections and several new members were elected. The King appointed Marich Man Singh, a Newari Shrestha, to be the new Prime Minister and Upadhyaya as the new Foreign Minister. It was evident that the new ministry would push forward the King's Chinese policy. A significant event of the year was the visit by Queen Elizabeth and Prince Philip to Nepal completely bye-passing India. Britain was patently encouraging Nepal's King in his foreign policy stand.

Visits by foreign dignitaries continued in 1987, the most important being those of West German Chancellor Helmut Kohl and Japanese Prince Hiro, grandson of Emperor Hirohito. King Birendra also paid a long visit to China in September meeting several top leaders there. This was his seventh visit to Beijing since his coronation in 1975.

Events moved faster in 1988. The trade and transit treaties negotiated with the Janata government in India in 1978 were expiring in March and India insisted that the two countries should revert to the pre-1978 regimen of one trade and transit treaty. About the same time, India came to know about purchases of surface missiles by the King from China, about which India was not briefed. Restrictions on entry of Indian goods were also ordered when simultaneously enormous favours were granted to Chinese and other third country imports. Indians were also required to obtain work permits in future. All these developments resulted in the expiry of the two treaties on 23rd March 1989 and of trade in coal, petroleum and kerosene on 31 March 1989. Nepal had not visualised that India would let the trade treaties expire and the Nepalese administration put pressure on India by calling it an economic blocade. The year 1989 ended with the eventual slow-down of the new industries in Nepal and the tourist inflow.

Note

1 Dr. Y.P. Pant, Finance Minister on the basic issues of the Economy in an interview to the Economic Times of India Supplement on Nepal dated December 29, 1982.

Twenty-two

A New Beginning

The change in global political relations brought about by the "New Thinking" in the U.S.S.R. had its fallout in Nepal also. With the withdrawal of Soviet forces from Afghanistan Chinese strategy in South Asia needed adaptation to the changed realities on the ground. The change became inevitable with the suppression of Muslim fundamentalists' revolt in Sin Kiang (modern Xinjiang Autonomous Region) and the events in Tien Main Square in Beijing. Towards the end of 1989, Li Peng the Chinese Prime Minister paid official visits to China's traditional friends in South Asia. The main purpose of his visits was to inform China's friends that Chinese armed intervention was not on the cards in future. However, he promised moral support and supply of material goods on payment. But the main thrust of his visit to Nepal was to terminate the promise of General Chen Yi of "two bullets for one" fired from the Indian side. After the landing of the Indian Air Force planes in Jaffna without meeting any opposition, King Birendra had decided to pre-empt such a contingency in Kathmandu by buying ground to air missiles and other military hardware from China. It was said that China was keen to replace its old missiles and other military hardware in Tibet with more modern types and the request by Nepal was welcome as China got rid of its old equipment at a handsome price.

Developments in India also affected Nepal in the aftermath of the arms purchases from China. India, however, did not press this issue openly. The purchases from China were against the 1965 exchange of letters in which the Nepalese ambassador confirmed that these letters constituted an agreement between the two countries. The understanding was that India would supply the entire requirement of the Nepalese army to the best of its ability, with Britain and the USA being allowed to step in only when India was unable to do so. Moreover, the agreement further stipulated that even when British and U.S. arms were permitted, they would have to be routed to the land-locked kingdom only through Indian territory. Thus arms purchases from China without India's knowledge and approval were implicitly ruled out. In July 1988, 500 trucks with Chinese arms rolled on the Chinese built Kodare-Kathmandu road to the airport to deliver ground to air missiles and other equipment. In September, when King Birendra as the outgoing Chairman of SAARC visited India, he skirted the issue when it was brought up by the Indian Prime Minister. There does not appear to have been any firm diplomatic protest but the events made India suspicious of Nepalese intentions. The result was a tough attitude by India on the question of renewal of trade and transit treaties. India refused to renew the special treaties and decided to abide by International trade and transit requirements only.

Thus in the closing years of the eighties, Nepal had to face, two developments in her international relations. Firstly, Nepal could not count on China's armed support in any confrontation with India brought about by Nepal's own actions. King Birendra's other friends like the U.K., the U.S.A. and Japan were too far away to be of much help because of geographical separation from the land-locked Kingdom of Nepal. Secondly, in March 1989, the trade and transit treaties with India lapsed and the world simply watched when India refused to allow Nepal any more benefits than what international practice and usage allowed. Even a change of government in Delhi made little difference. Shailendra Kumar Upadhyaya the Nepalese foreign Minister visited Delhi in the first week of January and foreign Secretary level talks were held towards the end of February 1990, but no early solution was expected. The economy of the country, however, was in disarray and the prices of essential goods like petrol, kerosene, sugar and salt made life expensive and troublesome for the common people. The citizens were unhappy with the outcome of the Marich Man Singh ministry's handling of the foreign and economic policies which were closely interlinked. The King and his ministers failed to appreciate the difficulties of the people who then became alienated from their government.

Apart from these international factors, the King lost completely on the information and media front. The political effect of the widespread use of the transistor radio was not noticed by the powers that ran the country. In Nepal, transistor radio sets were the cheapest as compared to other South Asian countries and were of superior quality. Many countries broadcast in the Nepali language and as every household in Nepal has a radio-set, every Nepalese citizen knew what was happening in eastern Europe, China, India, South Africa etc. as the broadcasts in Nepali kept him abreast of all political developments and thinking in these countries. It was said that the U.S.S.R. lost the media war with the U.S.A. In the same way, it was said that the Nepalese government lost on the media sector. It could ban Indian newspapers and books but it could not jam all the foreign broadcasts.

It was in this milieu that the Nepalese political parties were discussing the events in their own country. The success of V.P. Singh in building an anti-Congress front in India, in 1989, showed that centrist and leftist parties could join hands politically for a clear-cut objective. In Nepal, efforts had been made from time to time to get the Nepali Congress and the Leftist parties, consisting of different Communist groups, to work together, but they had always failed. In 1989, a common objective, however, attracted both the parties. It was to have a multi-party political system in Nepal in place of the partyless panchayat system which did not recognise officially any of the several political parties registered under legal cover names or otherwise. This also meant constitutional monarchy with all powers vested in the elected representatives of the people instead of the Maharajadhiraj. This was necessary as the Nepalese, by and large, were loyal to the monarchy and cherished the heritage of Prithvi Narayan Shah who had consolidated the kingdom in the second half of the eighteenth century. In 1989, the main Leftist parties formed a United Left Front and decided to cooperate with the Nepali Congress in asking for a multi-party political system in which the King was bound to appoint the leader of the majority party as his Prime Minister. This meant the new political grouping was intended to organise a political struggle for democracy. Ganesh Man Singh, the Nepali Congress leader, born 1915, had not favoured taking part in the 1980 national referendum and had not accepted its results for the partyless panchayat system by a 10% margin. After the death of B.P. Koirala in 1982, Ganesh Man Singh became the supreme leader of the Nepali Congress. In 1970, Pushpa Lal Shrestha had given a call for joint action by the Communists and the Nepali Congress to start a movement against the monarchy, but this was not acceptable to the Nepali Congress. During the referendum again the Communists wanted joint action but did not succeed in their efforts. In 1985, the Nepali Congress, on its own strength, had launched a satyagraha movement against the partyless system, but to no avail. By 1987, Ganesh Man Singh had come to the conclusion that if the King could not be persuaded to restore multiparty democracy, a mass movement jointly with like-minded parties was the only alternative left. In a last bid effort in 1989 Ganesh

Man Singh met King Birendra and urged him to abolish the partyless system, reinstate multiparty democracy and hold elections under a national government consisting of all parties in the country. It was said that the king who had been educated in the USA, Tokyo and Britain, was not averse to constitutional monarchy but that the queen mother and the queens vehemently opposed any dilution in the powers of the monarchy. It was evident that the king would not part with his absolute powers except under pressure. At this juncture Ganesh Man Singh thought that Mikhail Gorbachov's glasnost and perestroika had brought liberalisation all over the world and that these winds of change were bound to affect Nepal also. He thought that the external factors would definitely help Nepali movement for democracy. Previously, the Nepali Congress had kept aloof from the left parties but in 1989 Ganesh Man Singh actively supported the plan for a joint mass movement by the left parties and the Nepali Congress. The Nepali Congress agreed that its ideology was different from that of the United Left Front but a joint mass movement for political democracy had become a historical compulsion. The two groups agreed to work for certain common goals, namely, the restoration of a full-fledged democracy, amending the constitution, ushering in genuine parliamentary democracy and to that end holding general election, hopefully within a year. The alliance was to last till the dates of the election were announced and both parties decided to sincerely fulfil their promises.[1]

When the movement for democracy started on 18th February 1990, few thought that it would succeed. The Tribhuwan University had brought in a new generation of youngmen brought up on western concepts of democracy. Higher education through the English language brought British ideas with it. It would not possibly support the Nepal monarchy. Articles 20(2) of the old constitution said: "The sovereignty of Nepal is vested in his Majesty and all powers executive, legislative and judicial-emanate from him. These powers are exercised by His Majesty through the organs established by or under this constitution and other laws for the time being in force, keeping in view the interest and wishes of His Majesty's subjects according to the highest traditions of the Shah dynasty".

The aim of the movement was to change this constitution. The new middle class of doctors, lawyers, teachers, journalists, trade union leaders and industrialists joined the movement. The protagonists of the monarchy had been restricted to the operators amongst the top elite who in conjunction with black marketeers and smugglers cornered a good part of the national wealth for their own use. The petty government employees also sympathised with the movement. The monarch was left alone with his ministers, regional commissioners and the economic operators who made their living with the help of permits, quotas and licences.

In 1989-90, several east European dictatorships had submitted to democratic revolutions. Something similar happened in Nepal, but ultimately the innate tolerance of the Hindu mind prevailed and a peaceful solution was arrived at. We will now examine the course of the revolution in Nepal in greater detail to understand the issues involved and the working of the Hindu mind.

The movement was formally launched on 18 February, 1990. On the previous day the King's men had put Ganesh Man Singh and Krishna Prasad Bhattarai, top-most Nepali Congress leaders, under house arrest. Man Mohan Adhikari, a top leader of the United Left Front was arrested the same day. However, the left front's chairperson Sahana Pradhan went underground with most of her colleagues and a number of Nepali Congress activists. The Communists had learnt this disappearing trick through previous experience and it now came handy to Nepali Congress activists as well. The movement was intended to be a series of peaceful but assertive demonstrations by unarmed people for democracy. The demonstrations were small and passed off peacefully in Kathmandu but at Bhaktapur and Hetanda police opened fire to disperse the demonstrators and five persons were killed. A Nepal bandh was called by the underground leaders for 19th. In Bhaktapur, in the Kathmandu valley on that day 12 persons were killed in police firing, 33 persons were injured and the arrangements for treatment of the injured were negligible. On February 20, police bullets killed five un-armed demonstrators near Janakpur town on the Nepal-India border. When news of the deaths by police firing reached Kathmandu, the lawyers suspended work. On 23rd, the doctors of Bir-teaching Hospital at Kathmandu observed a two hour strike and a one hour strike on 25th, when they found 303 Dumdum bullets on autopsies.

In the meantime hundreds were arrested from amongst the peaceful demonstrators, which included even National Panchayat members.

On February 27, University teachers from all the degree colleges in the kingdom stayed away from work and supported the movement. The journalists also joined in and even a junior minister and another leading member of the National panchayat, resigned protesting against the police brutalities.

On March 2, the opposition called for a second bandh which was partly successful inspite of the authorities best efforts to curb it. Nepal Medical Association, Nepal Bar Association, Nepal Journalists Association and other organisations protested against the use of prohibited Dumdum bullets on unarmed crowds. On March 9, the underground leaders organised the burning of effigies of Panchayat system throughout the kingdom, and a third Nepal Bandh was called for March 14. The regional Commissioners or Mandaleys now got panicky and large scale arrests of students and teachers took place. They were sitting down in protest against the repression with black bands over their mouths in the campuses of the University. On March 18, however, King Birendra hinted at reform when he was addressing a rally at Pokhra. He had been away to Pokhra leaving the Marich Man Singh ministry to deal with the opposition movement in Kathmandu. This was the first clear indication that the King was not in complete agreement with his Prime Minister. His prolonged visit for official inspection to Pokhra at the commencement of the movement had left his stand unclear.

From March 23, the opposition started the "lights off" protests. The students promptly adopted this method of protest in all boarding schools. The lights would go off at night when the students would come out in protest marches. In sheer desperation the police clashed with demonstrators in day time and arrests were made indiscriminately. Several people also died or received injuries in police firing. The international media was reporting the events in Kathmandu and the valley. On March 30, called the black Friday by the opposition, police opened fire on pro-democracy demonstrators at Lalitpur, killing 2 and injuring 13. People came out of their homes with kitchen utensils and agricultural tools and drove away the police. On March 31, police opened fire again injuring the senior nurse of Bir Hospital.

Massive crowds now took over Lalitpur. This unnerved the Prime Minister. He reshuffled his cabinet on April 1 and decided to take a tougher line. On April 2, police firing killed 7 persons and injured 23 at Kirtipur and killed 3 in Kathmandu. The police was now in a vengeful mood and the officers were unable to control them. On the other hand, village panchayat pradhans in Kirtipur resigned en bloc and the electricity workers and Royal Nepal Airlines staff went on token strike on April 4. This became a difficult moment for King Birendra. The citizens of Kathmandu threatened to march to his palace in protest against his Prime Minister's government, who had lost control over the police. The army was mostly officered by Ranas but could be relied on to protect the palace at any cost. To stem the tide of resentment against the government the King on April 6 dismissed Marich Man Singh and reappointed Lokendra Bahadur Chand, an ex-Prime Minister, Prime Minister. The King directed the new Prime Minister to hold talks with the opposition leaders, promised to appoint a commission for reforms and another to enquire into the police firings. But it was already too late. The common people of the kingdom had now cast their lot with the movement and against un-bridled police repressions. As early as April 6, the people from all over the valley had already converged on Kathmandu and they mounted a massive demonstration at the open air theatre. The police and the army decided to deal with the demonstrations firmly. They opened indiscriminate fire on the crowds and killed more than 150 demonstrators and left more than 200 injured. In Butwal another 13 persons died in police firing. Next day April 7, curfew was imposed in Kathmandu. This was extended to April 8 and to other towns in the kingdom, while sporadic police firings and deaths continued. The King, however, did not want to fight a last ditch battle against his own people especially when he had no support internationally. Already on April 7, dialogues had started with the leaders of the Nepali Congress and the United Left front. Much blood had already been shed, with promises of much more, and King Birendra decided to capitulate. On April 8, a royal proclamation announced the dropping of the word "partyless" from the preamble to the constitution and the ban on political parties was lifted. This gesture from the King was reciprocated by the leaders of the opposition and they decided to withdraw the movement. The people, however, were greatly agitated by the brutalities of the armed police and the army and demonstrations continued throughout the kingdom. Ultimately on April 19, the revolution in Nepal celebrated its victory by the swearing-in of a new ministry by the King. The 11 member interim government included 2 nominees of the King also but Krishna Prasad Bhattarai, the Nepali Congress leader became the Prime Minister and Sahana Pradhan minister for industry and commerce.

An immediate result of the triumph of the opposition was discontent amongst the senior bureaucrats and the police and the army. But the calm understanding demonstrated by the new Prime Minister, his decision not to be vindictive and to work for reconciliation paid rich dividends. He was able to restore normalcy in a short time and was able to visit India from June 8 to 10 concluding new arrangements with India which were welcomed by both countries and their peoples.

Bhattarai's real triumph came on November 9, 1990 when the King formally promulgated the new constitution of Nepal. The new constitution changes Nepal from an absolute monarchy to a constitutional monarchy on the model of Great Britain.

The promulgation of the new constitution heralded the dawn of a new democratic era in Nepal. It was a domestic product of Nepalese wisdom, drafted by a committee with Justice Vishwanath Upadhyaya as Chairman, pressed for acceptance by Ganesh Man Singh, Krishna Prasad Bhattarai and Sahana Pradhan and accepted and proclaimed by the King. This amicable settlement of the political crisis became possible only because of the spirit of cooperation, toleration and compromise exhibited by all the parties concerned and in particular by the King and his council of ministers.

The new constitution envisages a multi-party constitutional monarchy for the country. Under the old constitution political parties had been banned and it was laid down that all powers-executive, judicial and legislative, emanated from the King. The new constitution says that Nepal's sovereignty is vested in the people, who are the source of power, and that the King is "the symbol of the Nepalese nation and the unity of the people of Nepal".

The King, in whom executive power is vested, acts on the advice and consent of his council of ministers, who, in turn, are responsible to the house of representatives. The constitution provides for a house of representatives or Prati Nidhi Sabha consisting of 175 members which will include elected representatives of various political parties. A 60-member "Rashtriya Sabha" (upper house) is also provided which will comprise representatives of various political, intellectual and social communities. Certain seats in the upper house are reserved for women, depressed and backward communities and regional groups. The "Prati Nidhi Sabha" will be elected every five years but the "Rashtriya Sabha" will be a permanent body with one third of its members completing their term every two years.

The preamble to the constitution forms an important part of the constitution. It ensures the fundamental rights of the people and empowers the supreme court to enforce them. Its provisions include the rights to education and culture, rights to secrecy, rights against custody, rights of information and provisions guaranteeing freedom of thought and expression. The constitution provides special rights to women, remaining backward financially and for various other reasons, and to the people of various castes and communities. The constitution also provides for enactment of laws for securing the sovereignty, unity and cooperation among the people as also social courtesy and discipline.

The new constitution continues Nepal's ban on religious conversion but unlike the old constitution, it guarantees freedom of worship for all faiths.

As regards treaties and agreements pertaining to "serious matters" reached by the government with foreign countries, they will all have to be ratified by two-third majority in the joint session of parliament.

The constitution also empowers the King to declare emergency in the country on the recommendation of the council of Ministers, if the kingdom is faced with external threats, armed revolt and for the maintenance of the integrity and sovereignty of the country. The proclamation of emergency would last upto six months at a stretch provided it was approved by parliament within a month of proclamation.

The supreme command of the Royal Nepal army is vested in the King but it is also laid down that the King shall appoint the commander-in-chief of the army on the recommendation of the Prime Minister, and that the King shall carry out the administration and deployment of the army on the recommendation of the National Defence Council, consisting of the Prime Minister, as chairman, and Defence Minister and Commander-in-chief, as members.

The multi-party elections under the new constitution were held on May 12, 1991. For nearly three decades elections were held in a partyless system of government with most of the functions of government being controlled by the monarch. There were more than 11 million voters and scores of parties came up in the wake of freedom for political activities in an environment of western style democracy. The Election Commission recognised 20 political parties but 12 of these failed to obtain a single seat. Out of the 205 seats, the Nepali Congress claimed 110 thus obtaining a simple majority on its own. Next came the United Marxist Leninist Party (UML) with 69 seats.

The party had been a constituent of the interim government that had wrested power from the King. The UML took full benefit of their acceptance as a political force in Nepal and are now hopeful of forming the government at the next election. Their success in Nepal proves that the anti-communist trend in Eastern Europe has little effect in South Asia. Though they were part of the government the communists had kept an independent profile and had decided to fight the election on their own. They went on demanding a constitution framed by a Constituent Assembly elected on the basis of universal adult franchice. They blamed the King and the Nepali Congress for all the difficulties faced by the masses. They actively opposed any close links with India and blamed the Nepali Congress for neglecting Nepalese interests. The voters missed their pro-China tilt but India baiting was welcome to a large extent. At the same time anti-Indian sentiment was not decisive. The National Democratic Party with its factions of Thapa and Chand groups fared poorly with just 4 seats and former Prime Minister Surya Bahadur Thapa, and Lokendra Bahadur Chand suffered defeat at the hands of communists. Even Marich

Man Singh Shreshta who contested as an independent was defeated by a Nepali Congress candidate. The Sadbhawana Party of the Madhesis which sought to represent the Nepalese of Indian origin mainly in the central Tarai region faired badly. It got only 6 seats. Broadly speaking the eastern regions and the Kathmandu Valley voted for the UML and the rest of the country for the Nepali Congress, thus providing the basis for a two party system in Nepal.

A sombre example of the success of democratic elections in Nepal was the defeat of the Prime Minister Krishna Prasad Bhattarai himself in Kathmandu-1 by a mere 751 votes to Man Mohan Adhikari UML general Secretary. The result was that G.P. Koirala of the Nepalese Congress became the Prime Minister and Adhikari the leader of the opposition. As Koirala formed his cabinet so did Adhikari form his shadow cabinet in Westminister style. The Nepalese voters by eliminating the panchayat politicians have put the communists on test as much as the Nepali Congress. Both these parties have in future to keep in close touch with public opinion and carry the peoples trust.

Although a democratic government has come to power after more than three decades, the new government has already displayed an affirmative and balanced approach to public administration. A three member Mallick Commission was set up shortly after the overthrow of the panchayat regime to report on the "atrocities and excesses" during the popular movement. The new government showed commendable restraint in not starting purnitive actions against public servants and public authorities. Instead the government in late July 1991, placed the 1100 page report on the table of the lower house along with the letter from the attorney general saying that "as the existing enactments are inadequate, punitive action can not be initiated against those found responsible for the activities calculated to suppress the popular movement."

Secondly, since June 30, 1991, the Nepal Civil Servants organisation, with tacit support from the left parties, began its total strike, ignoring the Prime Minister's appeal to all state employees to allow a moratorium for one year on strikes and protests to allow his government to study the issues involved and come with a long term plan to deal with their problem. However, the Nepal Civil Servants Association did not join the strike. On July 18, the government appointed a five member pay commission to review the current pay scales and recommend measures to redress the genuine grievances of the employees keeping in view the financial condition of the country. The commission is headed by a Former finance Secretary, Nara Kant Adhikari. On August 5, four government employees started a hunger strike unto death. After a week they were removed to the teaching hospital for intravenous feeding. Throughout this period the government stood firm and kept its offer of peaceful negotiations open. This firm attitude of the government brought the strike to an end after the Nepal Civil Servants Organisation which organised the strike unconditionally withdrew it after 55 days on August, 25.

It will be seen that the democratic government has strengthened its position with the administration and has shown a maturity of political perception which its detractors had not expected to find in its deliberations and action. But the coming years will pose their own problems and basic issues will come to the fore to be perceived and adequately dealt with. The geopolitical reality was clearly perceived by Prithvi Narayan Shah who compared Nepal to a tree between two giant rocks or in other words a sapling between two boulders. How does the sapling survive and keep away from any grinding of the two boulders, that has been the basic concern for Nepali rulers in the political and foreign affairs' domains ever since. At present four major political forces, can be seen working in Nepal. The King, the ruling Nepali Congress, the opposition Communists and the remnants of the panchayati system which had always had the King's backing. In Nepal, the King is not merely a constitutional figure head. He is essentially a Hindu monarch and the only Hindu monarch in the world. He is not only the symbol of the multi-national Nepali identity but also the head of the nation loved and respected by the citizens as a person above political parties and identified with the Nepali dreams of grandeur, prosperity and pride.

For the common people if the political administration is "teen (three) Sarkar", he in his person is "panch (five) Sarkar". Then with the recent multiparty elections Nepal has brought in a new type of the King's government and the King's opposition. The new system has an old political party as the government with a strong opposition working hard to win the next elections and form the government. Will the elections to follow in future years also bring in sustenable governments, will the King play a positive and national role in coming years and will the neighbours leave Nepal to sort out its problems in its own way, are the questions that are difficult to answer at present.

The greatest challenge to Nepal, however, is how to improve the living conditions of its citizens. Nepal has tremendous potential to generate hydro-electricity and its climate can provide ideal sanatoria and holiday facilities. But on both these counts its clientale is restricted. There is only one buyer for its hydro-power and the majority of the tourists coming to Nepal come from one and the same country.

This is the great dilemma for Nepal. This is common to any small country, with big and powerful neighbours. Any long term and especially a monopolistic arrangement puts definite restraints on one's economic and political decision-making. Examples of good neighbourly relations are Canada and the U.S.A. and Great Britain and Portugal. But examples of strained relationships are many, in Europe and the far East. This, then is the real test of Nepalese statesmanship. The relationships with Nepal's neighbours have to have the broad approval of the monarch, his people generally and both His Majesty's government and opposition. If this common national approach is not fostered and consummated, the national income can not grow and the common citizen can not improve his standard of living. The first part of this national approach is obvious, namely that the security interests of neighbours are properly taken into account and not hurt. The second part is more difficult, namely that economic agreements with neighbours must not give or appear to give undue economic advantages to the foreigner. Economic and legal planning in India has sometimes overlooked the interests of the poorer, the more honest and the more law abiding of its citizens which has led to protests, demonstrations and ultimately violence arising out of frustration.

In Nepal, efforts to avoid such unequal arrangements can certainly be made by statesmen on both sides with built-in cures to prevent the sophisticated and the unconventional elements from exploiting the simpler hillmen of Nepal who are nearer to basic human values and qualities than many other outcrops of a modern consumer society which keeps away from moral values and conduct. The rulers in Nepal, *i.e.* the King, his government and his opposition have to chart new policy frames with great care, take the common people in confidence and insist on preserving and promoting the national interests of its citizens. This is the first and foremost task for the new democracy in Nepal. Small beginnings have been made but the key to success lies in the confidence of the common people that what is done in their name is for their good and that their interests have been safeguared.

At the proclamation ceremony for the new constitution on November 9, 1990, Ganesh Man Singh said that "the constitution has opened a new era with vast possibilities of political, social and economic development of the country." It is with this bright prospect for the future that Nepal joined the comity of democratic nations. The future is just beginning and we think on hopeful signs.

Note

1 Interviews to the press by K.P. Bhattarai and Sahana Pradhan reported in *Front Line* April 28-May 11, 1990 issue. Sahana Pradhan widow of Pushpal Lal Shrestha, is the Chair-person of the United Left Front.

Appendix - I

Nepal's Relations with India

The contacts between Nepal and India are integral parts of Nepal's history, which we have described in detail in Chapter XIII. The Karnali river provided the shortest route from Benares to Mansarowar. According to several myths pre-Vedic Shiva who lived in the eternal city of Benares was wedded to Parbati, the daughter of the Himalayas. Shiva and Parbati stayed at Benares during day-time but left for Mansarowar every evening and returned to Benares at day-break next moring. This established the necessary harmony between the Vedic and the indigenous traditions or between the "Nigams and the Agamas" as the Hindu priests put it. Shiva also became the Pashupati Nath-Lord of all animals-of the Kirati rulers of the Kathmandu valley. At the same time Guhyeshwari temple became the link with the mother-cult of the pre-Vedic period that spanned Kamrup or Assam, Mithila or Bihar, Bengal and Orissa. These were the binding social links between the people of Nepal and early India.

Coming to facts established by archaeological findings we come to the time of Gautam Buddha. He was born at Lumbini in the Nepal Tarai and he spent a good deal of his wandering life near that area.

Then we come to the time of Ashok who built the stupas at Patan, and whose daughter Charumati dedicated her life to the spread of the 'Dharma' *i.e.* the Buddhist faith amongst the people of Nepal.

It is not necessary to recapitulate the interactions between the rulers and people of Nepal and India here. We have described it in detail in the body of the book. Suffice it to say that the Shah dynasty of Gorkha and later of Nepal claims descent from the Rajput ruling family of Chittor. Along with the Shah family came several collateral chiefs including Ranas, Kunwars and others. The family priests also accompanied them. This exodus occurred when Allauddin Khilji sacked Chittor. Like the Shah rulers of Gorkha, most of the other chiefs and rulers in Nepal in the medieval period were of Rajput descent and intermarriages between these families and collateral branches of the same families, in India were common.

We have discussed in detail the relations between Nepal and the East India Company in Chapter XV. The first treaty between Nepal and the East India Company was signed on 1 March 1792. It was a treaty of Commerce. In 1801, another treaty was signed which envisaged the appointment of vakils by the two powers at each other's courts. Both these treaties had been signed by Nepal under special circumstances, namely the Chinese-Tibetan invasion in 1791-92 and the presence of Ran Bahadur Shah at Benares. Neither of these treaties was implemented.

The relations between Nepal and the East India Company were later governed by the treaty of Segouli 1815-16 and the letters exchanged between the Resident and the King of Nepal, in December 1816. The treaty fixed the boundaries of Nepal in East, South and West. In the east, the Mechi river formed the boundary. In the south, all the low-lands between the rivers Kosi and the Kali in which the authority of the British Indian Government had been established or was going to be established were ceded by Nepal to the Company. In the west, the river Kali formed the boundary, thus separating Nepal from the Sikh State in the Punjab. Nepal had also to agree "never to take or retain in its service any British subject, nor the subject of any European or American State, without the consent of the British government". At the same time "accredited ministers from each State were to reside at the court of the other".

After the help rendered by Jung Bahadur to the company in fighting the Sepoy War of 1857-58, the British Government by the treaty of 1860 agreed to restore "in full sovereignty the whole of the low-lands between the rivers Kali and Rapti and the River Rapti and the district of Gorkhpur, which were in the possession of the Nepal State in the year 1815 and had been ceded to the British government by the treaty of Segouli in 1815".

(The texts of these treaties as well as those of the extradition treaties of 1855 and 1866 are given in Aitchison's Treaties, Engagements and Sanads; as also in the author's "Nepal and the East India Company"- Appendices 9 to 15).

After the First World War, the Indian government offered an annual "gift" to Nepal of Rs. 10,00,000 which went to Chandra Shamsher.[1] On 21 December 1923, a new treaty of perpetual peace and friendship was signed between Nepal and Great Britain. Under this treaty the British Indian Resident became the Envoy of Great Britain at the court of Nepal. At the same time all the previous treaties and agreements between Nepal and the British government in India were confirmed. Both parties were obliged to notify each other of any misunderstanding with neighbouring states likely to interfere with their friendly relations and to remove the cause of friction. Neither party was to permit its territory to be used to the detriment of the other.[2] Nepal was also to have the right to free and unrestricted import of goods and of arms and ammunition across India into her own territory provided the intentions of the Nepal government were friendly and there was no immediate danger to India from such importations.[3]

After Indian independence, on 31st July 1950, a treaty of Peace and Friendship was signed between Nepal and India. The two governments agreed to respect the complete sovereignty, territorial integrity and independence of each other. Nepal was also free to import from or through India, arms, ammunition or warlike material and equipment necessary for the security of Nepal. The two countries also agreed to give to each others' nationals facilities for industrial or economic development, concessions and countracts as to nationals of its own country. Pandit Nehru also made a statement that India would come to the help of Nepal if it was attacked. Nepal made no such commitment and stood aloof from India in all the wars that India fought with China and Pakistan since 1950. Similarly, while Nepalese citizens have the same rights as the Indians in India, the Nepalese government does not allow Indian citizens the same facilities in Nepal as given to its own citizens.

A trade and transit treaty was also signed later. In 1978 when it was due for renewal, India agreed to separate the arrangements and signed two treaties-one on general trade and another on transit matters. These were due for renewal in 1988 but as the perception of the two countries differed on their respective national interests, the two sides allowed the treaties to lapse on 23rd March 1989 after these had been extended on an *ad-hoc* basis for one year.

Even more basic was the issue of economic development of Nepal to which King Birendra had given the utmost priority. There was little foreign investment and all industrial development in Nepal was propped up on foreign loans and grants. Indian capital was also shy as the Nepalese government did not want that industries in Nepal should be controlled by Indian giants. This discrimination has halted investment by Indian industry in Nepal. At the same time no other country is interested in investing in Nepal in the expectation of obtaining even modest profit. This is because all industry in Nepal has to depend on raw materials and power (derived from coal or oil) which can be had only with the good will of India.

This is the big dilemma for Nepal. Geographical considerations dictate that economic growth in Nepal can only take place when Nepalese economy has a harmonious relationship with the gigantic Indian economy. Like the European Economic Community Nepal and India can have a common market, a common currency and a common trade, agriculture and industry policy. If and when such an understanding will develop, no one can predict convincingly.

Here the perception of Nepal's destiny by the monarch and the people of Nepal will determine the future course of history. The recent breakdown of trade and transit relationships between India and Nepal, point to the discordant elements in the relationship between the two countries. Sooner rather than later Nepal and India have to adjust to the realities of geography, communication-systems and mutually beneficial trade relations. The difficulties arise from national security interests. Nepal had recently brought assault rifles, missiles and anti-aircraft guns from China with which country India had recently fought a war. This was an extremely unfriendly act. Who can tell that Nepal will not buy more powerful missiles from China or elsewhere which can hit Calcutta, Delhi or the heart of the Indian industrial belt in South Bihar? How can India persuade Nepal not to go in for missiles that can only be aimed at India? Unless this is assured Nepal cannot expect India to forget the missiles that pose a great threat to its security and industrial strength. Further, India's assessment of Nepal's intentions turn sour when one finds that King Birendra did not permit Indians within a ten kilometre distance from the Nepal-Tibet border and at the same time purposefully invited Chinese nationals near to the Nepal Indian borders. This dangerous tilt against India had to be halted by all peaceful means. India cannot be blamed for withholding the enormous economic gifts it had been granting to Nepal. The lapse of the treaties proved to the King and the people of Nepal, if such proof was necessary, what unfriendliness with India would cost to Nepal. Nepal could not expect any help regarding trade and transit arrangements with India, from any other foreign country. Unfriendliness was returned with unfriendliness and friendship will be reciprocated. There is a saying in Hindi, "Bin bhya hohi na preeti". That stage had arrived in Nepalese and Indian relationship. Let us hope good sense will prevail in both countries and relations will return to those of King Tribhuwan's times.

Notes

1 *Nepal-Strategy for Surivial,*. Leo E. Rose, page 171.
2 *Gorkha*, Sir Francisi Tuker, pp. 201-2.
3 *Nepal,-Strategy for Survival.*, Leo E. Rose, page 172.

Appendix - II

Select Statistical Data

Membership of International Organisations:-

ILO, IMF, UN, WHO, Asian Development Bank, Colombo Plan, Economic and Social Commission for Asia and the Pacific, World Bank.

Development Plan 1980-85

Expenditure allocation for Public Sector NR. 20,490 million
Panchayat Sector NR 1,800 million
Private Sector NR 11,650 million
Total NR 33,940 million

Industry-The Public Sector manages sugar, jute and textile mills; cigarette, leather goods and brick and tile units, cement plant etc.
The Private Sector has sugar, cigarette, matches, liquor, soap, shoes, stainless steel utensils, straw board, beer, confectionaries and polythene pipes. Paper and lead and zinc smelting units are under construction-mid 1986.

Literacy-(estimated) 21%
Employment-(estimated) in agriculture 90%, industry 2%
Inflation-Consumer price index was rising annually at 5.2% (1975-80)
Currency-Money supply has risen annually (1975-80) by 16.2%
Agriculture-Food-grains output in 1982-83 (estimated) was app. 4 million metric tons. However, the average yield per hectare of paddy, wheat and maize, the staple crops was 1.92, 1.20 and 1.62 mts respectively during 61-62 to 70-71, and 1.88, 1.44 and 1.69 mts. during 71-72 to 80-81.

Glossary

Acharya- A learned man, well-versed in religious rites and ceremonies.

Arghun- Death ceremony.

Bandya- One worthy to be respected.

Bargha- Time cycle of twelve years, with animal or bird names for each year.

Bangar- Highland where canal irrigation is not possible, opposed to Khadar.

Banhra- Vernacular form of the Sanskrit word "Bandya" *i.e.* one worthy to be respected.

Bhabar- Waterless tract of land below the Himalayan foothills, twenty to thirty kilometres in width.

Bharadar- Important officers and noble-men.

Bhikshu- A Buddhist monk.

Bihar- See Vihar

Bodhisatwa- A person whose inner feelings are inclined towards enlightenment.

Brahmin- The learned caste of the Hindus.

Buddha- The enlightened one.

Chaitya- A Buddhist place of worship.

Chandravanshi raja- A raja claiming descent from the lunar line.

Dandi- See jhampan.

Dashera- Tenth day of the moon in the Hindu month after the rains when Ram is said to have killed Ravan.

Dharmadhikari- A judge of a Hindu religious court.

Dharmashastras- Codes of conduct prescribed by Hindu sages or preceptors.

Ditha- A magistrate presiding over a court dealing with criminal offences.

Doab- Land between two rivers.

Dun- A valley between the Himalayas and the Siwaliks.

Durbar- The court of a raja, open to the public.

Gotra- Descendents of a particular person or legendary sage.

Grihastha- A married person.

Hakim- Chief executive officer of a district or sub-district. A civil officer appointed by the government.

Jatra- Pilgrimage, outing. A religious celebration in which the idol from a temple is taken out for an outing and later brought back to the temple, as in Kathmandu and Puri (Orissa).

Jhampan- Or Dandi- A wooden carriage or couch for persons carried on the shoulders of four men; mostly used in the hills.

Kastura- The pod from the navel of the musk deer.

Kazi- A secretariate officer.

Khadar- Low-lying land, liable to floods.

Kshatriya- The warrior caste of the Hindus.

Khukri- A broad, light sword, typical of the Gorkhas.

Kumbha-biyah-Marriage of a girl with a pitcher of water.

Maharaja- A great raja.

Maharajadhiraj- A great raja. A title more high sounding than Maharaja.

Panch- A member of the panchayat or presiding council of a village or caste assembly.

Panchayat- A council of five; generally a village or caste assembly where the elders decide local matters by consensus or overwhelming majority.

Parishad- An association. A council. A league.

Pradhan- Leader, Chairman of a village council.

Praja- The common people. Citizens and villagers.

Pratima-biyah- Marriage of a girl with an idol.

Pundit- A Hindu learned man.

Raghuvanshi raja- A raja descended from Raghu-an ancestor of Ram.

Rajguru- The preceptor or religious priest of the raja.

Shaivism- Worship of Shiva.

Shakti- The consort of a deity. The spiritual power of a god or goddess.

Shravak- A Buddhist monk or apprentice monk.

Shudras- The fourth or service caste of Hindu society.

Smriti- Knowledge gained by listening to learned sages. Religious books of the Hindus prescribing codes of conduct, administration etc.

Subba- An officer heading the ministerial staff.

Suryavanshi raja- Raja claiming descent from the solar line.

Tanaka- A Buddhist religious painting on parchment, cloth or silk in the form of a scroll.

Tarai- Marshy land below bhabar, some times with artesian wells.

Tantra- Certain secret practices of Hindu and Buddhist religion.

Tantrik- One who follows tantras.

Thum- District or sub-district.

Toran- Central and topmost edifice of a temple.

Umra- Gorkhali word for amir. A person of noble birth. A high official.

Vaishya- The third caste of Hindu society, consisting of peasants and traders.

Vakil- Representative.

Vichari- A civil judge.

Vihar- Buddhist monastery.

Vikram era- The era starting from 58 B.C. based on lunar and solar movements and said to have been started by raja Vikramaditya of Ujjain.

Bibliography

Agarwal, Hem Narayan- *Nepal: A Study in Constituent Change*; New Delhi: Oxford & IBH, 1980.

Acharya, Balburam- *Shri 5 Bada Maharaja Prithvi Narayan Shah*: Vol (1-4). H.M.'s Principal Press Secretariate, Royal Palace, Kathmandu. (1967-69).

Bandopadhyaya, J.- *The Making of India's Foreign Policy*; New Delhi: Allied Publishers; Revised edition, 1980.

Banskota, N.P.- *Indo-Nepal trade and economic relations*; Delhi: B.R. Publishing Corporation, 1981.

Baral, Lok Raj- *Oppositional Politics in Nepal*; New Delhi: Abhinav Publication, 1977.

Bista, Dan Bahadur- *The People of Nepal*; Kathmandu: Ratna Pustak Bhandar, 1967.

Blackie, Piers, Cameron, John and Siddon, David- *Nepal in Crisis: Growth and Stagnation at the Periphery*: New Delhi: Oxford University Press, 1980.

Buchanan, Dr. Francis- *An Account of the Kingdom of Nepal*; Edinburgh: Constable, 1819.

Caplan, Lionel- *Land and Social Change in East Nepal. A Study of Hindu Tribal Relations*; London: Routledge and Kegan Paul, 1979.

Chatterjee, Bhola- *A Study of Recent Nepalese Politics*; Calcutta: World Press, 1967.

———— *Palace, People and Politics: Nepal in Perspective*; Delhi: Ankur Publishing House, 1980.

Chaudhuri, K.C.- *Anglo-Nepalese Relations*; Calcutta: Modern Book Agency Private Ltd., 1960.

Devkota, G. Bahadur- *Nepal Ko Rajnaitik Darpan* (in Nepali); K.C. Gautam, Kathmandu, 1960.

Furer-Haimendorf, Christoph Von- *The Sherpas of Nepal: Buddhist Highlanders*; Berkeley: University of California Press. 1964.

———— *Caste and Kin in Nepal, India and Ceylon: Anthropological Studies in Hindu-Buddhist contact Zones*; Bombay: Asia Publishing House, 1966.

———— *A Himalayan Tribe: From Cattle to Cash*; New Delhi: Vikas Publishing House, 1980.

Gibbs, H.R.K.- *The Gurkha Soldier*; Calcutta, 1949.

Gupta, Anirudha- *Politics in Nepal*; Bombay: Allied Publishers, 1964.

Hasraj, Bikram Jit- *History of Nepal*; Hoshiarpur: V.V. Research Institute, 1970.

Hagan, Toni- *Nepal*: New Delhi: Oxford and IBH Publishing Co., 1961.

Hodgson, Brian Houghton- *Essays on the Languages, Literature and Religion of Nepal and Tibet*; London: Trubner, 1874.

———— Miscellaneous Essays relating to Indian subjects, 2 Vols. London: Trubner, 1880.

Hunter, Sir W.W.- *Life of B.H. Hodgson*; London: Murray, 1896.

Jain, Girilal- *India Meets China in Nepal*; Bombay: Asia Publishing House, 1959.

Jain, S.C.- *Poverty to Prosperity in Nepal*; Delhi: Development Publishers, 1981.

Jayaswal, K.P.- *Chronology and History of Nepal* (600 B.C. to 880 A.D.); Varanasi: Bharati Prakashan, 1976.

Jnawali, Surya Bikram- *Amar Singh Thapa* (in Hindi); Darjeeling: Ratnakar Press, 1951.

———— *Nepal Vijeta Shri Panch Prithvi Narayan Shah Ko Jeevani* (in Nepali); Darjeeling, 1935.

———— *Nepal Upatyakako Madhya Kalin Itihas*; Kathmandu: Royal Nepal Academy, 1962.

Joshi, Bhuwan Lal and Leo E. Rose- *Democratic Innovations in Nepal: A Case Study of Political Acculturation*; Barkeley: University of California Press, 1966.

Kaiser, Bahadur, K.C.- *Nepal after the Revolution of 1950* (2 vols); Kathmandu: Sharda Prakashan Griha, 1976-77.

Karan, P.P. and Jenkins, W.M.- *A Cultural and Physical Geography of Nepal*; University of Kentucky Press, 1960.

———— *The Himalayan Kingdoms: Bhutan, Sikkim and Nepal*; Princeton: D. Van Nostrand & Co. Inc., 1963.

Khanal, Yadunath- *Reflections on Nepal-India Relations*; Delhi: Rakesh Press, 1964.

———— *Nepal, Transition from Isolationism*; Kathmandu: Sajha Prakashan, 1977.

Kirkpatrick, Captain William- *An Account of the Kingdom of Nepal*; London: W. Miller, 1811.

Kumar, D.P.- *Nepal Year of Decision*; Delhi: Vikas Publishing House, 1980.

Kumar, Satish- *Rana Polity in Nepal: Origin and Growth*; Asia Publishing House, 1967.

Landon, Perceval- *Nepal*, 2 Volumes; London: Constable, 1928.

Levi, Sylvain- *Le Nepal*, (in French) 3 volumes; Paris 1905-08. (type written translation in English. Indian Council of World Affairs Library, New Delhi).

Mihaly, E.B.- *Foreign Aid and Politics in Nepal. A Case study*; New York: Oxford University Press, 1965.

Narayan, Shriman- *India and Nepaul: An Exercise in Open Diplomacy*; Bombay, Popular Prakashan, 1970.

Nath, Tribhuwan- *The Nepalese Dilemma*; New Delhi, Sterling Publishers, 1975.

Nepali, Chitta Ranjan- *Janaral Bhim Sen Thapa ra Tatkalin Nepal* (in Nepali); Kathmandu: Jorganesh Press, 1957.

Northey, W.B.- *The Land of the Gurkhas*. Cambridge, 1938.

Northey, W.B. and Morris, C.J.- *The Gurkhas; Their Manners, Customs and Country*; London, 1928.

Oldfield, H.A.- *Sketches from Nepaul*; 2 vols. London, 1880.

Pant, Y.P.- *Economic Development of Nepal*; Allahabad: Kitab Mahal, 1965.

Pant, Y.P.- *Nepal's Economic Development on International Basis: An Analysis of Foreign Aid Utilization*; Kathmandu: Educational Enterprise, 1962.

Pant, Y.P.- *Problems in Fiscal and Monetry Policy*; Kathmandu: Sahayogi Prakashan, Kathmandu, 1970.

Patterson, George- *Peking versus Delhi*; London: Faber and Faber, 1963.

Petch, Luciano - Medieval History of Nepal; Rome, 1958

Rana, Pashupathi S.J.B. & Kamal P. Malla- *Nepal in Perspective*; Kathmandu: Centre for Economic, Development and Administration, 1973.

Regmi, D.R.- *Medieval Nepal*; 3 volumes. Calcutta: Firma K.L. Mukhopadhyay, 1965-66.

————*Modern Nepal*; Calcutta: Firma K.L. Mukhopadhyay, 1961.

———— *A Century of Family Autocracy in Nepal*; Nepal National Congress; Benares, 1950.

Rose, Leo E. i)- *Strategy for Survival*; Oxford University Press; Delhi: 1973.

ii) and Margaret W. Fisher- *The Politics of Nepal*; Ithaca: N.Y. Cornell University Press, 1970.

iii) and Sholz, John T- *Nepal: Profile of a Himalayan Kingdom*. Select Service Syndicate, New Delhi, 1980.

Sanwal, B.D.- *Nepal and the East India Company*; Bombay: Asia Publishing House, 1965.

Shaha, Rishikesh- *Nepal and the World*; Kathmandu: Nepali Congress Publication, 1955.

———— *Heroes and Builders of Nepal*; London: Oxford University Press, 1965.

————*An Introduction to Nepal*; Kathmandu: Ratna Pushtak Bhandar, 1976.

———— *Essays in the Practice of Government of Nepal*; New Delhi: Manohar Book Service, 1982.

———— *Modern Nepal- A Political History*; vol. I & II. New Delhi. Manohar Publishers and Distributors 1990.

Shrestha, B.P.- *The Economy of Nepal or a Study in Problems and Processes of Industrialization*; Bombay: Vora, 1967.

———— and Jain S.P.- *Regional Development in Nepal*; Patna: Development Publishers, 1975.

———— *Monetary Policy in an Emerging Economy: A Case Study of Nepal*, Kathmandu: Ratna Pushtak Bhandar, 1965.

Shrestha, S.M.- *Modern Geography of Nepal*; Kathmandu: Vishwakrama Press, 1968.

Singh, S.K.- *The Fiscal System of Nepal*; Kathmandu: Ratna Pushtak Bhandar, 1977.

Slusser, Mary Shephard- *Nepal Mandala. A Cultural Study of the Kathmandu Valley*; 2 Vols, Princeton 1982.

Tandukar, Gopal Man- *Kiratas at a Glance*; Kathmandu: International Standard Books & Periodicals Store, 1980.

Temple, Sir R.- *Journals Kept in Hyderabad and Nepal*; 2 volumes,

London, 1887.

Thapa, Netra B.- *A Short History of Nepal*; 5th edition, Kathmandu: Ratna Pushtak Bhandar, 1981.

Tucci, Giuseppe- *Nepal, The Discovery of the Malla*; New York: Dulton, 1962.

Tuker, Sir Francis- *Gorkha- The Story of the Gorkhas of Nepal*; London: Constable, 1957.

Tuladhar, Daman Raj- *Contemporary Nepal, 1945-55*; Kathmandu: Laxmi Publication, Kathmandu, 1980.

Tuladhar, Tirth R.- *Partyless Democracy, Its Basis and Background*; Kathmandu: Royal Palace Secretariat, 1962.

Tyagi, Sushila- *Indo-Nepalese Relations*; Delhi: D.K. Publishing House, 1974.

Upadhyaya, Yogeshraj- *Facts about Nepal.* His Majesty's Government; Kathmandu, 1980.

Wright, Daniel- *History of Nepal*; Cambridge University Press, 1879.

May also see-

American University, Washington D.C. Foreign Area Studies Division: Area Handbook for Nepal. U.S. Department of the Army. Washington D.C. 1964.

Several studies issued by

i) Centre for Agricultural Projects Services

ii) Centre for Economic and Development Administration

iii) Centre for Nepal and Asian Studies, Kathmandu.

IBRD- Nepal, Development, Performance and Prospects, Washington, 1971.

United Nations:

Social and Economic Commission for Asia and Pacific: Population of Nepal, Bangkok, 1980.

INDEX